IMAGES
of America

IDAHO FALLS POST REGISTER

ON THE COVER: The automated typesetter revolutionized the newspaper industry, making it possible to produce larger papers on a more frequent publication schedule and at lower cost. This photograph shows a string of typesetters at the *Post-Register*'s composing room on Capital Avenue in the late 1930s or early 1940s; the center operator sawed off the back legs of a wooden chair to ease his back during what were often long hours of casting hot lead galleys. Linotypes were in use at the *Post-Register* from 1904 until about 1977. (*Idaho Falls Post Register.*)

IMAGES
of America

IDAHO FALLS POST REGISTER

William Hathaway

ARCADIA
PUBLISHING

ISBN 978-0-7385-5968-1
Published by Arcadia Publishing
Charleston SC, Chicago IL, Portsmouth NH, San Francisco CA

Printed in the United States of America

Library of Congress Control Number: 2008928808

For all general information contact Arcadia Publishing at:
Telephone 843-853-2070
Fax 843-853-0044
E-mail sales@arcadiapublishing.com
For customer service and orders:
Toll-Free 1-888-313-2665

Visit us on the Internet at www.arcadiapublishing.com

This book is dedicated to J. Robb Brady, to Jerry M. Brady, and to the employee-owners of the Post Register, *who at 128 years and counting still put out an excellent locally owned, independent newspaper every day.*

Contents

ACKNOWLEDGMENTS

For nearly 130 years, the history of the region has been told in the pages of the *Idaho Register*, the *Times*, the *Daily Post*, the *Times-Register*, and the consolidated *Post-Register*. The late Joe Marker was the *Post-Register*'s history editor and author of *Eagle Rock, U.S.A.* He leads a legion of reporters whose decades of newspaper accounts form the backbone of this book. This book also draws on the weekly "Looking Back" columns of Paul Menser and *Post Register* executive editor Dean Miller's work for the newspaper's 125th anniversary edition, published in 2005.

Thanks to the Bonneville County Historical Society and Museum of Idaho for providing some photographs and to the aid of LaDean Harmston and Judy House of the museum's reference department. This book and all other local histories are indebted to Mary Jane Fritzen, whose 1991 Bonneville County Historical Society publication *Idaho Falls, City of Destiny* preserved a detailed outline of events that shaped Idaho Falls. William Stibal Pettite has also done much to preserve the facts surrounding local events, especially the history of local newspapers and newspapermen. Edith Haroldsen Lovell's 1963 book *Captain Bonneville's County* is a trove of first-person accounts from the area's pioneers. The work of Fritzen, Marker, and Lovell, and former Idaho Falls mayor Barzilla Clark's *Bonneville County in the Making*, were printed, published, or partly supported by the *Post Register.*

Special thanks to *Post Register* researcher Linda Metcalf and to Jan Blickenstaff, the grant administrator for the Idaho Falls Historic Preservation Commission, for his knowledge of local downtown landmarks and help in obtaining pictures from the Perk's Photo collection.

Thanks also to Roger Plothow, J. Robb Brady, Jerry M. Brady, and Marty Trillhaase for offering valuable comments and guidance. Unless otherwise noted, photographs are from the *Post Register*'s files and its talented staff of photojournalists.

And a short note: In 1990, the *Post-Register* changed the name on its masthead to remove the article and hyphen noting a contraction of two newspapers. Subsequent notations follow the newer spelling.

INTRODUCTION

JOURNALISM AT THE END OF THE TRACKS

When an uncommonly well-dressed newspaperman stepped off the train at Blackfoot, there were only a couple of newspapers in the vast and empty Idaho Territory. Indian uprisings were still common, and most of the settlers who would build eastern Idaho had not yet arrived. William Edward Wheeler's arrival in June 1880 was accompanied by the offloading of printing equipment and a press at the very end of the railroad's line of tracks.

Another Blackfoot arrival about a month later was Fred T. Dubois, a recent Yale graduate who came to Idaho to visit his brother, a doctor on the nearby Fort Hall reservation. Both arrivals changed the face of the Western landscape in the course of a few years.

Dubois became the U.S. marshal, then the territory's representative to Congress, and finally a U.S. senator. In the course of a decade, he was instrumental in pushing statehood through for Idaho, largely at the expense of the region's Mormon population.

Wheeler became a newspaper publisher the hard way. He was born in Vermont in 1843 and served as a private in the Union army during the Civil War. He completed one year of college before heading west as a representative for Bluff City Printing Company of Council Bluffs, Iowa. Wheeler started the *Evanston Age* in 1871. The coming of the Union Pacific in 1869 had brought prosperity to the Midwest, but Wyoming's cattle boom of the 1870s did not cause the territory to flourish, forcing Wheeler to think of moving farther down the tracks. His departure exasperated Laramie editor J. H. Hayford, whose paper labeled him "a drunkard, a pimp, a whoremonger, a dead beat, a man on whom nature or education never fooled away a moment's time"—harsh words for a war veteran whose household included a widowed mother and younger sister.

Wheeler had decided on Blackfoot because it was the county seat for sprawling Oneida, which extended from Utah to the Montana–Wyoming borders. Blackfoot was the most populated city in the sparse territory—it boasted a cafe, hotel, four general merchandise stores, four saloons, two blacksmith shops, a wagon shop, a lumber yard, a jewelry store, and a doctor.

A small settlement to the northeast, Eagle Rock, also was considered, but it had little to offer in comparison: Anderson's store, Dick Chamberlain's saloon, and Matt Taylor's toll bridge were hardly enough to support a newspaper.

FIRST EDITION

On July 10, 1880, a handset newspaper was printed on a foot-powered press in a small frame building. A one-year subscription cost $3. Virtually the whole town showed up to get a copy. It was a sign of progress and a source of pride.

In an introduction, Wheeler proclaimed his passionate commitment to political independence, local news over national issues, and greed—or, as it was called then, capitalism. "We have . . . one main object in view, and that is to secure as large an amount of the filthy lucre as possible," he wrote.

The major social issues in Oneida were treatment of Native Americans and Mormons, two points that convened in the interests of both Wheeler and Dubois.

Dubois took a job as a stockman at the reservation, and Wheeler started a newspaper and became a member of the Independent party, formed to counter the tendency of members of the LDS Church to vote as a bloc, usually for Democrats.

The *Register* took an instant dislike to chief reservation agent John A. Wright, calling him a "liar" and "sanctimonious." The charges gained strength when eight agency employees, including

Dubois, added charges of dishonesty and neglect. When Wright resigned, the *Register* accused him of setting his successor up for failure by throwing open the doors of the reservation's food warehouse to the Native Americans. Wheeler then defended Dubois when Wright charged him with being a drunkard in an attempt to block Dubois's appointment as U.S. marshal; Wheeler wrote a letter to Washington that claimed "unanimous" support in Blackfoot for Dubois's appointment.

Only a few months before Wheeler's arrival, the last of Idaho's two major Native American wars was concluded to the detriment of the Bannocks, a tribe of Northern Paiute who had lived in peace with the Shoshones but objected to their own shoddy treatment by Fort Hall's Indian agent. Bannock leaders continued to object to the whites' theft of water, land, and cattle from the Native Americans, but the 1878 war ended when most Bannocks returned to the reservation, and the rest simply disappeared into the wilderness.

Dubois consistently supported the interests of white settlement over that of Native Americans trying to adapt to reservation life. Wheeler and his newspaper seemed more interested in promoting economic expansion than in bettering the plight of the Bannocks and Shoshones. An article in the *Register* in 1882 suggested that the reservation be reduced to 10 square miles and the rest of what was originally a 1.8-million-acre reserve should be thrown open to mining and settlement.

Moving North with the Railroad

Wheeler produced the newspaper in Blackfoot for more than three years, until the small town to the northeast began to look more lucrative. The railroad had taken a different route and named Eagle Rock its Idaho headquarters. Blackfoot, meanwhile, had been passed over by the Idaho Territorial Legislature as well, losing the opportunity to become the capital by a single vote. In Eagle Rock, more shops appeared; when the Utah and Northern established a switchyard and car shops at Eagle Rock, and Mormon settlers came to the Upper Snake River Valley en masse during the spring of 1883, it was clear the town was becoming the leading economic center in the area.

During that winter, the longtime bachelor made two momentous decisions: He married Elizabeth Macey Daugherty on December 19, 1883, in Denver; and in April 1884, Wheeler again loaded up his press and a few personal belongings on a flat car to start over. His new home was a building on the corner of Capital Avenue and Cliff Street in Eagle Rock.

The last edition of the *Blackfoot Register* published on March 22, 1884. Wheeler wrote, "We had contemplated skipping the next issue in consequence of the change we are about to make enlarging the paper, etc. . . . The *Idaho Register* will be the name of the first issue in April—a larger and greatly improved paper."

"Eagle Rock's first newspaper equipment, crated in rickety, old boxes, arrived in 1884 aboard a puffing, steam-spitting, old, narrow-gauge train of the Utah and Northern Railway," Sam Dennis, the first printer of the *Idaho Register*, wrote in a 1932 article. "Although the equipment was anything but pretentious, it was an eager and happy, though small, crowd that watched William E. Wheeler superintend the unloading of the small presses and a few cases of type at the old wooden station."

The couple made an annex adjoining the building into their home. The front room was Wheeler's office. Elizabeth was an excellent proofreader and learned to hand-set type. Wheeler made his move at an opportune time. Even though the turbulent Snake River had not yet been diverted into canals for irrigation, several were begun; fields and fruit orchards were planted, and settlers who had arrived in March had their first harvest by fall.

The area grew quickly for three years, so Wheeler's heart must have sunk in 1887 when he first heard rumors, confirmed by a clipping from another newspaper, that the railroad would move its headquarters to Pocatello.

Wheeler did not believe it but saw the need to print the news in the *Register*, despite the possible ruin such a move could mean to his own business. He ran the article with an editor's note at the end that said, "It is not worth mentioning except that it has been copied in other papers." The railroad proved Wheeler wrong and moved to Pocatello, taking shops, personnel, and a good portion of the community wealth with it. Almost overnight, the town of 1,500 dwindled to about 500. The railroad superintendent offered to move Wheeler's print shop and home to Pocatello free of charge and provide him with $1,000 in startup money, but Wheeler decided to stay in Eagle Rock.

Dennis wrote later that the "*Register* had a stormy and somewhat difficult existence in its early years." But Wheeler mounted an energetic campaign to focus attention on the water resources of the area. Soon canals and ditches were formed and the desert began to bloom into one of the country's richest agricultural areas, aided by the 1902 Reclamation Act, which opened up vast tracts. The *Register* was saved. In fact, it prospered for several years in spite of labor troubles and economic downturns, enabling Wheeler to install a mechanical typesetter in 1904 and a new cylinder press and other new Linotypes in 1909.

THE MORMON QUESTION

Dubois biographer Deana Lowe Jensen identified the *Register* as a "very popular and vociferous newspaper, non-Mormon in philosophy." But non-Mormon wasn't synonymous with anti-Mormon, even in those troubled times.

Wheeler became involved with the Independent party and for a time served as Oneida County chairman. The party was founded in the anti-Mormon movement, but Wheeler was "disinclined to be anti-Mormon," historian Merrill D. Beal recorded.

Wheeler objected to church members' tendency to vote en bloc, often at the urging of church leaders, but he saw little danger in the LDS Church's other practices and consistently supported its right of religious freedom. "Neither do we care to what religious sect a man may be affiliated with," the *Register* declared in its inaugural edition on July 10, 1880.

Wheeler also supported Dubois's political goals, lauding his appointment as U.S. marshal and even traveling with the young lawman to Boise to inspect the prison, since at that time the territorial marshal was also the warden. Dubois's immediate goal was statehood for Idaho, and that could not be accomplished, in his view at least, unless Mormons were restrained. But the Mormon matter later caused a rift between Wheeler and Dubois.

In October 1880, the *Register* and several other papers published a statement that it was "not the purpose of the Independent party to make war upon the honest religious convictions of any people, but that we will fight to the bitter end . . . the efforts of any religious sect to trail a free people in the dust of the wheels of a priestly chariot." Not much later, Wheeler abandoned the Independents and became an active Republican, where he stayed.

As U.S. marshal, Dubois spent a lot of time trying to enforce the recently passed Edmunds Act, rounding up Mormons who practiced plural marriage (only about a quarter of the church members at that time were practicing polygamists) and taking them to trial at Blackfoot. Local juries declined to convict for unlawful cohabitation until Dubois, with the help of local judge D. W. Standrod, introduced the open venire process, giving Dubois almost unlimited powers to select jurors from any district. He then filled juries with non-Mormons or even (in some cases) with excommunicated Mormons and others who had an outright grudge against the church.

What began as a political fight to keep Mormons from electing Democrats became a religious crusade in the courtroom, but it was good for business. A reporter for the November 5, 1887, *Salt Lake Herald* described the scene at district court in Blackfoot as "Sage brush and hotels, restaurants and camping grounds . . . Thoroughly impregnated with accused Mormons."

It's a fact that Idaho officials were much harsher in their treatment of Mormon polygamists than either Utah or Arizona. Some eastern Idaho Mormon leaders were singled out for special treatment—instead of paying a fine or spending a few months in the territorial prison, they were sent to federal penitentiary in South Dakota for terms up to three years. Idaho polygamists were "three or four times as likely to be arrested, tried and sentenced" as their Utah counterparts (*South*

Dakota History, Vol. 27, Nos. 1 and 2). "In such a vengeful judicial climate, it can be claimed that the last four Idaho polygamists sent to federal prison out of state were essentially victims of civil persecution."

After Dubois succeeded in getting the Test Oath passed, denying the vote to anyone who belonged to an organization that practiced or advocated polygamy, anti-Mormons in Rexburg renamed the town Kain and the county Tuck. Wheeler started up a newspaper in Rexburg, the *Kaintuck Bugle*, sending C. E. Arney and then Sam Dennis up to edit. But Dennis quit and returned to Idaho Falls to copublish a new rival paper, the *Idaho Falls Times*. Neither the *Bugle* nor Kain-Tuck stuck for very long. Church leaders agreed to disavow plural marriage and cease advising members how to vote. Mormon leader Ben E. Rich soon started a pro-LDS newspaper in Rexburg, the *Silver Hammer*, which became the *Rexburg Standard*.

The *Register* did little to calm anti-Mormon sentiments, but Wheeler never did join with Dubois in attacking Mormon beliefs. And when Dubois tried to use plural marriage once again as a political issue in 1904—this time as a Democratic candidate for the Senate—Wheeler editorialized against him and supported his GOP opponent.

One

SIGN OF THE TIMES

On July 10, 1890, another weekly paper was started in Idaho Falls. Noting the success of the *Register* and observing that the Idaho and New Sweden Canals were going to expand the already large agricultural business, Sam Dennis and Rufus C. Bonney put together a few hundred dollars, sold about $2,000 in stock, and started the *Times* with a printing plant purchased from Oklahoma.

Bonney was Eagle Rock's telegraph operator, and Dennis had just returned from a stint editing the *Kaintuck Bugle* in Rexburg after working as a printer with the *Register*. Hard times struck in 1891, and the *Times* announced it was "ready to receive grain, potatoes, wood or anything else it can use, on subscription." Under the heading "A Delicate Subject," Dennis and Bonney admitted that they were "very much embarrassed financially, and as free from money as a frog is of feathers."

The *Times* established a controversial reputation. After 18 months, Bonney and Dennis lost a libel suit, the result of an editorial attack on a court clerk, and faced a $3,000 judgment. Bonney left town and hired James W. Lamoreaux to edit the paper. After six months, Grant U. Hess took over as editor, but in January 1892 Lamoreaux bought Bonney's interest and returned to the helm. Dennis characterized the two as gypsy printers who wanted to try their hands at editing. Lamoreaux sold out a few months later and moved to St. Anthony. He died of consumption in January 1895 at Albion.

It appeared the newspaper was about to fold when George Chapin, who had just sold his ranch near Albion, came looking for an investment and purchased Lamoreaux's and Dennis's shares "at a real bargain price," paying off the libel judgment. Chapin had worked as an editor in New York City, and by April 6, 1893, he was listed as the editor of the *Times*.

But hard times persisted, and the *Times* passed through a series of ownership changes. The April 18, 1901, issue announced a sale to Charles P. Diehl. "The best interest of the town, community and Democratic party will be upheld," the new *Times* owner declared, but Diehl's tenure was also short-lived. He sold out to F. A. Darc in 1903. Darc immediately changed the paper's support to the Republican party but lasted only about a year, selling to Bert P. Mill, who in turn sold out in 1915 to William S. Snyder and one of the newspaper's original founders, Sam Dennis.

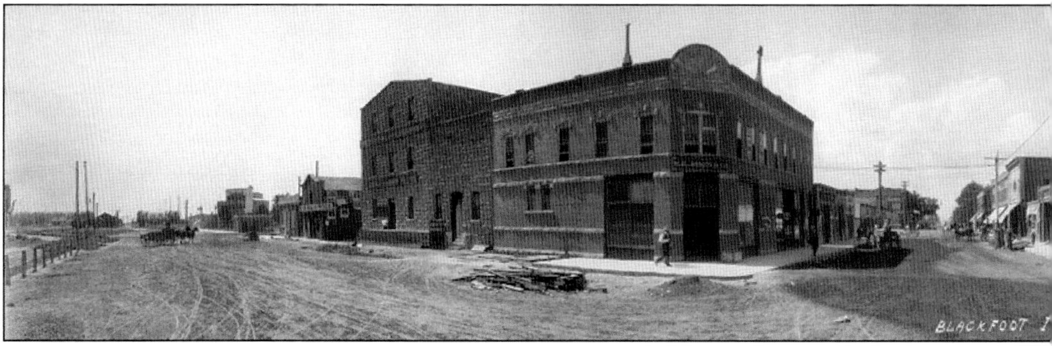

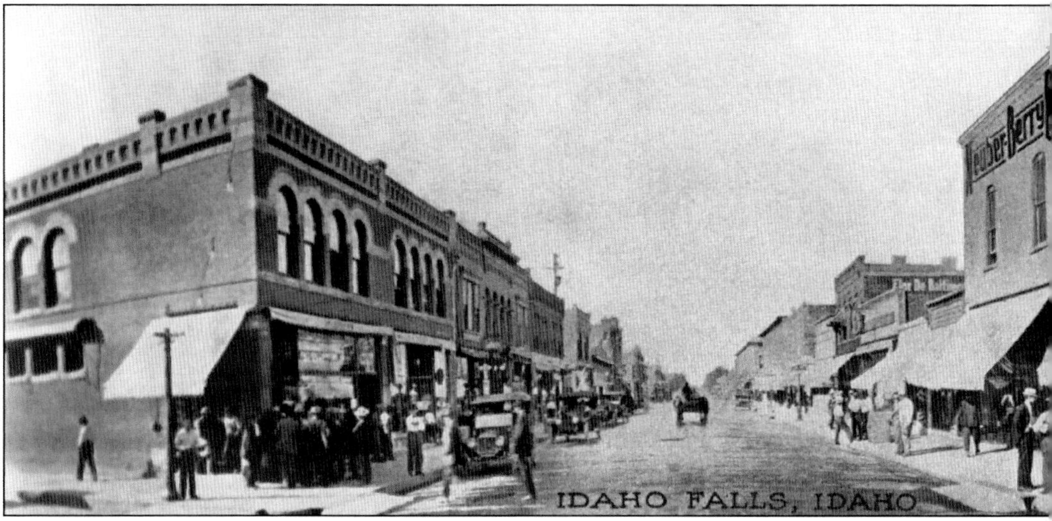

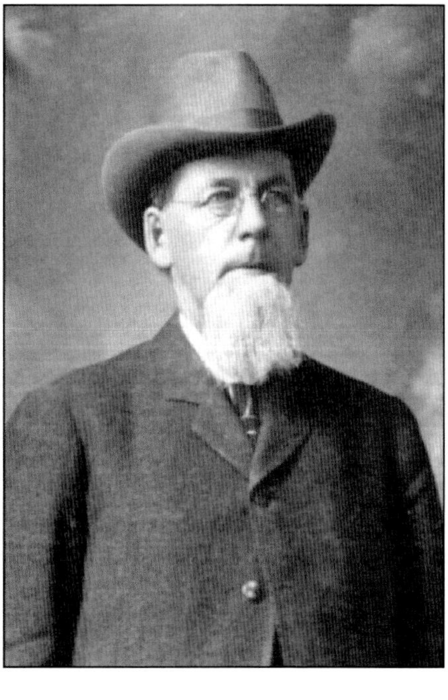

This studio portrait of *Register* editor William Wheeler shows him as he appeared about the time he was serving as Idaho Falls postmaster.

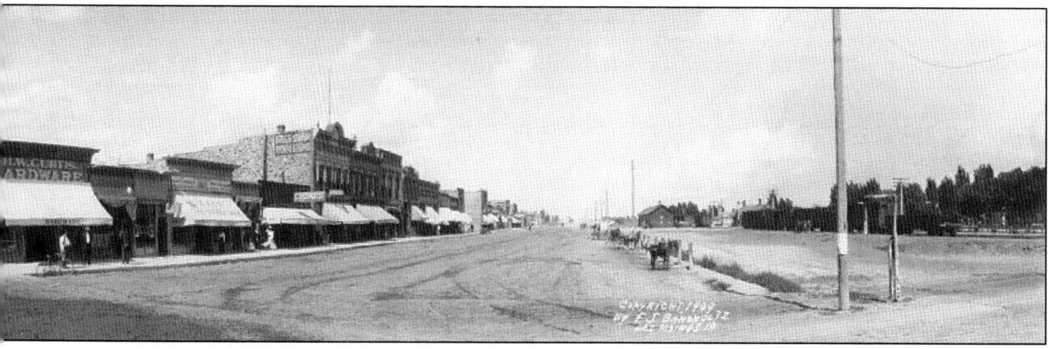

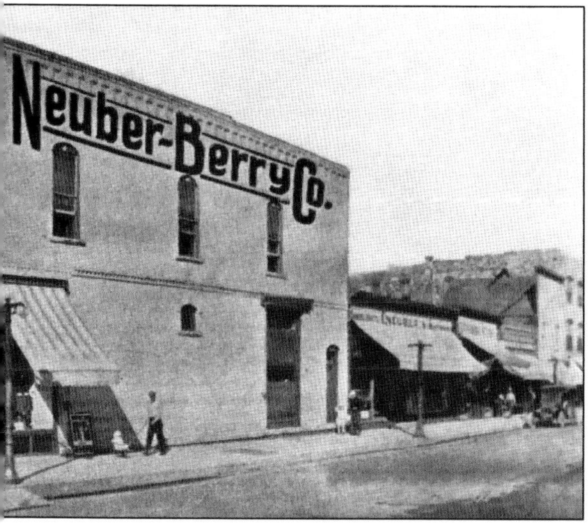

The above panoramic view of Blackfoot was taken about 1909. When the railroad arrived in 1880, the town was already well established while Eagle Rock was little more than a toll bridge. A similar panoramic view of Idaho Falls, on the left, was also taken in about 1909 and shows that by then the town had caught up with Blackfoot and surpassed it. (National Archives and Records Administration.)

Elizabeth Macey Daugherty was teaching school in Denver when she met William E. Wheeler. This photograph was taken for the newspaper's 50th anniversary Golden Jubilee edition in 1934. "She was a quiet-spoken, kindly soul who always surprised people not well-acquainted with her by the keen Irish wit and humor behind her sweet smile," according to an unsigned manuscript at the Museum of Idaho. The couple had no children but offered lodging so students could attend school in town. The boys often worked at the newspaper office. According to a contemporary account, Wheeler would tell them on their first Saturday night in town, "Tomorrow is Sunday and Mrs. Wheeler and I go to Sunday school and church. As long as you are with us we will expect you to attend some Sunday school."

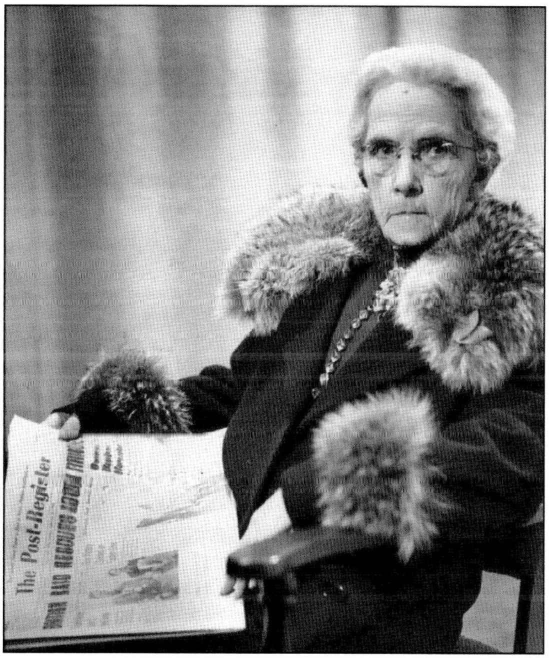

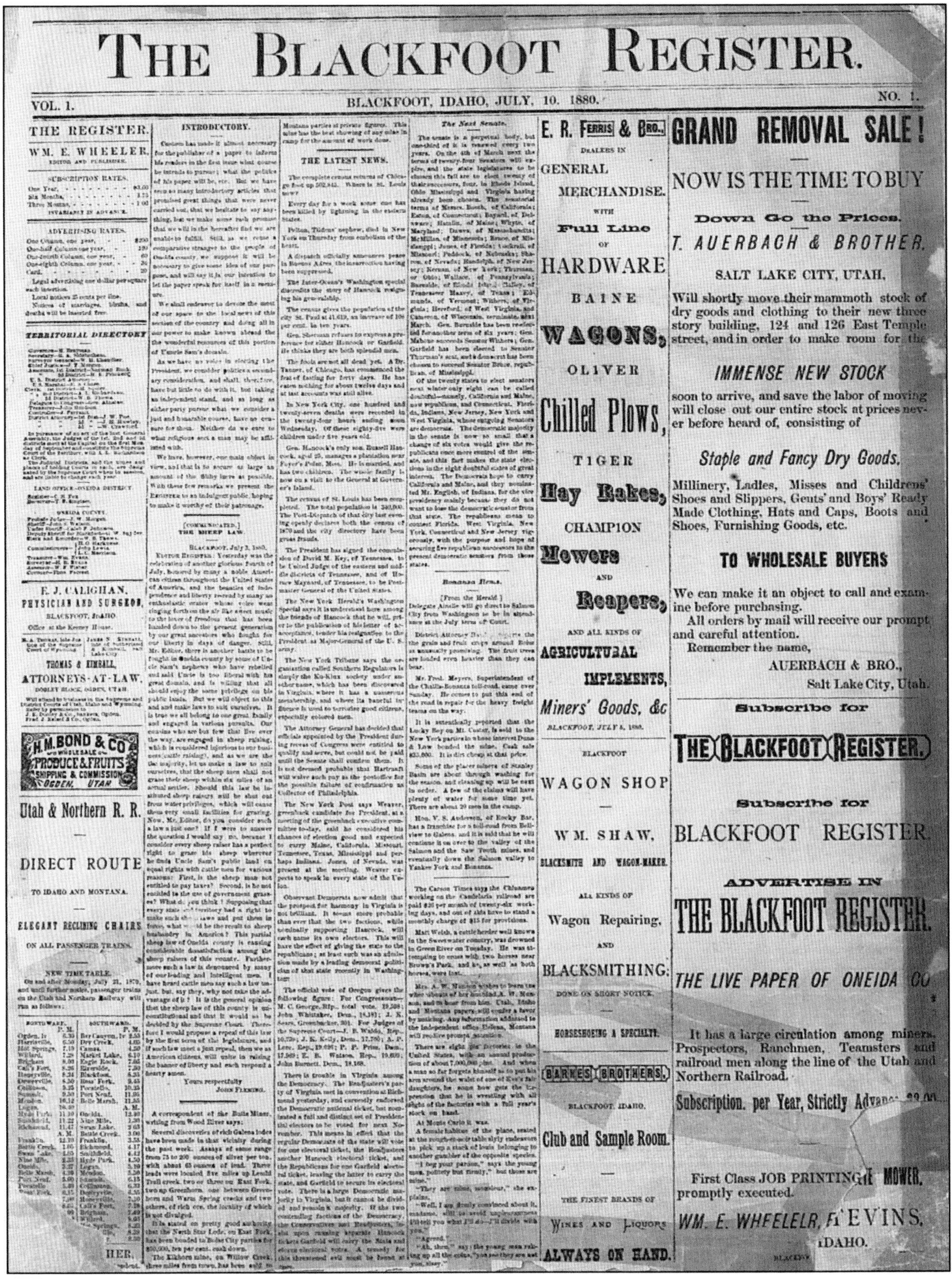

THE BLACKFOOT REGISTER.

VOL. 1. BLACKFOOT, IDAHO, JULY, 10. 1880. NO. 1.

THE REGISTER.

WM. E. WHEELER,

EDITOR AND PUBLISHER.

SUBSCRIPTION RATES.

ADVERTISING RATES.

TERRITORIAL DIRECTORY

INTRODUCTORY.

THE LATEST NEWS.

The Next Senate.

E. J. CALIGHAN,

PHYSICIAN AND SURGEON,

BLACKFOOT, IDAHO.

THOMAS & KIMBALL,

ATTORNEYS-AT-LAW,

H. M. BOND & CO

WHOLESALE

PRODUCE & FRUITS

SHIPPING & COMMISSION

OGDEN, UTAH

Utah & Northern R. R.

DIRECT ROUTE

TO IDAHO AND MONTANA.

ELEGANT RECLINING CHAIRS

ON ALL PASSENGER TRAINS.

NEW TIME TABLE.

THE SHEEP LAW.

Bonanza Items.

E. R. FERRIS & BRO.

DEALERS IN

GENERAL

MERCHANDISE.

WITH

Full Line

OF

HARDWARE

BAINE

WAGONS,

OLIVER

Chilled Plows,

TIGER

Hay Rakes,

CHAMPION

Mowers

AND

Reapers,

AND ALL KINDS OF

AGRICULTURAL

IMPLEMENTS,

Miners' Goods, &c

BLACKFOOT

WAGON SHOP

WM. SHAW,

BLACKSMITH AND WAGON-MAKER.

ALL KINDS OF

Wagon Repairing,

AND

BLACKSMITHING.

DONE ON SHORT NOTICE.

HORSESHOEING A SPECIALTY.

BARNES BROTHERS,

BLACKFOOT, IDAHO.

Club and Sample Room.

THE FINEST BRANDS OF

WINES AND LIQUORS

ALWAYS ON HAND.

GRAND REMOVAL SALE!

NOW IS THE TIME TO BUY

Down Go the Prices.

T. AUERBACH & BROTHER,

SALT LAKE CITY, UTAH,

Will shortly move their mammoth stock of dry goods and clothing to their new three story building, 124 and 126 East Temple street, and in order to make room for the

IMMENSE NEW STOCK

soon to arrive, and save the labor of moving will close out our entire stock at prices never before heard of, consisting of

Staple and Fancy Dry Goods,

Millinery, Ladies, Misses and Childrens' Shoes and Slippers, Gents' and Boys' Ready Made Clothing, Hats and Caps, Boots and Shoes, Furnishing Goods, etc.

TO WHOLESALE BUYERS

We can make it an object to call and examine before purchasing.

All orders by mail will receive our prompt and careful attention.

Remember the name,

AUERBACH & BRO.,

Salt Lake City, Utah.

Subscribe for

THE BLACKFOOT REGISTER.

Subscribe for

BLACKFOOT REGISTER.

ADVERTISE IN

THE BLACKFOOT REGISTER.

THE LIVE PAPER OF ONEIDA CO

It has a large circulation among miners, Prospectors, Ranchmen, Teamsters and railroad men along the line of the Utah and Northern Railroad.

Subscription, per Year, Strictly Advance

First Class JOB PRINTING promptly executed.

WM. E. WHEELER, [illegible] IDAHO.

The first edition of the *Blackfoot Register* was printed on July 10, 1880, just a few weeks after William E. Wheeler arrived by train from Evanston, Wyoming.

The press room at the *Register* is pictured with compositors—including Elizabeth Wheeler in the center—setting type by hand.

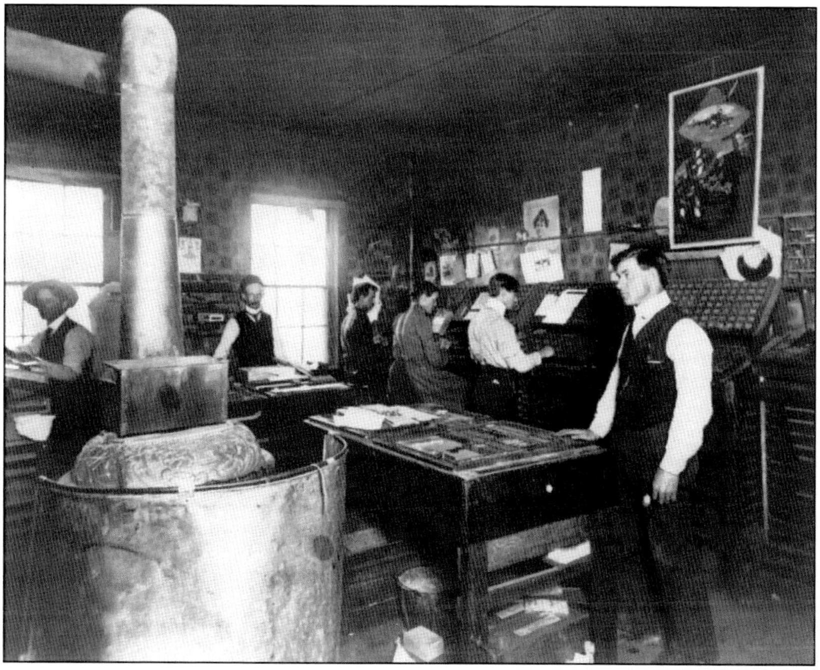

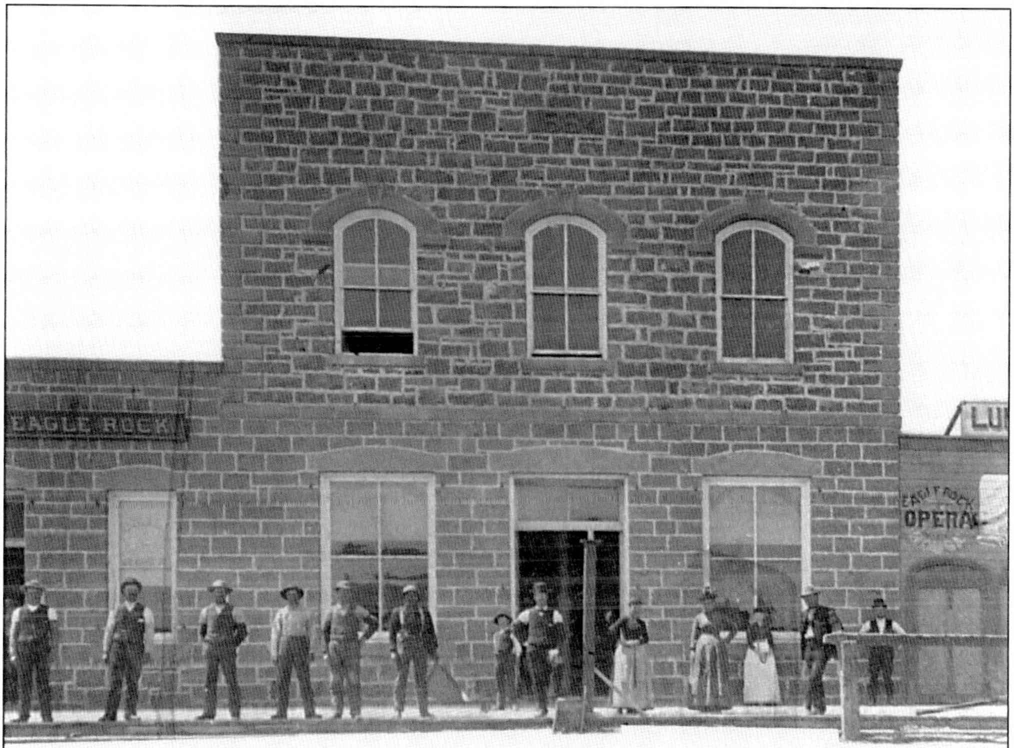

By about 1900, Idaho Falls boasted a bank and an opera. The basalt two-story building was built in 1884, but names on the bank and opera house say "Eagle Rock," not Idaho Falls, as the town was called by 1891. (Benneville Historical Society.)

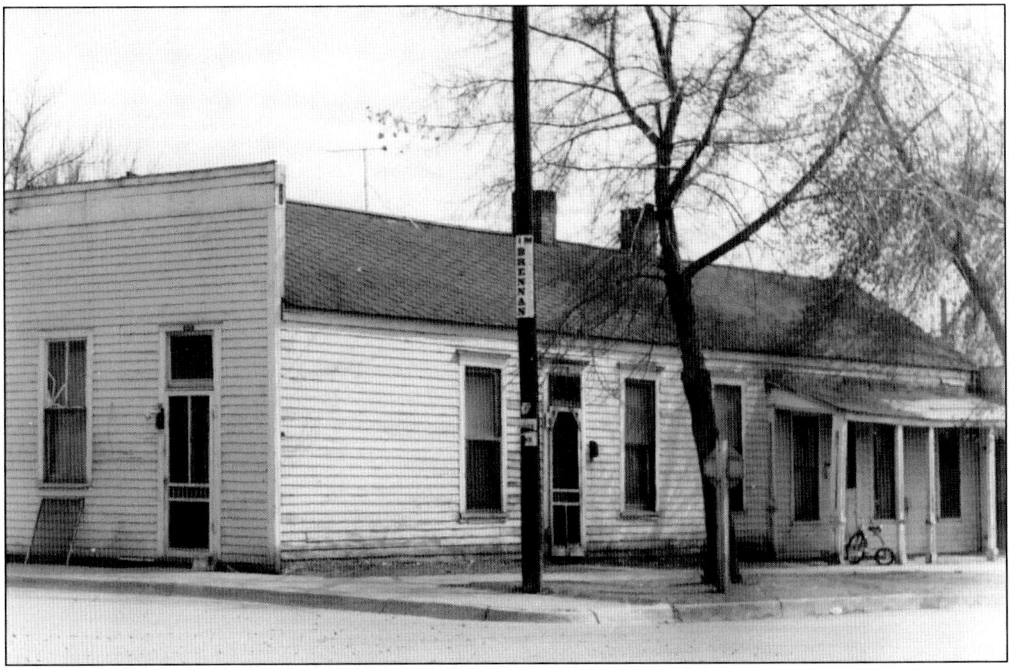

The *Register* building was on Cliff Street near the end of Capital Avenue. The Wheelers lived and worked here until moving into a larger building in about 1904.

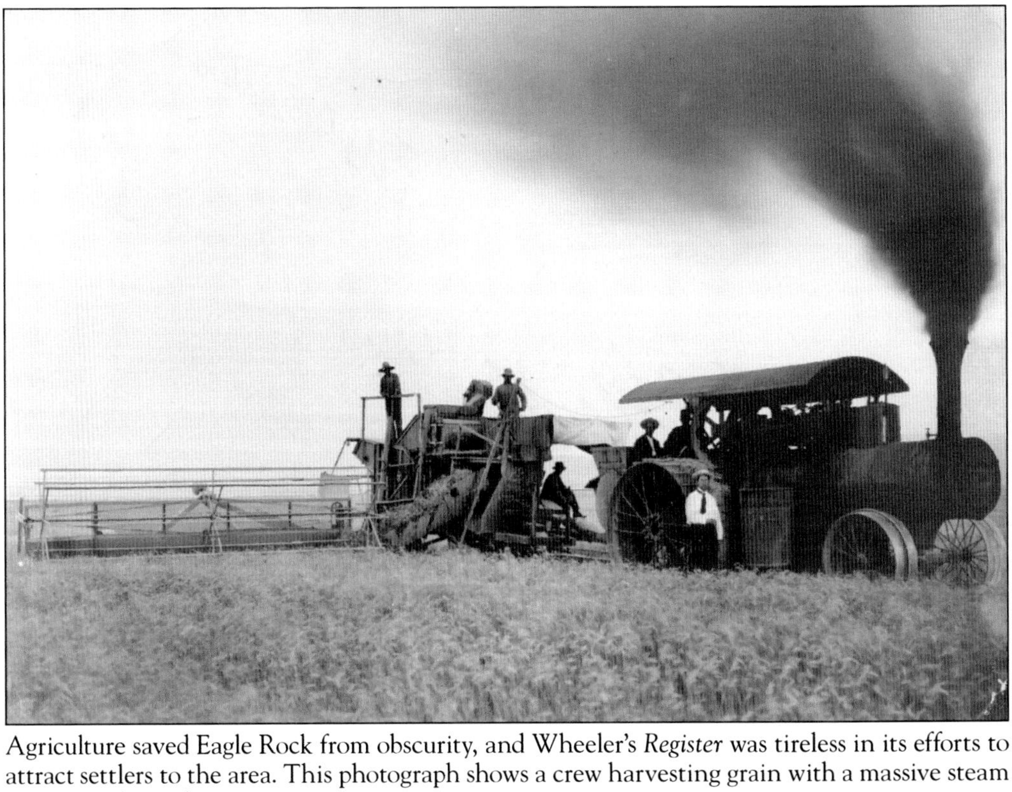

Agriculture saved Eagle Rock from obscurity, and Wheeler's *Register* was tireless in its efforts to attract settlers to the area. This photograph shows a crew harvesting grain with a massive steam tractor in the early 1900s.

These hunters gathered around a fireplace near Henry's Lake in Island Park were photographed by William Henry Jackson in 1872. Outfitters made money guiding hunting trips in the Island Park and Jackson Hole areas around the park, but friction developed between them and Native Americans from Fort Hall who had treaty rights to hunt in these areas as well. In 1895, outfitters concocted a story about a Native American massacre at Jackson Hole.

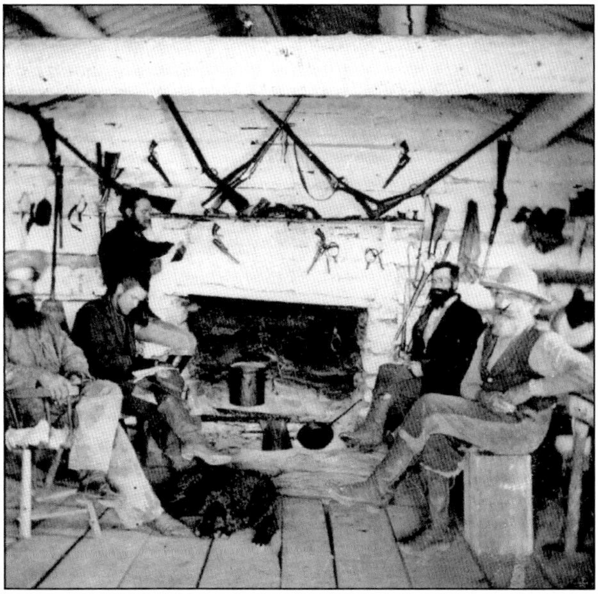

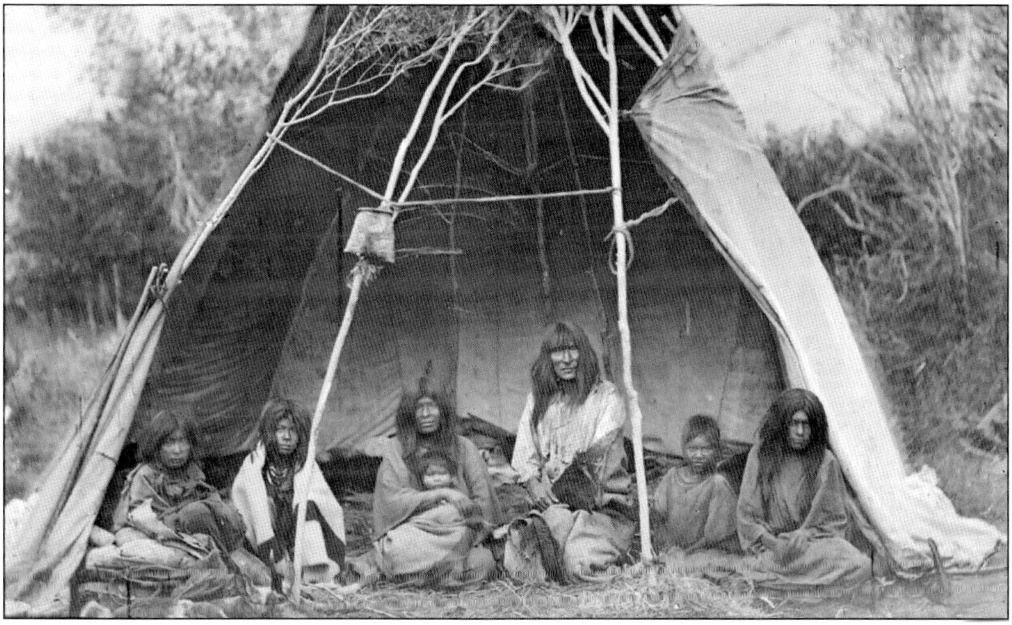

Bannock Indians of eastern Idaho and extreme western Wyoming used teepees like this or grass huts. Suffering from starvation and neglect at the Fort Hall reservation, the Bannocks and a few others left in 1878 and fought several battles with the U.S. Cavalry before survivors returned to the reservation. Hostilities broke out again in 1895, when a group of outfitters concocted a story about a massacre at Jackson Hole. "EVERYONE IS KILLED," announced the *Chicago Inter-Ocean*; "Indians commit wholesale murder at Jackson's Hole." "Bannocks Kill a Settler, His Wife and Child, and They are Pursued," announced the *Omaha World Herald*. There was no massacre. The outfitters had arrested nine Native Americans from Fort Hall at Jackson Hole, disarmed them, and killed one at the end of a day's march in what was reported as an escape attempt. During the melee, another was seriously wounded and two children were lost; one was never found. The *Idaho Register* ridiculed the trumped-up war.

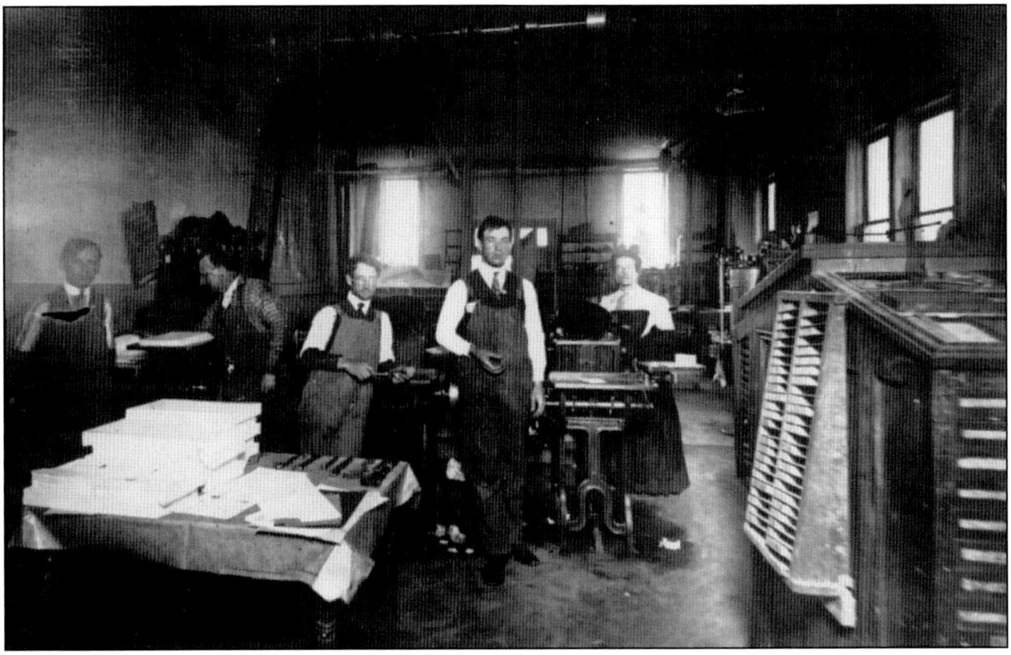

Wheeler (center) and his assistants hand-set type out of so-called California type cases in an early photograph of the newspaper. "At that time printers were mostly transients, out to see the country and would stay a few days or perhaps one day and be gone," Elizabeth Wheeler recalled years later. "Although it was easy to get others to take their places, I insisted to Mr. Wheeler that we learn to set type so that if the time came when we should find ourselves without help we could get out a paper of some kind. That time came too," she said in 1934.

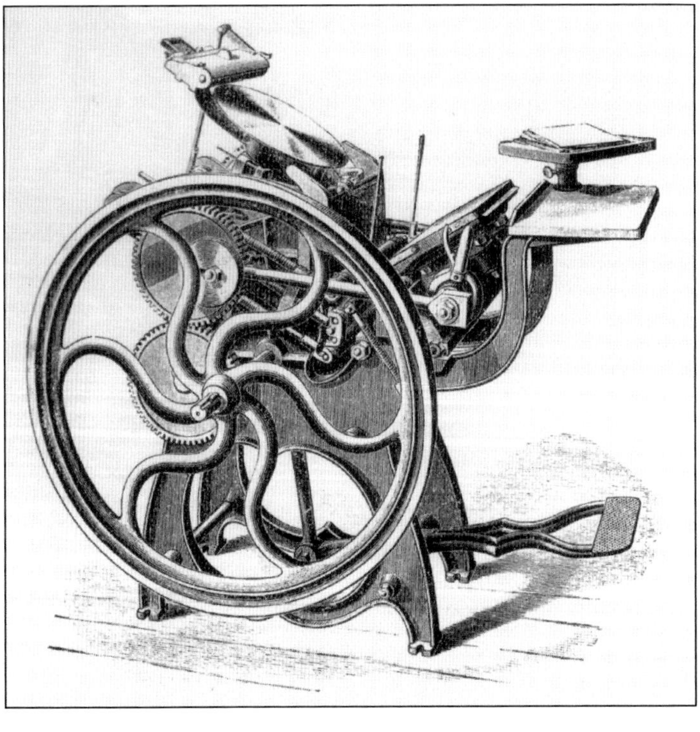

The *Register*'s first presses were simple foot-powered models like this *c.* 1900 Eclipse, a clamshell job press popular in the West because it was easy to operate and repair. They were not designed specifically for newspaper production, but most of the *Register*'s business came from its print shop: fliers, letterhead, butter wrappers, and occasional circus posters. These presses were slow and could only produce a two-page single-sheet edition at one run. Newspapers quickly outgrew these all-purpose job presses.

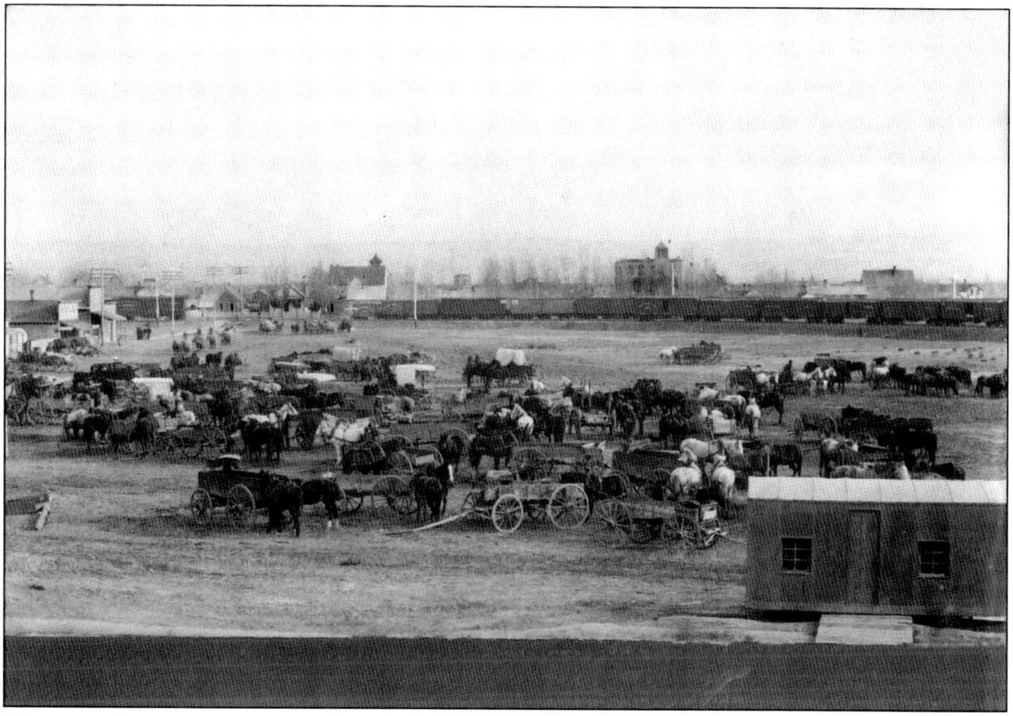

Horse-and-wagon teams gather for unloading near the railroad yards in Idaho Falls. (Perk's Photo collection.)

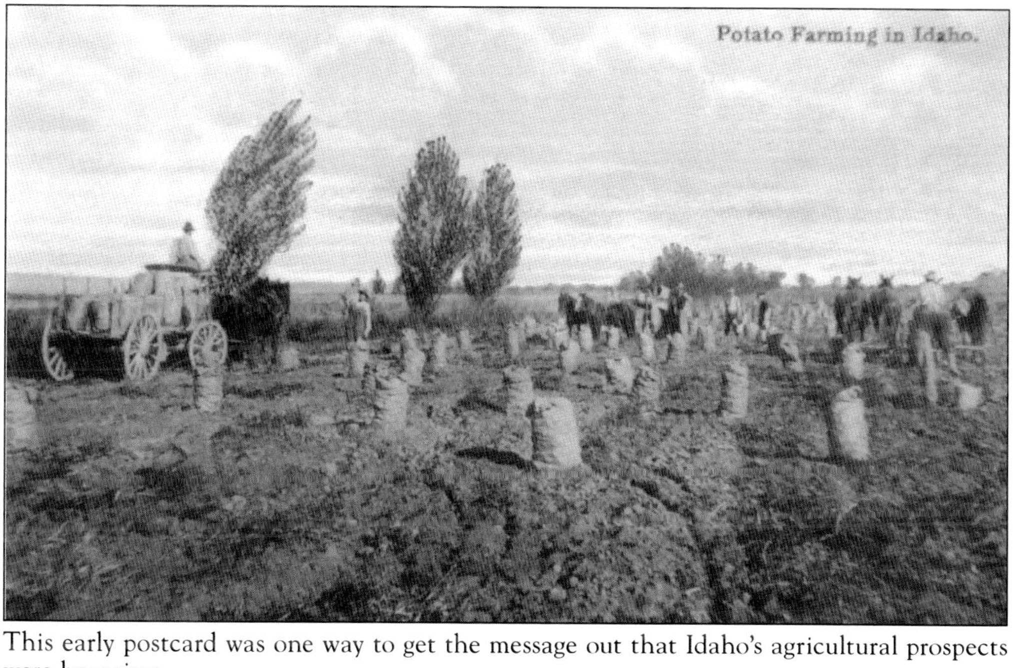

This early postcard was one way to get the message out that Idaho's agricultural prospects were booming.

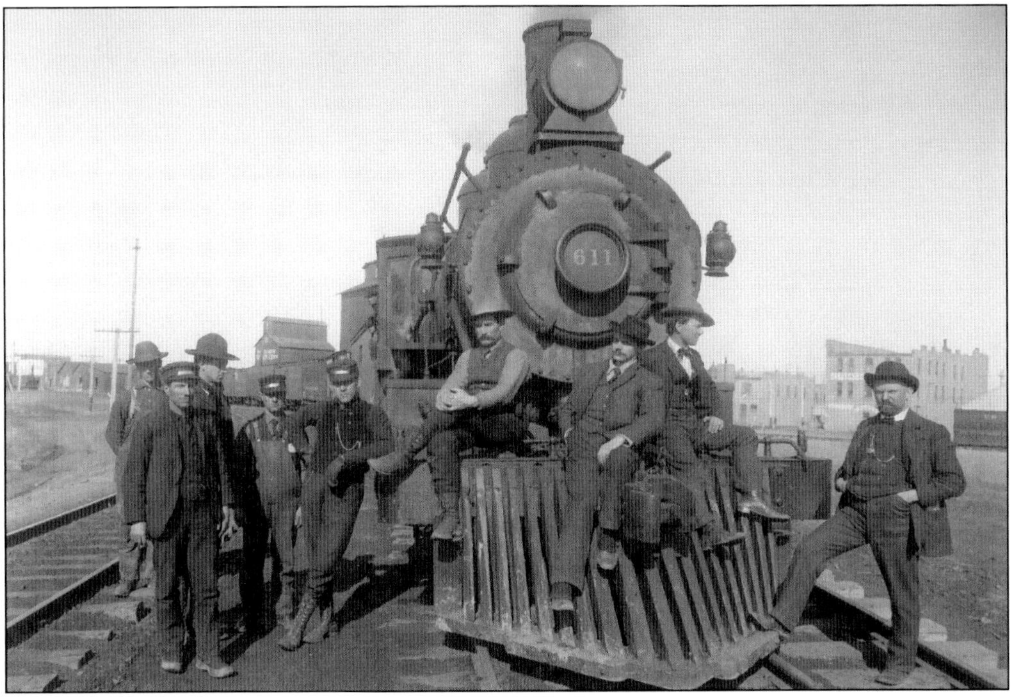

The *Register* was often at odds with the railroad and its often high-handed superintendents. These two photographs from the early 1900s were recently found behind a filing cabinet at the *Post Register*. The above photograph shows the back of Broadway (right side); the photograph below was taken in front of the town's first passenger depot at Yellowstone and Broadway. For a time, the railroad provided most of the town's law enforcement under a cooperative agreement with the city.

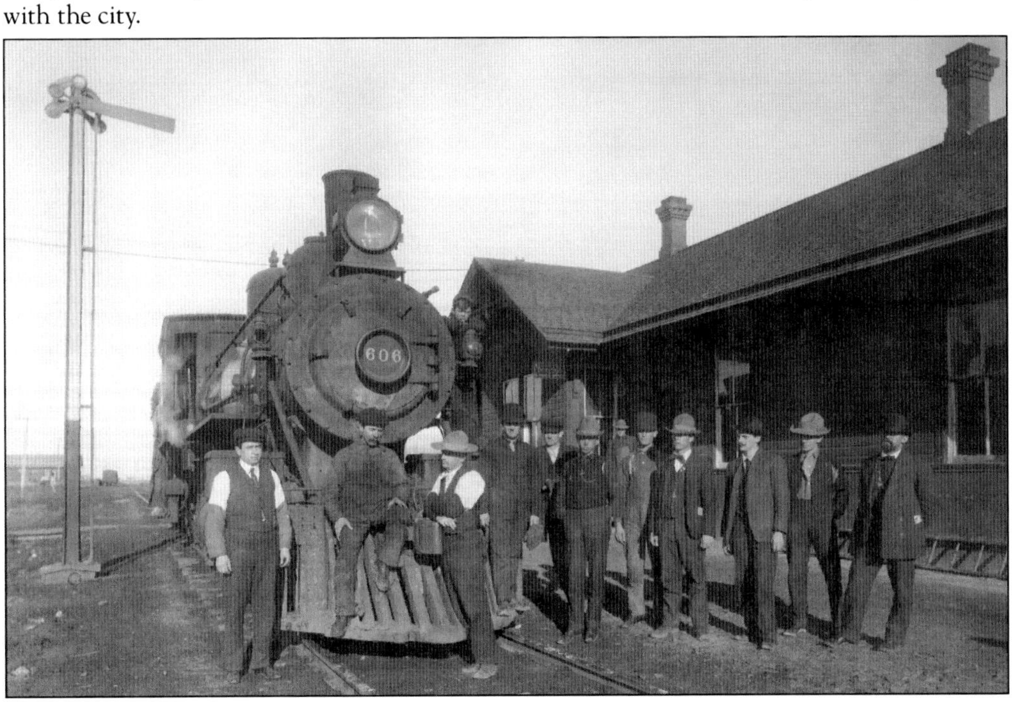

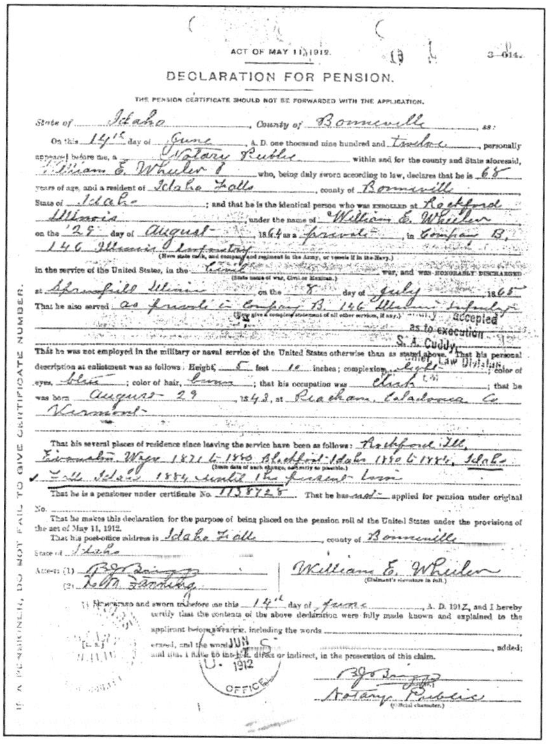

ACT OF MAY 11, 1912. 3-614.

DECLARATION FOR PENSION.

THE PENSION CERTIFICATE SHOULD NOT BE FORWARDED WITH THE APPLICATION.

State of Idaho, County of Bonneville, ss:

On this 14th day of June, A. D. one thousand nine hundred and twelve, personally appeared before me, a Notary Public within and for the county and State aforesaid, William E. Wheeler, who, being duly sworn according to law, declares that he is 68 years of age, and a resident of Idaho Falls, county of Bonneville, State of Idaho; and that he is the identical person who was ENROLLED at Rockford Illinois under the name of William E. Wheeler on the 29 day of August, 1864, as a private in Company B, 146 Illinois Infantry (Here state rank, and company and regiment in the Army, or vessels if in the Navy.) in the service of the United States, in the Civil war, and was HONORABLY DISCHARGED at Springfield Illinois on the 8 day of July, 1865.

That he also served as private in Company B 146 Illinois Infantry (Here give a complete statement of all other services, if any.)

Accepted as to execution S. A. Cuddy, Chief Law Division

That he was not employed in the military or naval service of the United States otherwise than as stated above. That his personal description at enlistment was as follows: Height, 5 feet 10 inches; complexion, light; color of eyes, blue; color of hair, brown; that his occupation was clerk; that he was born August 29, 1843, at Peacham, Caledonia Co. Vermont.

That his several places of residence since leaving the service have been as follows: Rockford Ill, Evanston Wyo 1871 to 1880 Blackfoot Idaho 1880 to 1884, Idaho Falls Idaho 1884, until the present time (State date of each change, as nearly as possible.)

That he is a pensioner under certificate No. 1158728. That he has not applied for pension under original No.

That he makes this declaration for the purpose of being placed on the pension roll of the United States under the provisions of the act of May 11, 1912.

That his post-office address is Idaho Falls, county of Bonneville, State of Idaho.

Attest: (1) B. J. Briggs (2) [illegible]

William E. Wheeler (Claimant's signature in full.)

Subscribed and sworn to before me this 14th day of June, A. D. 1912, and I hereby certify that the contents of the above declaration were fully made known and explained to the applicant before swearing, including the words ... erased, and the words ... added; and that I have no interest, direct or indirect, in the prosecution of this claim.

JUN 5 1912 OFFICE

B. J. Briggs, Notary Public (Official character.)

IF A PENSIONER, DO NOT FAIL TO GIVE CERTIFICATE NUMBER.

Pictured is William E. Wheeler's 1912 application for a Civil War pension when he was 68 and already retired from his newspaper. The application shows that he served as a private in the 146th Illinois Infantry. Capt. Dick Chamberlain, who ran the town's first saloon, declined a pension even when he was in some financial difficulties. (William Stibal Pettite.)

This photograph of the *Register* office shows an older Wheeler in beard and cutaway coat, probably taken prior to the *Register*'s move to Broadway in 1904. Hot lead for casting type was heated on a pot-bellied stove (left). No wonder Wheeler was concerned about the fire hazard posed by weak water pressure and wood-frame buildings in downtown Idaho Falls.

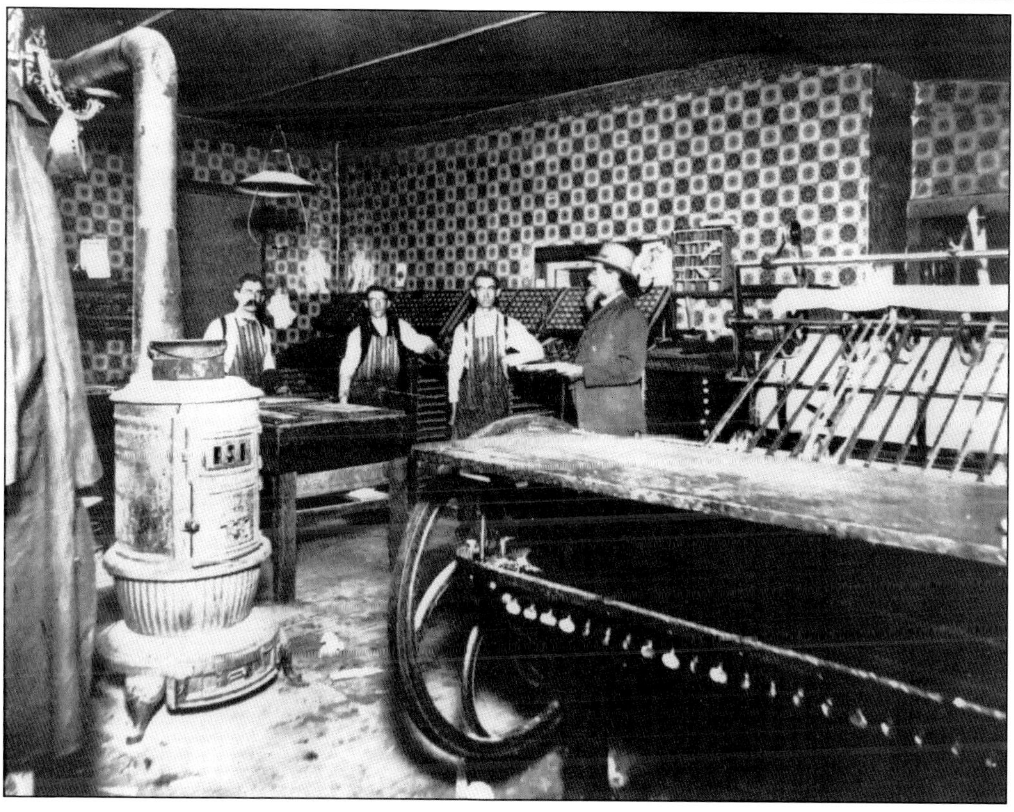

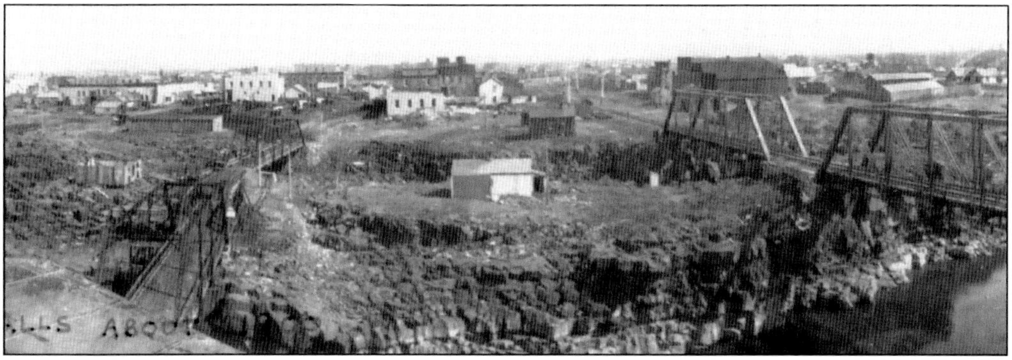

Just prior to the dawn of the 20th century, a small group of Idaho Falls women formed the Village Improvement Society with the goal of cleaning up the town. Led by Kate Curley, Rebecca Mitchell, Minnie Hitt, and Elizabeth Wheeler, the VIS bought the rocky outcroppings along the river (above) where brothels were located from the city for $1, razed the houses, and forced out the so-called "obnoxious element." It did not stop the trade. (Bonneville County Historical Society.)

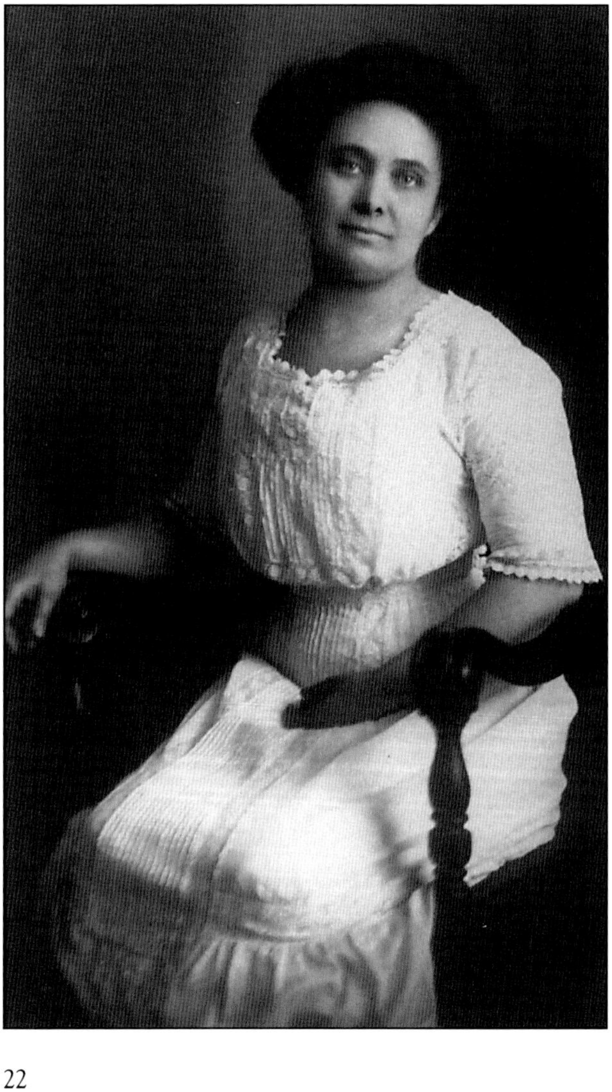

Minnie G. Hitt, who started out as a clerk at C. C. Anderson's store, became a banker who helped many of the town's early businesses thrive. (Bonneville County Historical Society.)

VIS member Rebecca Mitchell was a Baptist missionary credited with starting the town's first school and church and, with her daughter, launching the city's first library. She was pro-temperance and wrote a weekly column in the *Idaho Falls Times*. She used her column to highlight other early settlers to the area and to promote the reform platform of the *Times*.

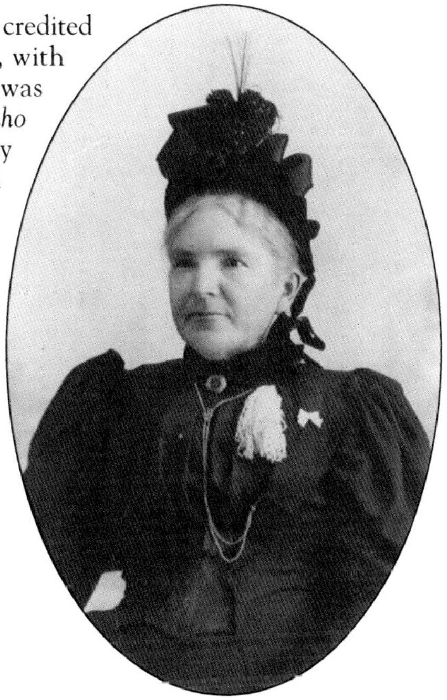

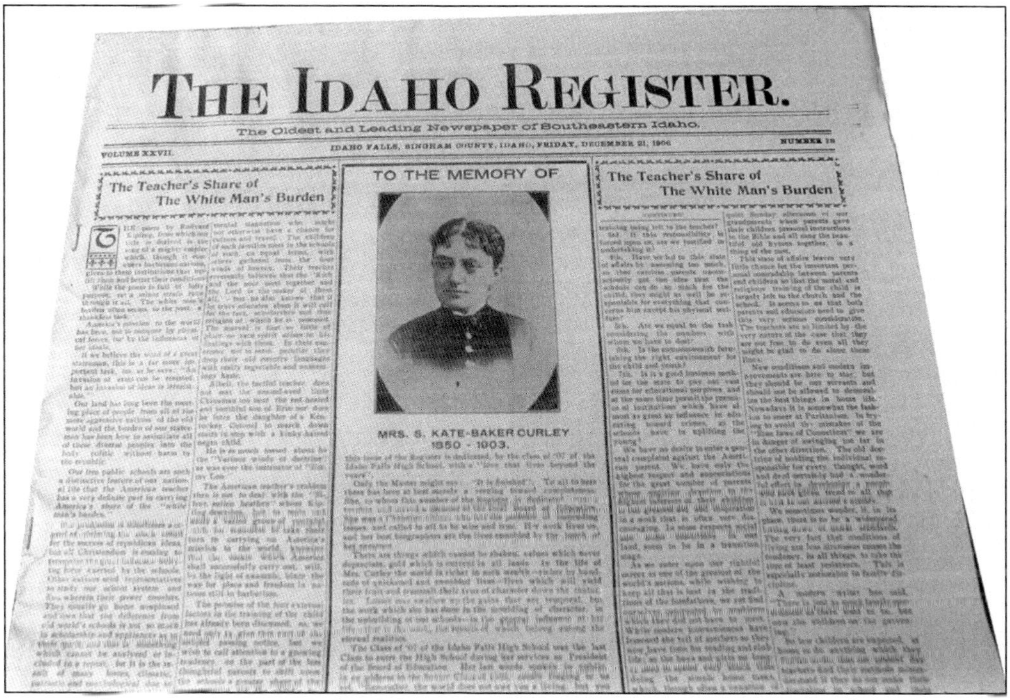

THE IDAHO REGISTER.

The Oldest and Leading Newspaper of Southeastern Idaho.

VOLUME XXVII. IDAHO FALLS, BINGHAM COUNTY, IDAHO, FRIDAY, DECEMBER 21, 1906

The Teacher's Share of The White Man's Burden

TO THE MEMORY OF

MRS. S. KATE-BAKER CURLEY 1850 - 1903.

The Teacher's Share of The White Man's Burden

Kate Curley was a mainstay behind formation of the VIS, which put out litter boxes, founded parks, planted flowers, and imported thousands of hardwood seedlings. The society spearheaded a decade-long fund drive culminating in creation of the Carnegie Library, now the Museum of Idaho. The *Register* memorialized her contributions in a special edition published three years after her 1903 death from cancer. Kate Curley Park became one of the VIS's projects, with donations from Curley's husband, Bowen, a local banker.

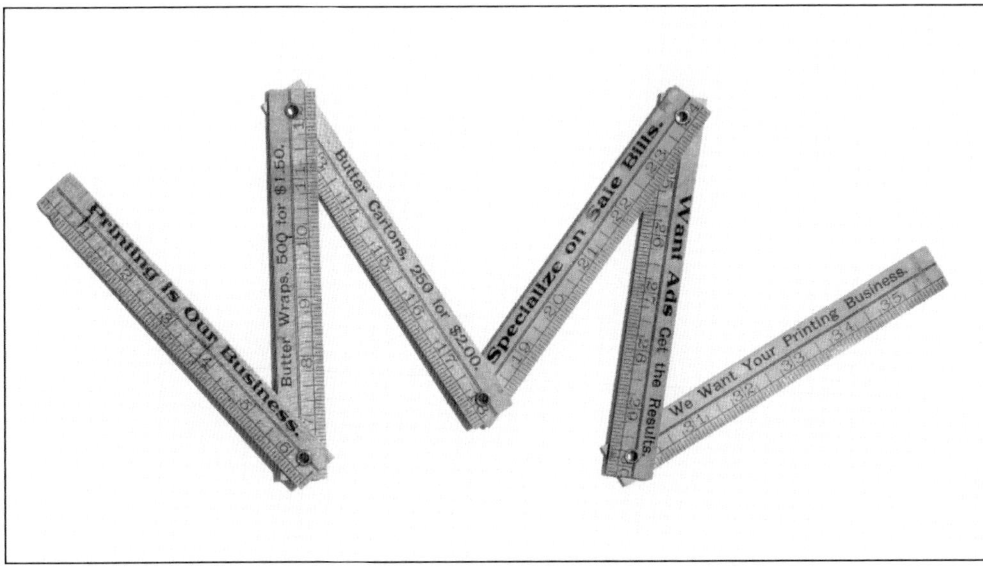

The front and back of this folding wooden ruler offers some information about the newspaper, which gave it out as a subscription incentive or as a gift to loyal customers. The front declares that "Printing is our business" and lists prices for butter wraps and cartons. The back of the ruler gives the *Register*'s location as 256 Broadway and notes subscriptions at the time were $2 for a Tuesday–Friday edition. The rulers were handed out sometime after 1904, when the newspaper moved to its location at the end of Broadway (near the present-day bridge), and before 1920, when the *Register* merged with the *Times*.

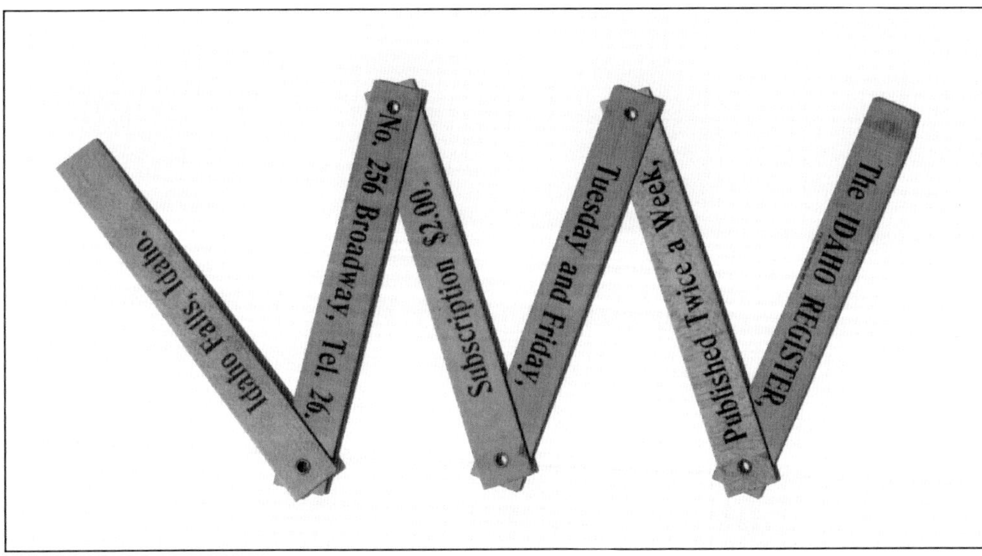

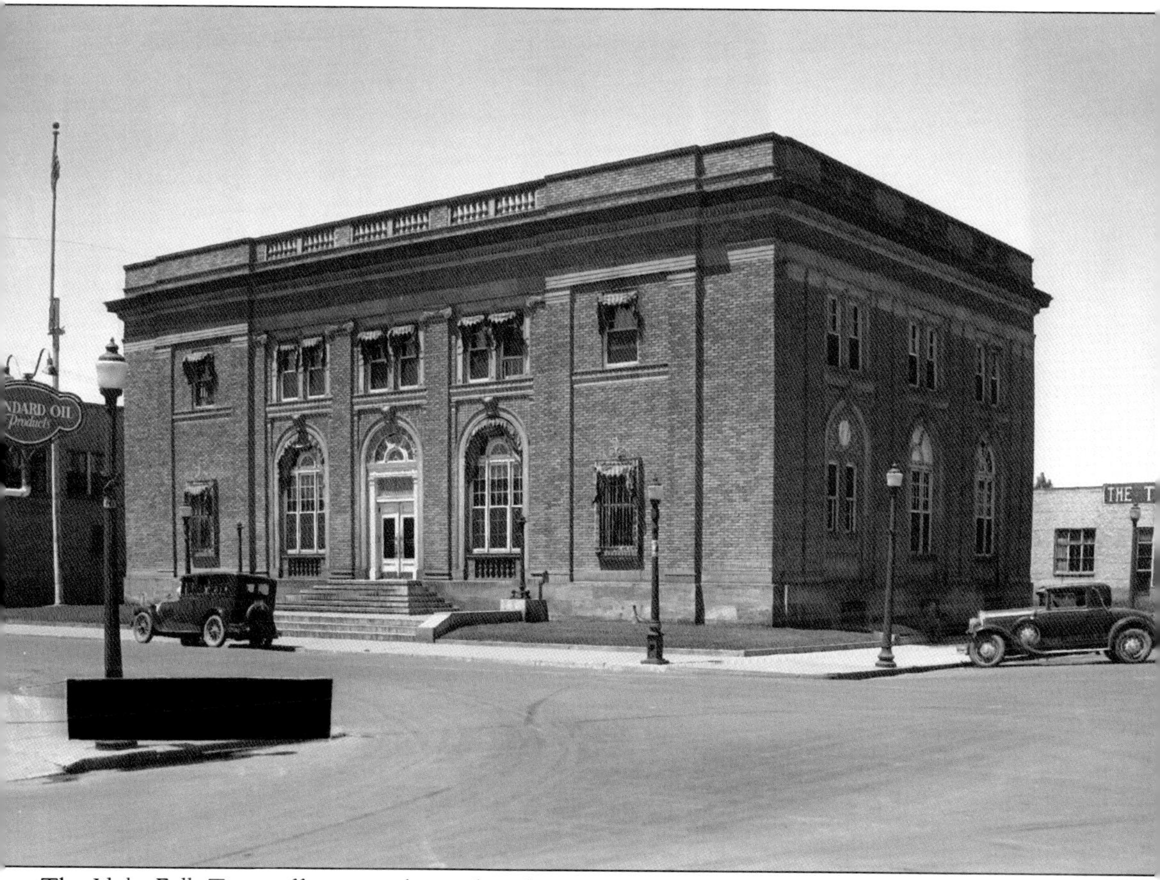

The *Idaho Falls Times* offices were located in the American Legion Hall, 485 Constitution Way, just behind the post office and federal building at 591 North Park Avenue. Newspapers were typically located close to post offices to hasten the sometimes hectic process of mailing papers to subscribers. When the *Register* constructed its new building at 256 Broadway, it housed the post office. For a time, editor William E. Wheeler was also the town's postmaster.

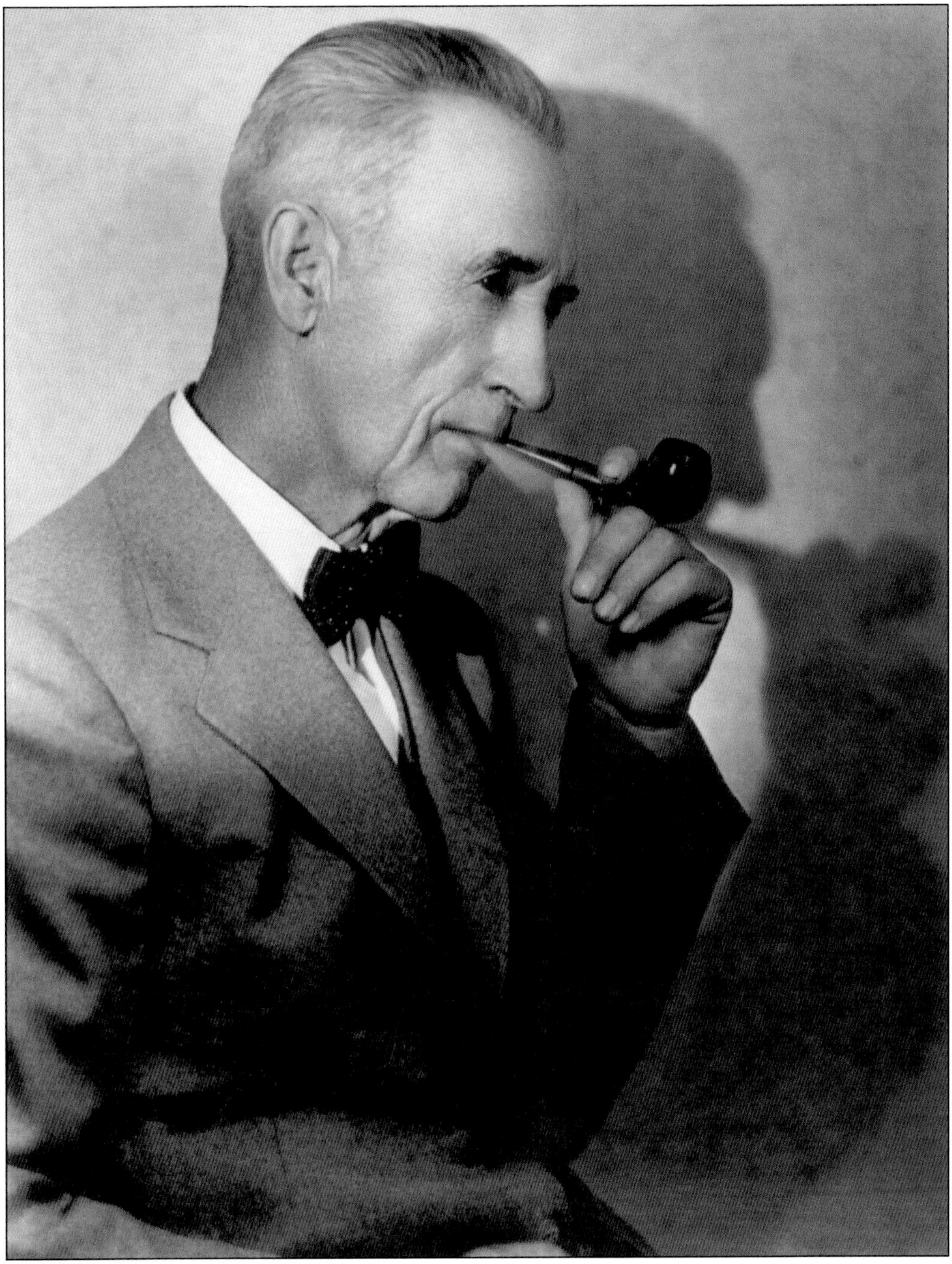

Sam Dennis began as a printer with William Wheeler and launched the rival *Idaho Falls Times* in 1890 with Rufus Bonney. The paper did not thrive, and Dennis took up farming with his wife, Sarah, and their 12 children. He also went back to the *Register* from time to time, and one contemporary account says he edited the *Post* for about a year and a half. Dennis returned to the *Times* as co-owner with William S. Snyder in 1915, and the pair bought the *Register* from M. B. Yeaman in 1920, merging to become the daily *Times-Register*. Dennis retired from newspapers when the *Times* merged with the *Post* in 1931. He was a probate judge when he died on May 31, 1949.

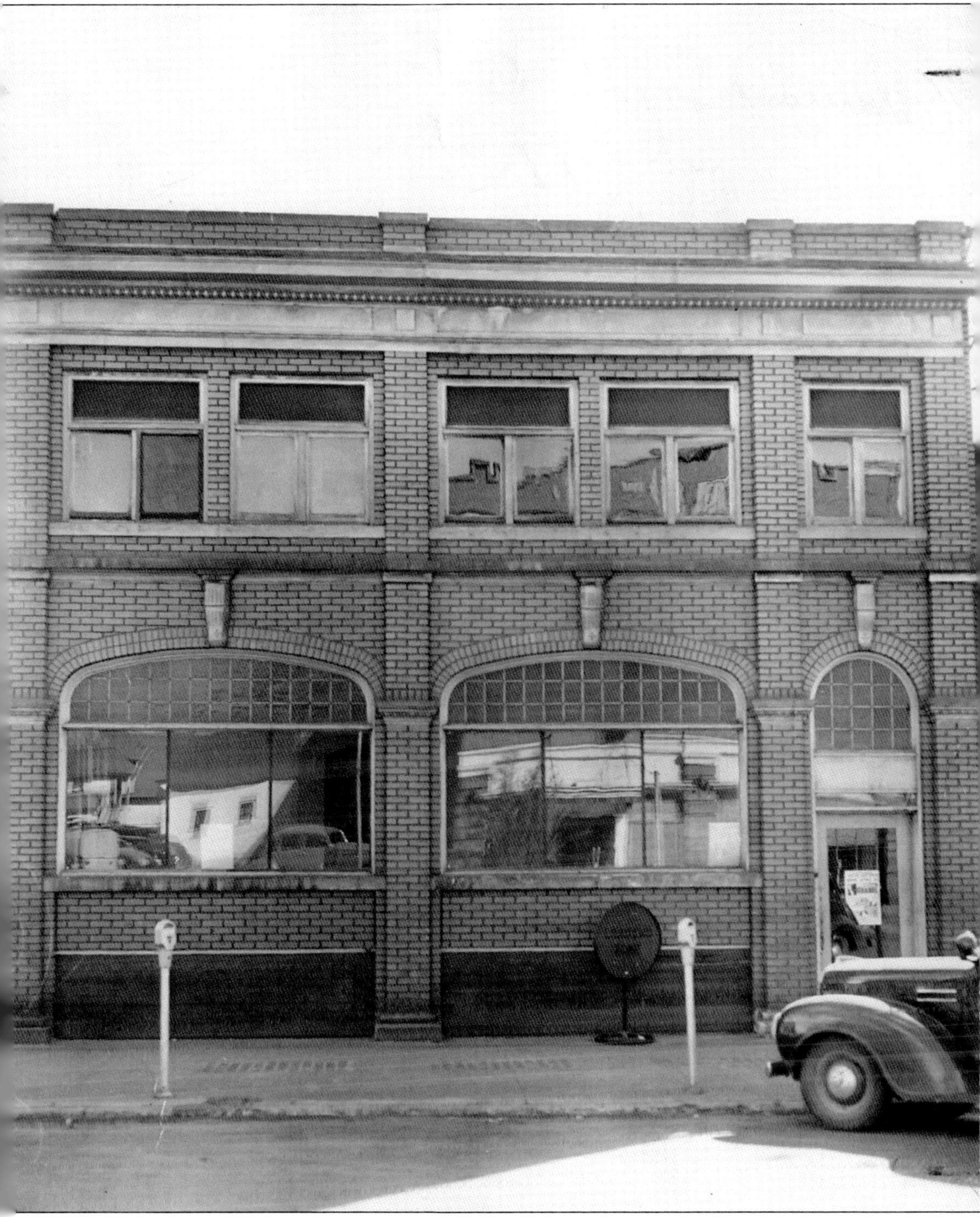

Most of the facade of the American Legion Building shown in this 1949 photograph by Rex Nield is covered now, but the building served as headquarters of the *Idaho Falls Times* from the early 1900s through its merger with the *Register* in 1920 and with the *Post* in 1931. The *Times* occupied the corner offices on the left.

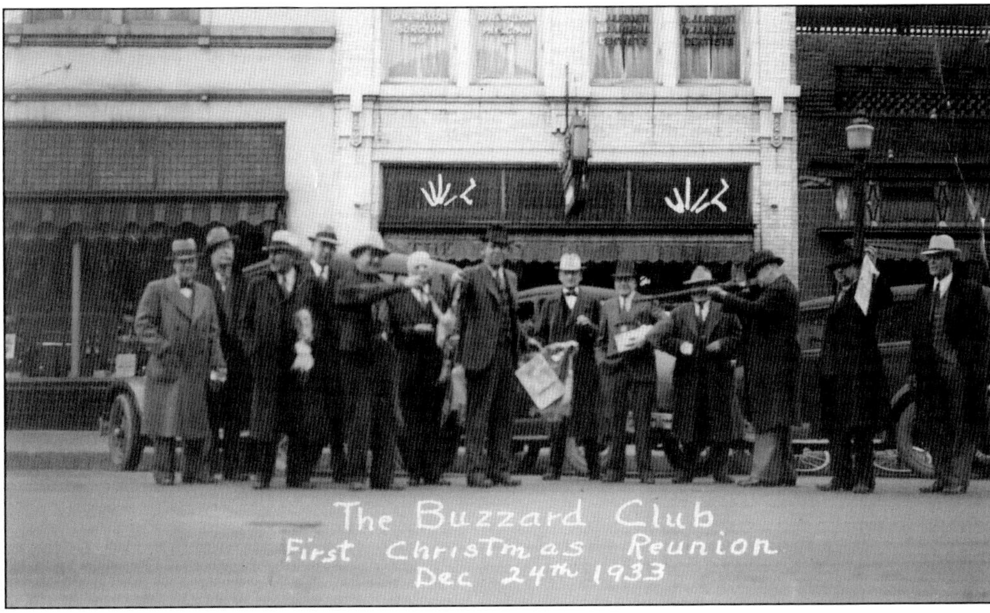

Idaho Falls Times copublisher William S. Snyder (above, far right) was part of the first annual Buzzard Club Christmas Reunion on December 24, 1933. The Buzzard Club was apparently a group of older Rotary Club members. The photograph of the December 25, 1937, reunion (below) shows the familiar Rotary Club gear emblem, right. (Bonneville County Historical Society.)

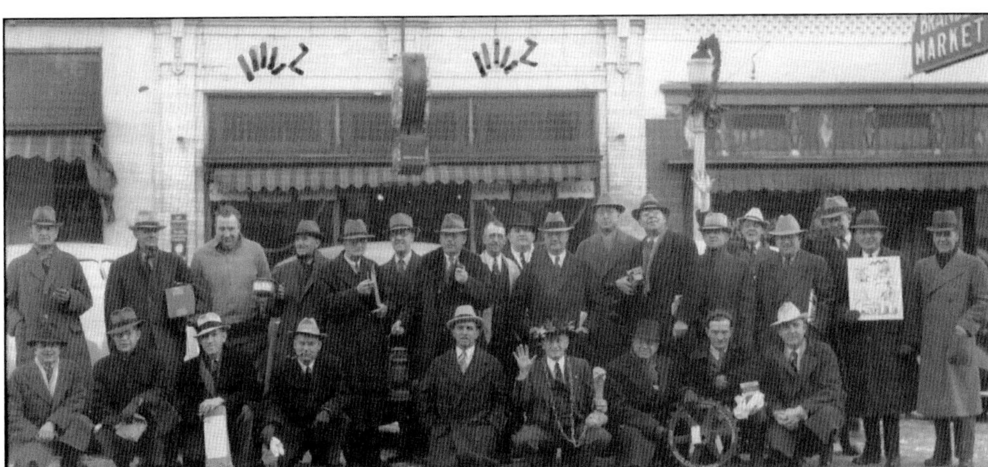

Two

Three-Ring Circus

The competing papers were often at odds. Wheeler's *Register*, usually an ardent civic booster, waged a fight against the city's first power plant, urging the city to concentrate its resources on improving the town's water system. In September 1904, a fire started in a bakery on the north side of Broadway and spread rapidly. Firemen could only stand by and watch, with water pressure capable of shooting water only 20 to 30 feet. Many of the wooden structures along Broadway and Park Avenue almost back to the river were leveled, but the *Times* and the new *Register* offices were only singed. The *Register*'s headline hinted at unheeded warnings: "The Long Predicted Happens."

The same year, Wheeler had purchased the first Simplex automated typesetter. In a front-page story on January 8, 1904, the paper claimed the new machine "will enable us to set much more type for each issue . . . and to do it at less expense, and much faster."

The *Register* upgraded its press and equipment again in 1909, about the time Wheeler retired at age 65. By this time, he had served on the city's first school board, as postmaster, and as a justice of the peace. He was often called "Judge Wheeler" or "Colonel Wheeler," a reference either to his appearance or to his former status as commandant of the Joe Hooker Post of the Grand Army of the Republic.

He and Elizabeth supported a number of civic causes. Elizabeth had been active in the Village Improvement Society, and there were numerous notices in newspaper's columns detailing the latest VIS project and urging participation. She was active in the Presbyterian Church; he was never a member but did attend services regularly.

Marshall Brotherton Yeaman bought a half-interest in the *Register*, continuing Wheeler's strong support of Republican ideals and civic-mindedness. He was active in the chamber of commerce, the Elks, and the Rotary Club, served nine years in the Idaho Legislature, and played an important role in securing better roads and bridges for eastern Idaho.

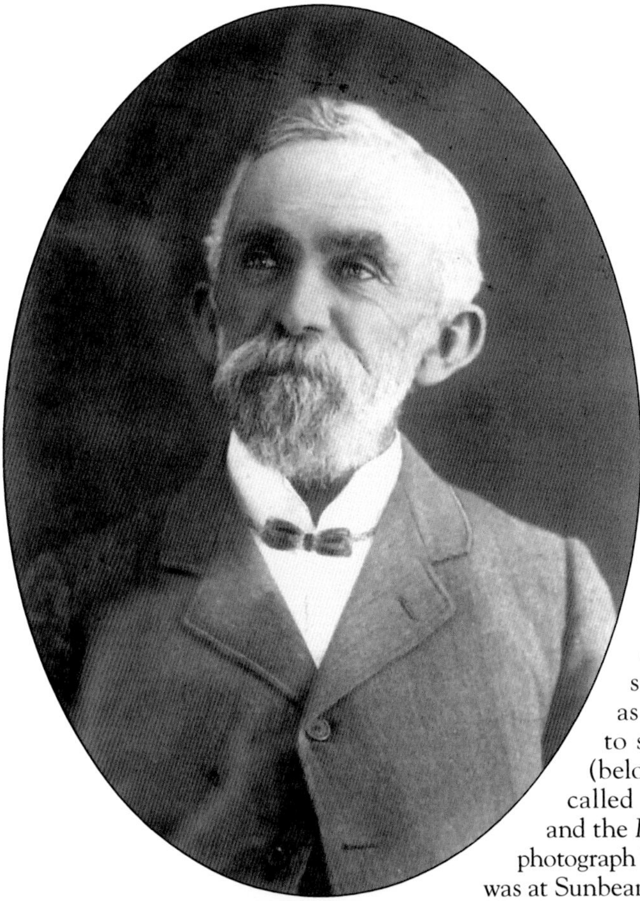

The *Register* opposed Joseph Clark's scheme to bring electricity to Idaho Falls in 1900. Clark, the city's first mayor, died in 1905. Two sons, Barzilla and Chase, served as Idaho Falls mayor. Both went on to serve as governor. Barzilla Clark (below) wrote a self-published history called *Bonneville County in the Making*, and the *Post-Register* printed it in 1941. The photograph below was taken in 1916 while Clark was at Sunbeam.

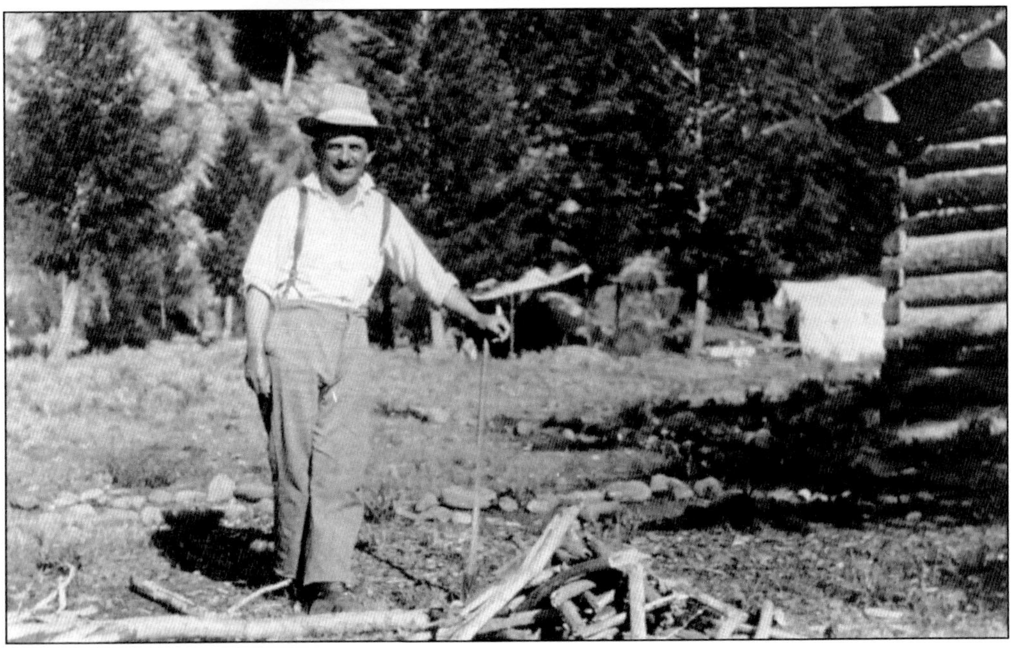

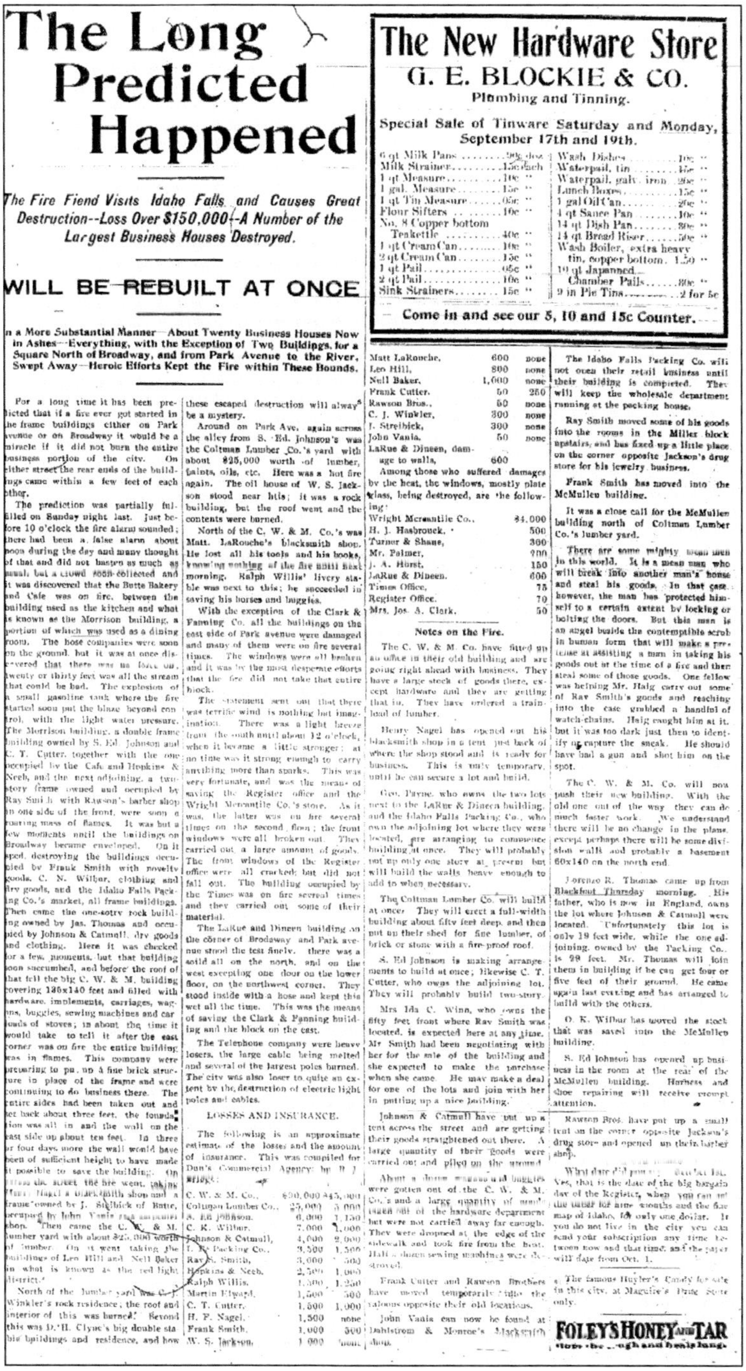

The Long Predicted Happened

The Fire Fiend Visits Idaho Falls and Causes Great Destruction--Loss Over $150,000--A Number of the Largest Business Houses Destroyed.

WILL BE REBUILT AT ONCE

[I]n a More Substantial Manner—About Twenty Business Houses Now in Ashes—Everything, with the Exception of Two Buildings, for a Square North of Broadway, and from Park Avenue to the River, Swept Away—Heroic Efforts Kept the Fire within These Bounds.

For a long time it has been predicted that if a fire ever got started in the frame buildings either on Park avenue or on Broadway it would be a miracle if it did not burn the entire business portion of the city. On either street the rear ends of the buildings came within a few feet of each other.

The prediction was partially fulfilled on Sunday night last. Just before 10 o'clock the fire alarm sounded; there had been a false alarm about noon during the day and many thought of that and did not hasten as much as usual, but a crowd soon collected and it was discovered that the Butte Bakery and Cafe was on fire, between the building used as the kitchen and what is known as the Morrison building, a portion of which was used as a dining room. The hose companies were soon on the ground, but it was at once discovered that there was no force on. Twenty or thirty feet was all the stream that could be had. The explosion of a small gasoline tank where the fire started soon put the blaze beyond control, with the light water pressure. The Morrison building, a double frame building owned by S. Ed. Johnson and C. T. Cutter, together with the one occupied by the Cafe and Hopkins & Neeb, and the next adjoining, a two-story frame owned and occupied by Ray Smith with Rawson's barber shop on one side of the front, were soon a roaring mass of flames. It was but a few moments until the buildings on Broadway became enveloped. On it sped, destroying the buildings occupied by Frank Smith with novelty goods, C. N. Wilbur, clothing and dry goods, and the Idaho Falls Packing Co.'s market, all frame buildings. Then came the one-sotry rock building owned by Jas. Thomas and occupied by Johnson & Catmull, dry goods and clothing. Here it was checked for a few moments, but that building soon succumbed, and before the roof of that fell the big C. W. & M. building covering 136x140 feet and filled with hardware, implements, carriages, wagons, buggies, sewing machines and car loads of stoves; in about the time it would take to tell it after the east corner was on fire the entire building was in flames. This company were preparing to put up a fine brick structure in place of the frame and were continuing to do business there. The entire sides had been taken out and set back about three feet, the foundation was all in and the wall on the east side up about ten feet. In three or four days more the wall would have been of sufficient height to have made it possible to save the building. On [illegible] the street the fire went, taking Henry Nagel's blacksmith shop and a frame owned by J. Streibick of Butte, occupied by John Vania [illegible] shop. Then came the C. W. & M. lumber yard with about $25,000 worth of lumber. On it went taking the buildings of Leo Hill and Nell Baker in what is known as the red light district.

North of the lumber yard was C. J. Winkler's rock residence; the roof and interior of this was burned. Beyond this was D. H. Clyne's big double stable buildings and residence, and how these escaped destruction will always be a mystery.

Around on Park Ave. again across the alley from S. Ed. Johnson's was the Coltman Lumber Co.'s yard with about $25,000 worth of lumber, paints, oils, etc. Here was a hot fire again. The oil house of W. S. Jackson stood near this; it was a rock building, but the roof went and the contents were burned.

North of the C. W. & M. Co.'s was Matt. LaRouche's blacksmith shop. He lost all his tools and his books, knowing nothing of the fire until next morning. Ralph Willis' livery stable was next to this; he succeeded in saving his horses and buggies.

With the exception of the Clark & Fanning Co. all the buildings on the east side of Park avenue were damaged and many of them were on fire several times. The windows were all broken and it was by the most desperate efforts that the fire did not take that entire block.

The statement sent out that there was terrific wind is nothing but imagination. There was a light breeze from the south until about 12 o'clock, when it became a little stronger; at no time was it strong enough to carry anything more than sparks. This was very fortunate, and was the means of saving the Register office and the Wright Mercantile Co.'s store. As it was, the latter was on fire several times on the second floor; the front windows were all broken out. They carried out a large amount of goods. The front windows of the Register office were all cracked, but did not fall out. The building occupied by the Times was on fire several times and they carried out some of their material.

The LaRue and Dineen building on the corner of Brodaway and Park avenue stood the test finely. there was a solid all on the north, and on the west excepting one door on the lower floor, on the northwest corner. They stood inside with a hose and kept this wet all the time. This was the means of saving the Clark & Fanning building and the block on the east.

The Telephone company were heavy losers, the large cable being melted and several of the largest poles burned. The city was also loser to quite an extent by the destruction of electric light poles and cables.

LOSSES AND INSURANCE.

The following is an approximate estimate of the losses and the amount of insurance. This was compiled for Dun's Commercial Agency by [illegible]:

	Loss	Insurance
C. W. & M. Co.,	$90,000	$45,000
Coltman Lumber Co.,	25,000	5,000
S. Ed Johnson,	6,000	1,150
C. K. Wilbur,	7,000	1,000
Johnson & Catmull,	4,000	2,000
I. F. Packing Co.,	3,500	1,500
Ray S. Smith,	3,000	500
Hopkins & Neeb,	2,500	1,000
Ralph Willis,	1,500	1,250
Martin Elward,	1,500	500
C. T. Cutter,	1,500	1,000
H. F. Nagel,	1,500	none
Frank Smith,	1,000	500
W. S. Jackson,	1,000	none
Matt LaRouche,	600	none
Leo Hill,	800	none
Nell Baker,	1,000	none
Frank Cutter,	50	250
Rawson Bros.,	50	none
C. J. Winkler,	300	none
J. Streibick,	300	none
John Vania,	50	none
LaRue & Dineen, damage to walls,	600	

Among those who suffered damages by the heat, the windows, mostly plate glass, being destroyed, are the following:

Wright Mercantile Co.,	$4,000
H. J. Hasbrouck,	500
Turner & Shane,	300
Mr. Palmer,	200
J. A. Horst,	150
LaRue & Dineen,	600
Times Office,	75
Register Office,	70
Mrs. Jos. A. Clark,	50

Notes on the Fire.

The C. W. & M. Co. have fitted up an office in their old building and are going right ahead with business. They have a large stock of goods there, except hardware and they are getting that in. They have ordered a train-load of lumber.

Henry Nagel has opened out his blacksmith shop in a tent just back of where the shop stood and is ready for business. This is only temporary, until he can secure a lot and build.

Geo. Payne, who owns the two lots next to the LaRue & Dineen building, and the Idaho Falls Packing Co., who own the adjoining lot where they were located, are arranging to commence building at once. They will probably put up only one story at present but will build the walls heavy enough to add to when necessary.

The Coltman Lumber Co. will build at once. They will erect a full-width building about fifty feet deep, and then put up their shed for fine lumber, of brick or stone with a fire-proof roof.

S. Ed Johnson is making arrangements to build at once; likewise C. T. Cutter, who owns the adjoining lot. They will probably build two-story.

Mrs Ida C. Winn, who owns the fifty feet front where Ray Smith was located, is expected here at any time. Mr Smith had been negotiating with her for the sale of the building and she expected to make the purchase when she came. He may make a deal for one of the lots and join with her in putting up a nice building.

Johnson & Catmull have put up a tent across the street and are getting their goods straightened out there. A large quantity of their goods were carried out and piled on the ground.

About a dozen wagons and buggies were gotten out of the C. W. & M. Co.'s and a large quantity of goods [illegible] of the hardware department but were not carried away far enough. They were dropped at the edge of the sidewalk and took fire from the heat. Half a dozen sewing machines were destroyed.

Frank Cutter and Rawson Brothers have moved temporarily into the saloons opposite their old locations.

John Vania can now be found at Dahlstrom & Monroe's blacksmith shop.

The Idaho Falls Packing Co. will not open their retail business until their building is completed. They will keep the wholesale department running at the packing house.

Ray Smith moved some of his goods into the rooms in the Miller block upstairs, and has fixed up a little place on the corner opposite Jackson's drug store for his jewelry business.

Frank Smith has moved into the McMullen building.

It was a close call for the McMullen building north of Coltman Lumber Co.'s lumber yard.

There are some mighty mean men in this world. It is a mean man who will break into another man's house and steal his goods. In that case, however, the man has protected himself to a certain extent by locking or bolting the doors. But this man is an angel beside the contemptible scrub in human form that will make a pretense at assisting a man in taking his goods out at the time of a fire and then steal some of those goods. One fellow was helping Mr. Haig carry out some of Ray Smith's goods and reaching into the case grabbed a handful of watch-chains. Haig caught him at it, but it was too dark just then to identify or capture the sneak. He should have had a gun and shot him on the spot.

The C. W. & M. Co. will now push their new building. With the old one out of the way they can do much faster work. We understand there will be no change in the plans, except perhaps there will be some division walls and probably a basement 60x140 on the north end.

Lorenzo R. Thomas came up from Blackfoot Thursday morning. His father, who is now in England, owns the lot where Johnson & Catmull were located. Unfortunately this lot is only 19 feet wide, while the one adjoining, owned by the Packing Co., is 29 feet. Mr. Thomas will join them in building if he can get four or five feet of their ground. He came again last evening and has arranged to build with the others.

C. K. Wilbur has moved the stock that was saved into the McMullen building.

S. Ed Johnson has opened up business in the room at the rear of the McMullen building. Harness and shoe repairing will receive prompt attention.

Rawson Bros. have put up a small tent on the corner opposite Jackson's drug store and opened up their barber shop.

What date did you say? October 1st. Yes, that is the date of the big bargain day of the Register, when you can get the paper for nine months and the fine map of Idaho, for only one dollar. If you do not live in the city you can send your subscription any time between now and that time, and the paper will date from Oct. 1.

The famous Huyler's Candy for sale in this city, at Maguire's Drug Store only.

FOLEY'S HONEY AND TAR

stops the cough and heals lungs.

The New Hardware Store

G. E. BLOCKIE & CO.

Plumbing and Tinning.

Special Sale of Tinware Saturday and Monday, September 17th and 19th.

6 qt Milk Pans	90c doz	Wash Dishes	10c "
Milk Strainer	15c each	Waterpail, tin	15c "
1 qt Measure	10c "	Waterpail, galv. iron	25c "
1 gal. Measure	15c "	Lunch Boxes	15c "
1 qt Tin Measure	05c "	1 gal Oil Can	20c "
Flour Sifters	10c "	4 qt Sauce Pan	10c "
No. 8 Copper bottom Teakettle	40c "	14 qt Dish Pan	30c "
1 qt Cream Can	10c "	14 qt Bread Riser	50c "
2 qt Cream Can	15c "	Wash Boiler, extra heavy tin, copper bottom	1.50 "
1 qt Pail	05c "	10 qt Japanned Chamber Pails	80c "
2 qt Pail	10c "	9 in Pie Tins	2 for 5c
Sink Strainers	15c "		

Come in and see our 5, 10 and 15c Counter.

The *Register*'s front page records the devastation from a 1904 fire that burned a block of downtown Idaho Falls from Park Avenue and Broadway north and west almost to the river. "About Twenty Business Houses Now in Ashes," the subhead proclaims. The Consolidated Wagon and Machine Company, having moved to Broadway, was one of those burned but opened the next day out of the original store, a lava-rock building on the river's west side that was demolished early in 2008 to make room for a new hotel.

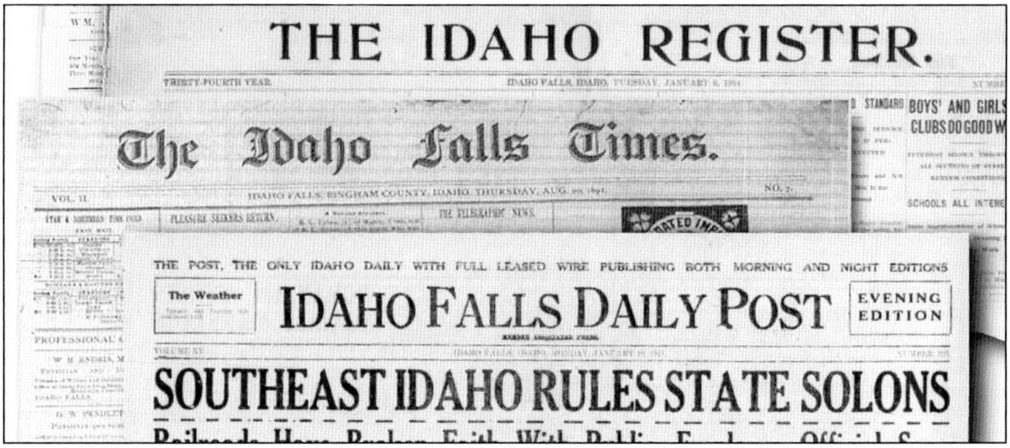
THE IDAHO REGISTER.

The Idaho Falls Times.

THE POST, THE ONLY IDAHO DAILY WITH FULL LEASED WIRE PUBLISHING BOTH MORNING AND NIGHT EDITIONS

The Weather

IDAHO FALLS DAILY POST

EVENING EDITION

SOUTHEAST IDAHO RULES STATE SOLONS

By 1905, Idaho Falls had three newspapers. The *Register*, a Republican weekly, was started in 1880 by William E. Wheeler; the *Times* began in 1890, begun by a former telegraph operator and a former Wheeler employee, and also published weekly. Over its 30-year life, the *Times* switched back and forth between Democratic and Republican leanings. The progressive, pro-labor *Idaho Falls Daily Post* arrived in 1905 but struggled as a morning edition and did not print on Mondays. Later on, it had both morning and evening editions. The Democratic *Times* bought the Republican *Register* in 1920 to form a semiweekly, the *Times-Register.* The paper tried twice to go daily before the *Post* bought it to become the *Post-Register* in 1931.

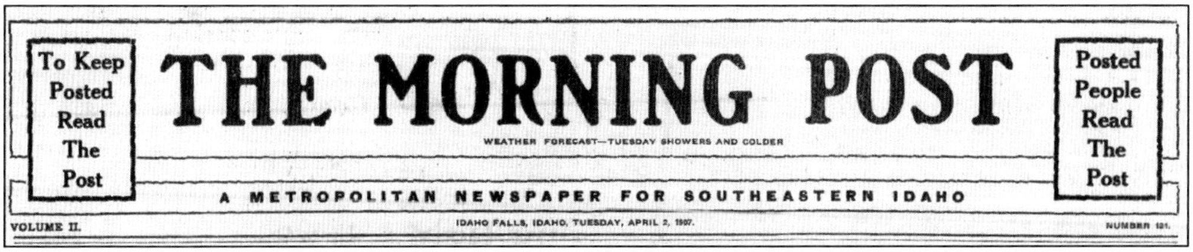
To Keep Posted Read The Post

THE MORNING POST

Posted People Read The Post

WEATHER FORECAST—TUESDAY SHOWERS AND COLDER

A METROPOLITAN NEWSPAPER FOR SOUTHEASTERN IDAHO

VOLUME II. — IDAHO FALLS, IDAHO, TUESDAY, APRIL 2, 1907.

Shown here is the masthead of the *Morning Post* of April 2, 1907. The *Post* did not publish on Mondays and was often late in delivering its morning edition.

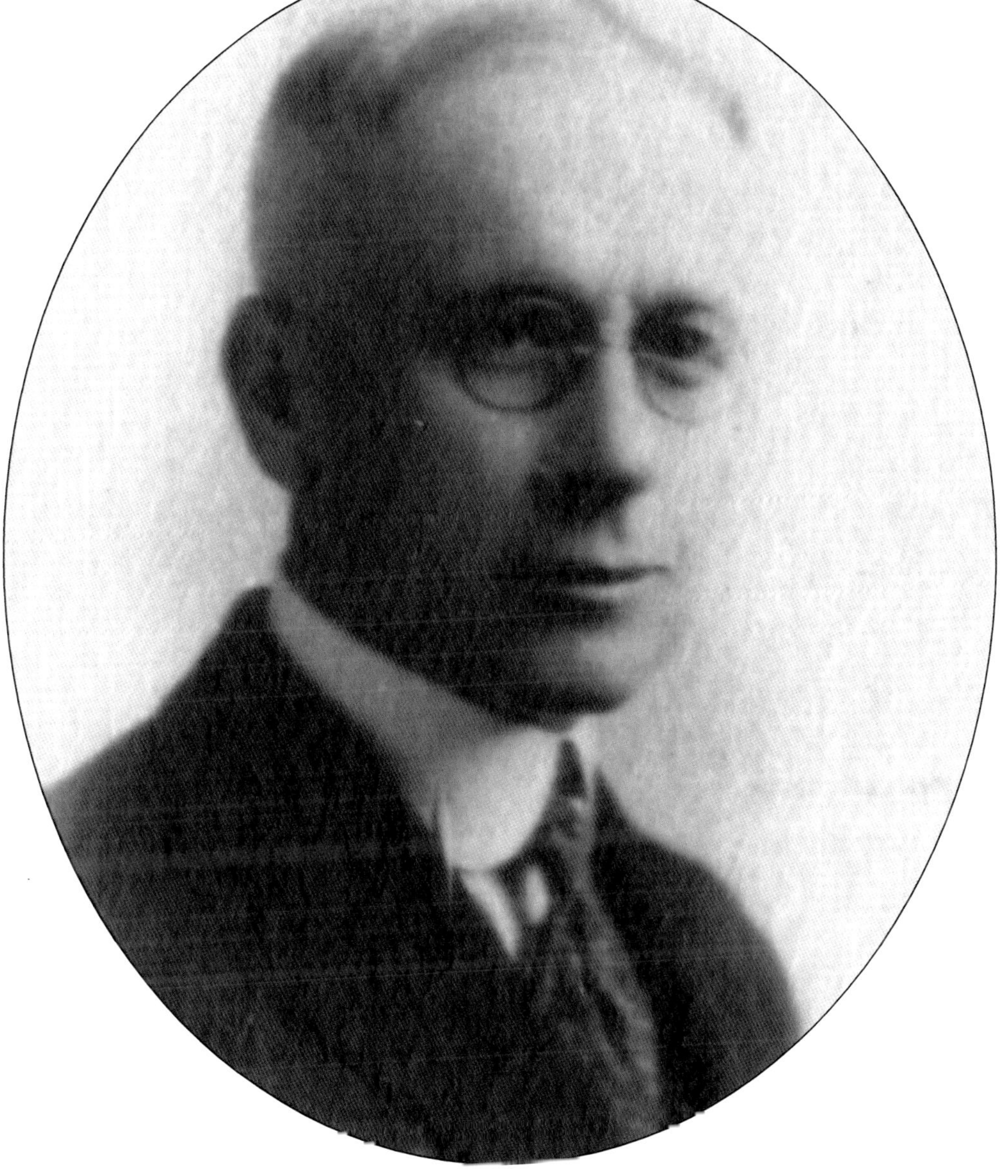

M. B. Yeaman bought half the *Register* in 1909, when Wheeler retired, and was the paper's sole owner by 1919. Originally from St. Louis, Yeaman had edited a weekly in Arkansas for 11 years; his career included 27 years of newspaper work in Idaho Falls. "His editorials were important in overcoming opposition and educating the public" for a Utah–Idaho Yellowstone Highway, according to Otto McCutcheon, the first president of the Utah–Idaho Yellowstone Highway association. A decade after Wheeler died, Yeaman sold the paper to Sam Dennis and William S. Snyder, who formed the *Times-Register* in 1920. Yeaman served as editor of the *Times-Register* and was the first editor of the *Post-Register* after a merger in 1931. He was a Republican legislator from 1919 to 1929 and increased state support for public libraries. He was offered the nomination for lieutenant governor in 1924 but declined. He moved to Boise in 1935 to serve four years on the state liquor control board and died on January 5, 1940, after a long illness.

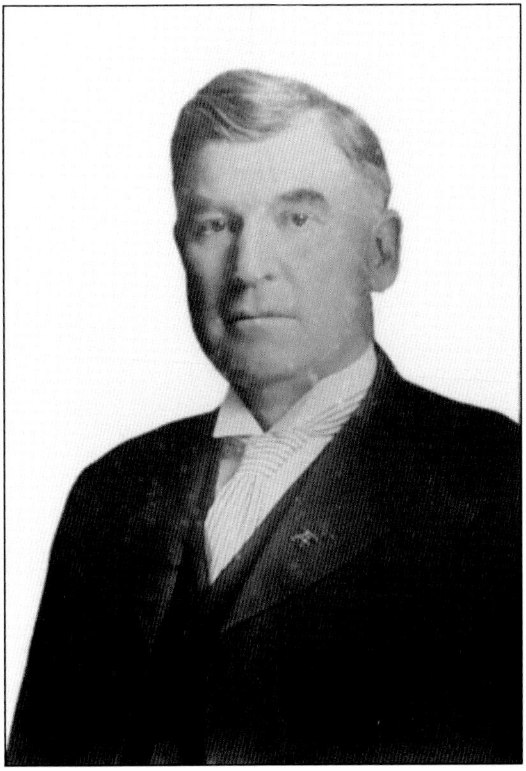

There is some indication that real estate developer James H. Brady was the financial backer behind eastern Idaho's first daily newspaper in 1905. Twenty years later, after Brady's death while serving in the U.S. Senate, Brady's son, J. Robb Brady Sr., bought the *Post* with money from his father's estate.

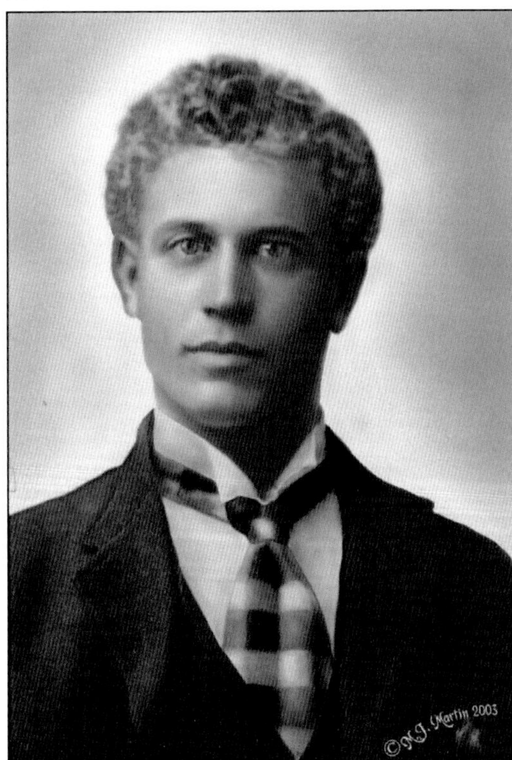

Charles Sumner started the town's first daily newspaper, the *Daily Post*, in 1905. The *Post*, according to a public library anthology, was referred to as the "Morning Jest"—mostly because it would often not be delivered until noon or after. Maybe this was the reason why it was changed to an evening paper. It was a four-page broadsheet, and news in it "was rare and scarce," according to the library record. Sumner, a miner's son, came here from Colorado, where as co-owner of the *San Miguel Examiner* he ran into trouble with mine owners who had him arrested and his paper closed. He and his younger brother Ernest lasted in Idaho Falls about five years before selling out; Charles edited the *Pocatello Tribune* in 1910 and lived there until at least 1930. (Copyrighted portrait from a 1903 newspaper photograph, courtesy MaryJoy Martin.)

Three

THE BATTLE GOES DAILY 1905–1931

In 1905, brothers Charles G. and Ernest Sumner and printer Henry Gabbe founded a morning newspaper, the *Idaho Falls Morning Post*. All three were experienced newspapermen.

Charles was the editorial leader, though younger brother Ernest did a little reporting. Charles was slim and curly-haired, friendly, and likable, and had a penchant for loud ties. "His most serious failing was a latent prejudice against Chinese and Native Americans, an attitude that seemed to fade as he grew older," biographer MaryJoy Martin reports in her book *The Corpse on Boomerang Road*.

It was a matter of speculation where Sumner got the money to mount eastern Idaho's first daily. Idaho Falls postmaster Ed F. Winn is the probable author of an anonymous ode, found among Winn's papers, that strongly indicates James H. Brady, head of the state's Republican party and soon to be elected governor, may have been Sumner's silent partner:

Brady had a little lamb
It's name is Charley Sumner
And every time he lets it blat
It blats and blats like thunder
He bought the Morning Post one day
And Sumner told to edit (?)
He also flashed a little coin
To help on Sumner's credit.

No records exist connecting Brady directly with Sumner and the *Post*. But it would not be unusual for Brady; he was a developer and occasionally used surrogates to purchase land on his behalf, such as a huge tract near Mountain Home in 1910 he bought through the highest bidder, Harry Watkins, at an extremely low price, his interest only surfacing after the sale.

A newspaperman in Kansas before moving out to Idaho in 1895, Brady had invested in Boise's Democratic paper, the *Capital News*, according to J. Anthony Lukas in his period study of Idaho politics, *Big Trouble*. "Since the paper was chronically short on cash, Republican politicians—notably Sen. Borah and James Brady, the [Republican party] chairman—provided the *Capital News* with desperately needed loans, thus buying support for themselves and grief for their enemies," Lukas reported. Consequently, the *News* was so lethargic in backing Democratic candidates that "the party suffered acutely from the lack of a vigorous flagship paper."

In Idaho Falls, Sumner paid union wages while Wheeler did not, and Sumner's "fairly fast press" shipped in from Colorado made it possible for the *Post* to print a daily edition, which eventually spelled doom for the *Register* and *Times*.

AN ODE

Dedicated to Dad Ledford
By the Author

Brady has a little lamb
Its name is Charley Sumner
And every time he lets it blat
It blats and blats like thunder

He bought the Morning Post one day
And Sumner told to edit (?)
He also flashed a little coin
To help on Sumner's credit

And when the eager creditors found
That this was really true
With all their might and main they ran
To get what was their due

Now Sumner is a foxy lamb
And tried hard to elude
Many of the eager ones
Who hotly him pursued
~~Amo~~
Among the first to reach his side
Was Ledford stern and big
And Charles began to realize
'Twas time for him to dig

But as he parted from his pelf
He kissed the coin goodbye
"And though I'm forced to do it Dad
I'll do you yet or die"

"I'll roast you to a turn he said
"Singe you of hair and horn
"And leave you a disfigured maverick
"On the desert Dad forlorn

"All of your ilk will get a roast
"Coltman, Porter, Winn
"Me and Brady, we're the stuff
"Just wait till I begin

"My editorials keen and sharp
Will cut like two edged swords
"Just kindly watch my smoke dear Dad
"Watch for my stinging words

Started? Yes. He's shot his wad
His wad of shameless bits
Like the little fly that sits all day
And ... and... and ...

What makes the lamb love Brady so?
Ah pity 'tis, 'tis true
Brady has such winning ways
Of coughing up the sou

An anonymous 11-stanza "ode" found among the papers of Ed F. Winn accuses Sumner and the *Post* of attacks on E. P. Coltman, but Sumner supported Coltman as the Progressive candidate in the 1907 election. The ode is dedicated to a liquor retailer who advertised in the *Post*. (Museum of Idaho/Bonneville County Historical Society.)

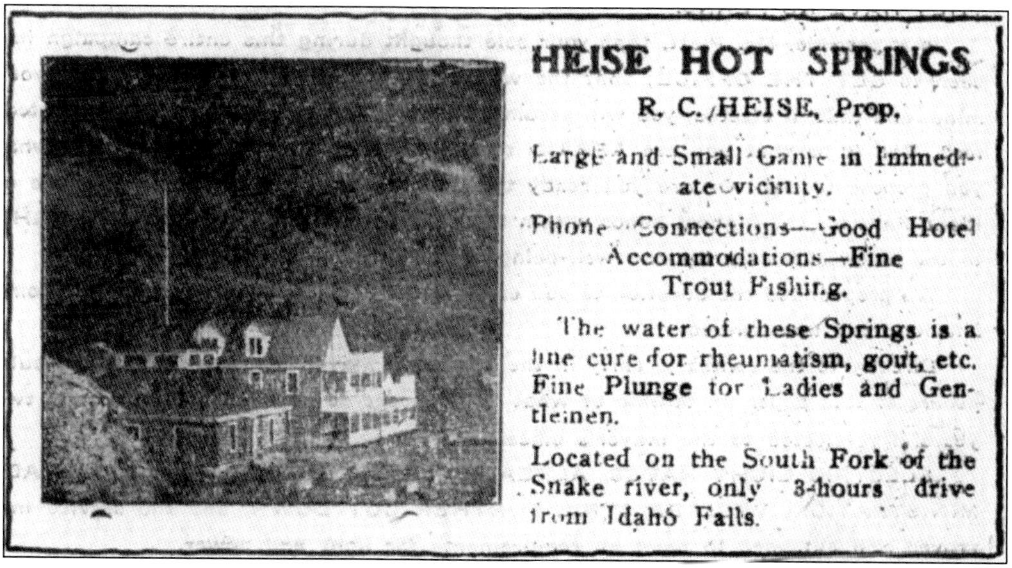

This 1907 *Post* advertisement for Heise Hot Springs is one of the first uses of photographs in that paper. The *Register* used photographs beginning in about 1903. Heise promised that "the water of these springs is a fine cure for rheumatism, gout, etc."

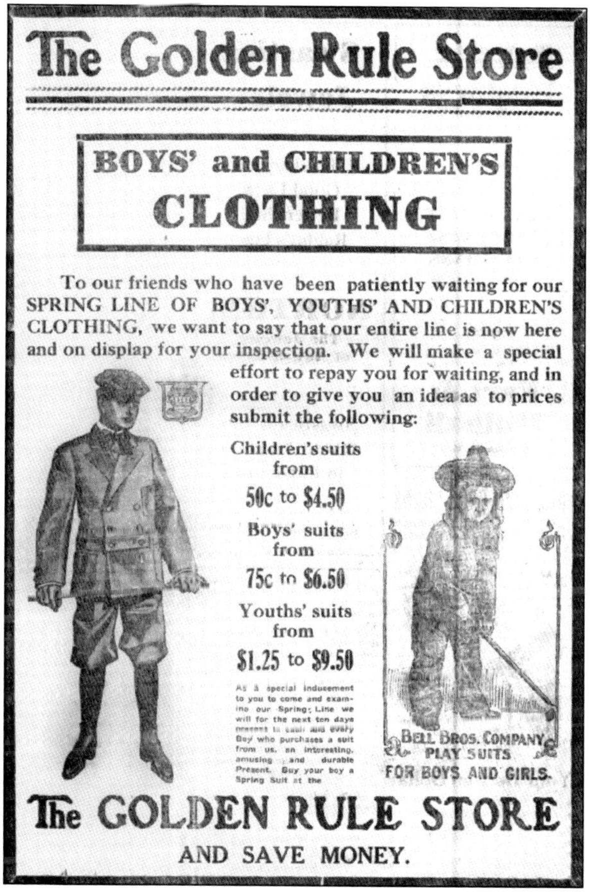

James Cash Penney started his first Golden Rule Store in 1902 in Kemmerer, Wyoming, and by 1907, Idaho Falls had its branch. Penney's dual philosophy—cash only and "do unto others as you would have them do unto you"—caught fire in the West and spread nationwide as J. C. Penney Company. The present store is located in the Grand Teton Mall.

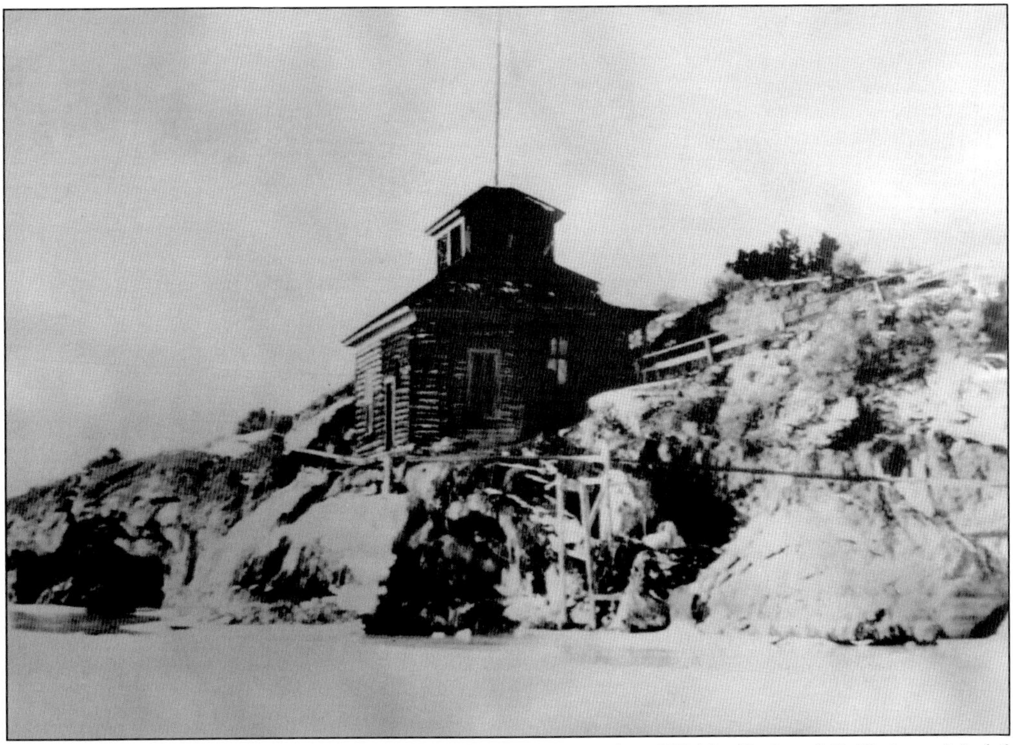

Eastern Idaho's earliest resort was Heise Hot Springs, started in 1894 by Richard C. Heise, a Medal of Honor winner in the Apache Wars of the 1870s who came through the area as a traveling salesman. Advertisements for the resort appeared in the *Post* as early as 1907, but it was difficult to get to Heise by ferry during high water until a bridge was built in 1938. Over the years, the resort passed ownership several times and has added outdoor pools, a nine-hole golf course, a pizza parlor, and picnic-camping areas. The photograph above shows the first Heise health baths as they appeared about 1900; the photograph below shows the resort as it grew during the 1920s.

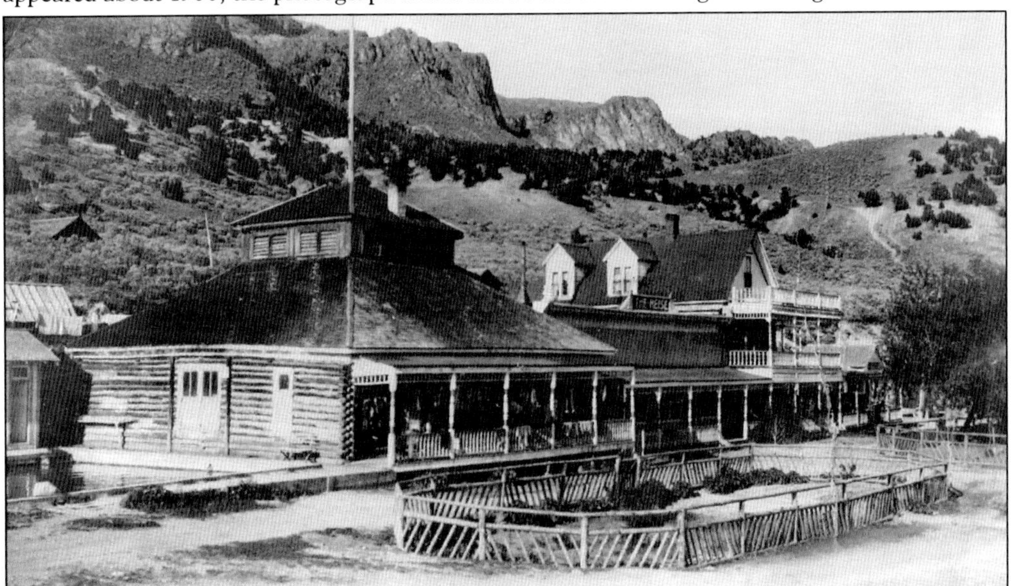

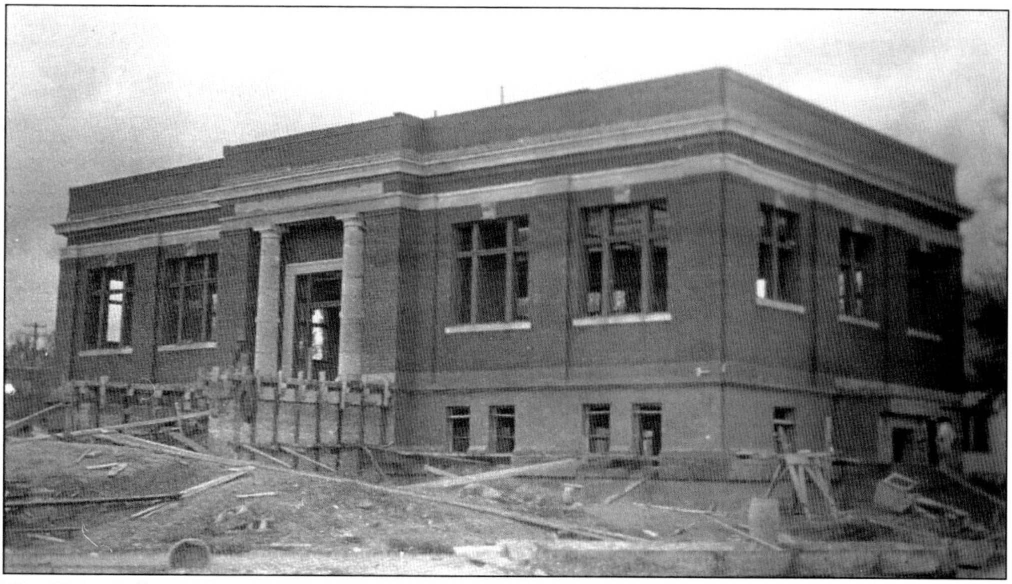

The Idaho Falls Carnegie Library is shown under construction in 1910. The library was a city landmark from the moment it opened at the head of Broadway in 1914. Two publishers of the *Register*, William Wheeler and M. B. Yeaman, were actively involved in fund-raising for the library.

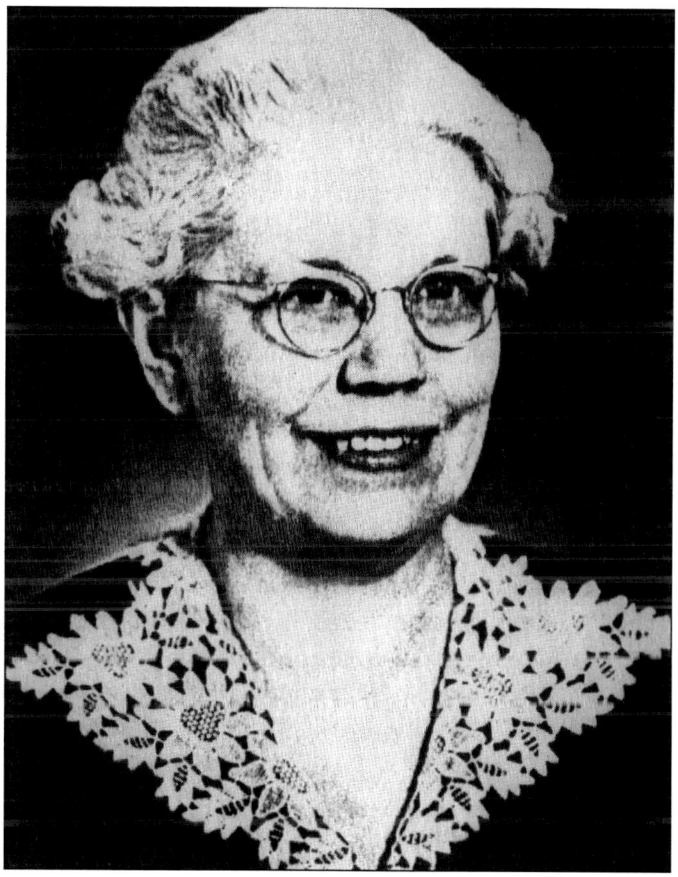

Marion C. Orr was city librarian from 1917 to 1954. Following the merger of the *Times* and *Register* in 1920, "a truck arrived at the Library one afternoon and the driver asked what he should do with the papers," according to a typewritten manuscript probably written by Orr. "We didn't know of the merger which had not been announced," the article recalled. "We were surprised to find it was their file of the *Idaho Falls Times*. While it was far from complete and badly mutilated, we were glad to receive it. No other exists. We have had them microfilmed in order to preserve them." Today neither the city library nor the Museum of Idaho has been able to locate these original newspaper files, so full of the history of the region.

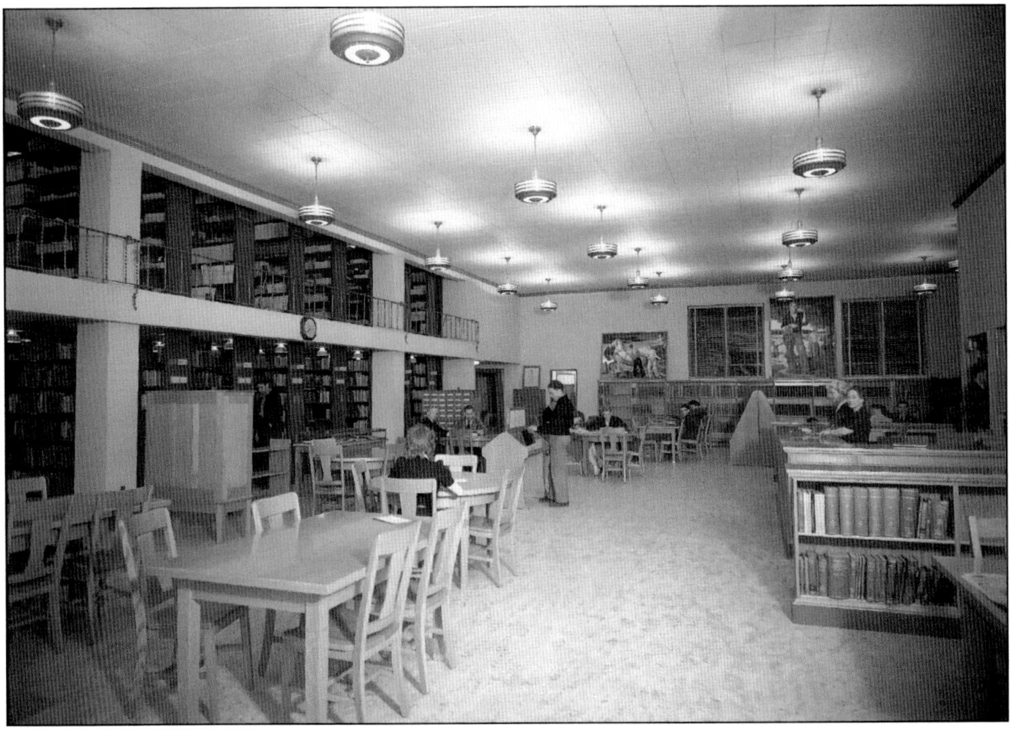

Pictured is the interior of the Idaho Falls Carnegie Library, which is now part of the Museum of Idaho. Longtime librarian Marion Orr is at the desk.

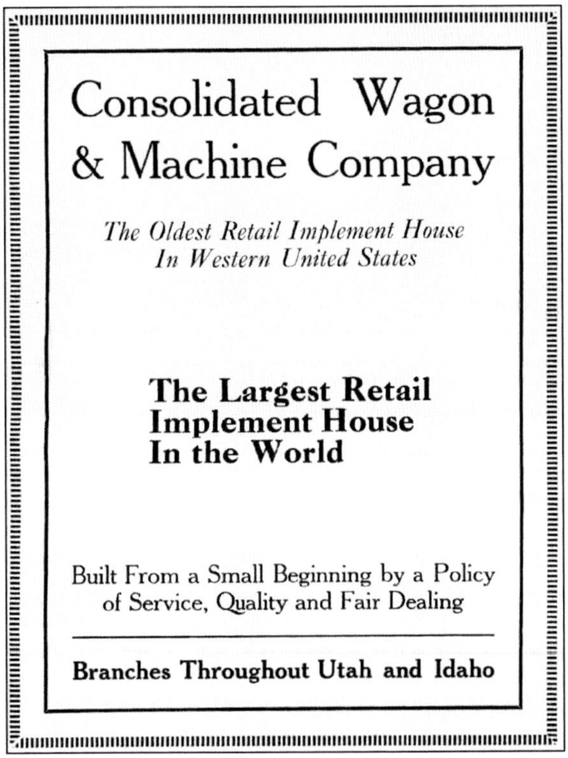

One of the West's first department stores, the Consolidated Wagon and Machine Company was also one of the first newspaper advertisers. The long lava-rock structure that originally housed the CW&M warehouse just south of the Broadway Bridge was demolished in the spring of 2008 to make way for a new hotel. This advertisement appeared in the *Post* in 1919.

Four

The Local Option

Since Eagle Rock's earliest days, fees paid by saloons were major contributors to the village budget. During city elections of 1904, saloonkeepers complained they might go out of business if they were going to be "regulated" so much. So a new ordinance allowed saloons to remain open all night. Three years later, the *Times* printed a series from the Civic League backing a reformer, city clerk D. G. Platt. "It is well-known that an enormous corruption fund has been collected for the saloons, breweries, gamblers and the immoral contingent on the river front," the League proclaimed in the *Times* on March 5. "Two newspapers have already been subsidized to do the bidding of the morplots in the personal abuse of respectable citizens." The League labeled the *Post* as know-nothing newcomers and claimed Wheeler had secured city printing contracts through graft. City attorney Arthur Holden was accused of allowing bawdy houses and gamblers to operate above the law.

When Platt narrowly defeated incumbent E. P. Coltman, he appointed a new police chief and several other city posts, and the *Times* was named the official newspaper of Idaho Falls.

By July, the *Register* reported the city council had taken "drastic measures," ordering enforcement of an ordinance "keeping the saloons closed within hours, closing down the so-called 'red light' district and compelling drug stores not to sell liquor . . . lest they fall under the extreme penalty of the law."

But when towns used a new local option law to ban liquor sales, customers went where they could still get a drink. E. P. Coltman was returned as mayor in 1909, and the statewide backlash caused Gov. James H. Brady to lose his bid for a second term. Brady favored closing the doors of every saloon permanently while his opponent, Democrat James Hawley, was "wet." Since two-thirds of the counties had held local-option elections and all but two had gone "dry," forecasters predicted Brady would win. But the GOP was split. The *Post* backed Brady to the bitter end. "It was a peculiar campaign," it reported as votes were tallied. Accusing Republicans who did not vote for Brady of "the rankest kind of disloyalty," the paper hoped "everything will turn out in good shape—which it will—and that the splendid business administration of Governor Brady will be continued."

Brady lost by 900 votes and returned to Pocatello. The same year, Charles Sumner sold the *Post*. He became editor of the *Pocatello Tribune* in 1910.

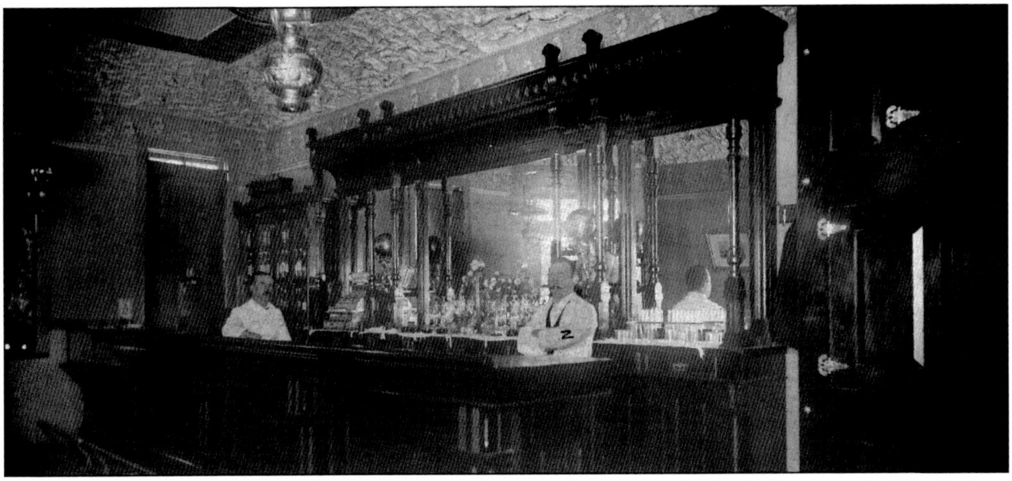

Ed F. Winn (left) stands behind the bar of his saloon in downtown Idaho Falls around 1905. He had earned a tough reputation as a lawman with a Parker shotgun and twin pistols mounted in swivel holsters. Winn went into the saloon business around 1883 with partner Dick Chamberlain, who was known for brewing up a popular local whiskey called "Chamberlain's Old Twenty-Year-Old." Over the years, Winn ran several saloons, was partners with his brother Ed in a drugstore, and built the Winn-Dill building on Park Avenue. After Bingham County became a dry county and Bonneville was formed from the northern part of Bingham in 1911, Winn assumed Idaho Falls would be "wet." When he opened another saloon, he was convicted of bootlegging.

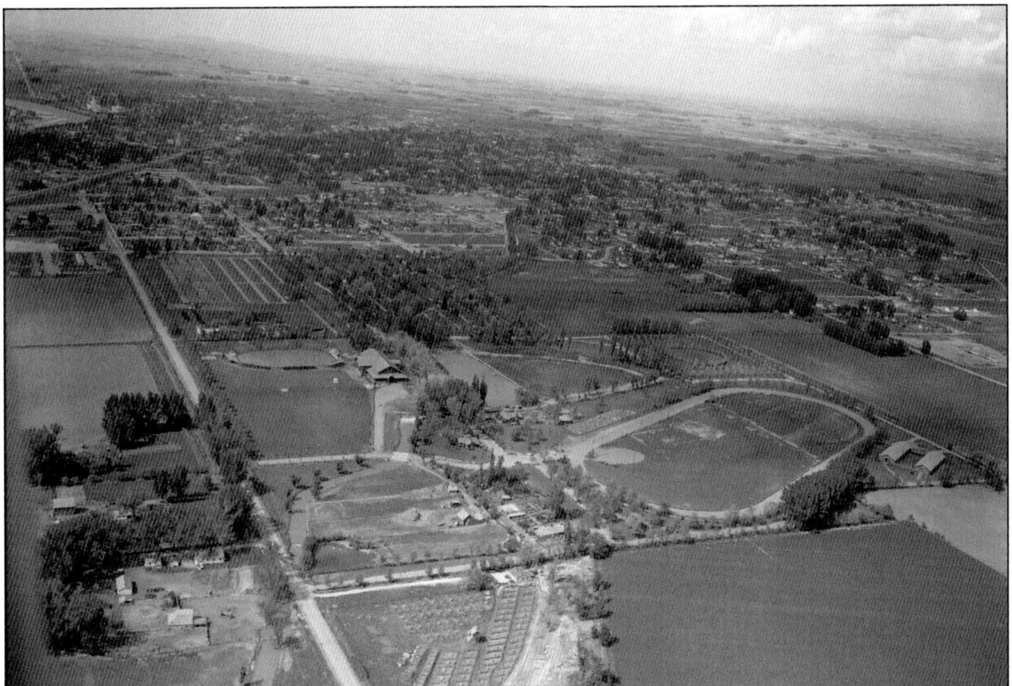

Two Idaho Falls newspaper publishers, *Register* owner M. B. Yeaman and *Post* founder Charles Sumner, served on the 15-member boosters group that raised money to buy the Tautphaus homestead for a city park by selling lapel pins for $1 each. The park developed around a rodeo grounds and racetrack, shown in this early aerial photograph.

In a Populist era, the Fair Store in Idaho Falls laid claim as "The Famous Store Where You get Your Money's Worth or Money Back."

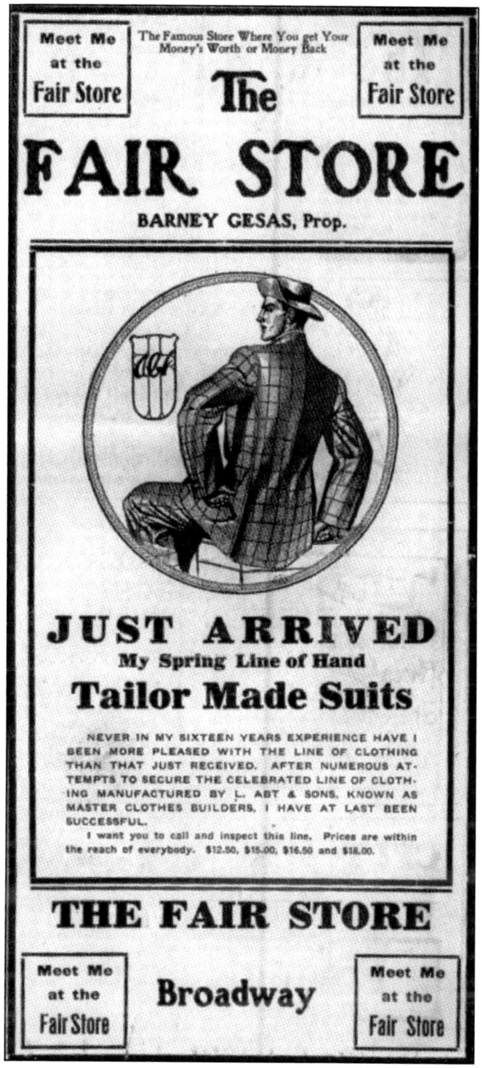

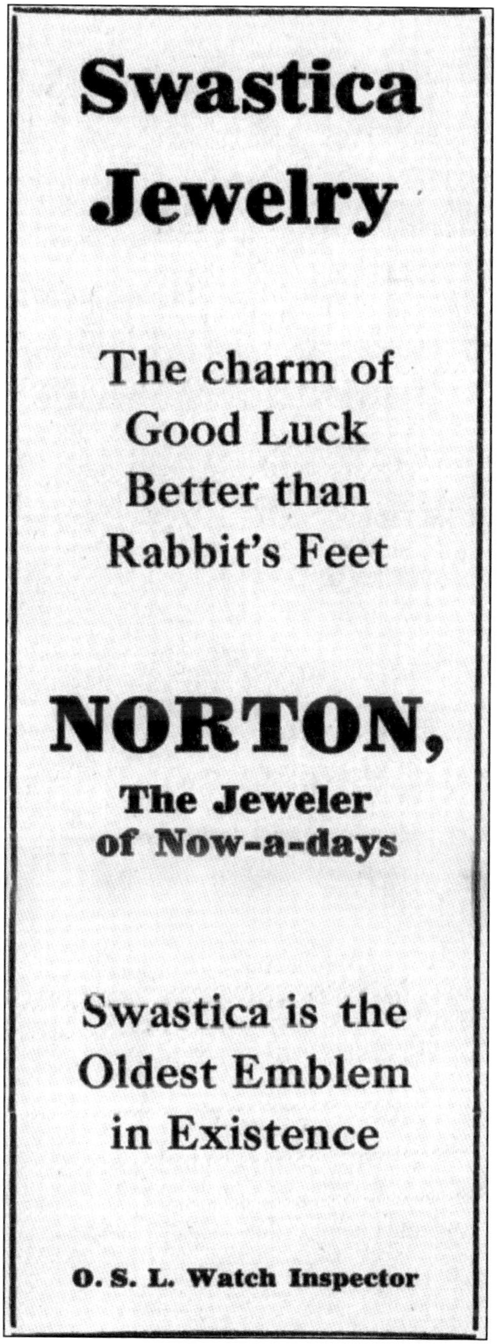

This 1907 advertisement for Swastica Jewelry in Idaho Falls predated the World War II era when swastikas became a malign symbol of Nazi oppression.

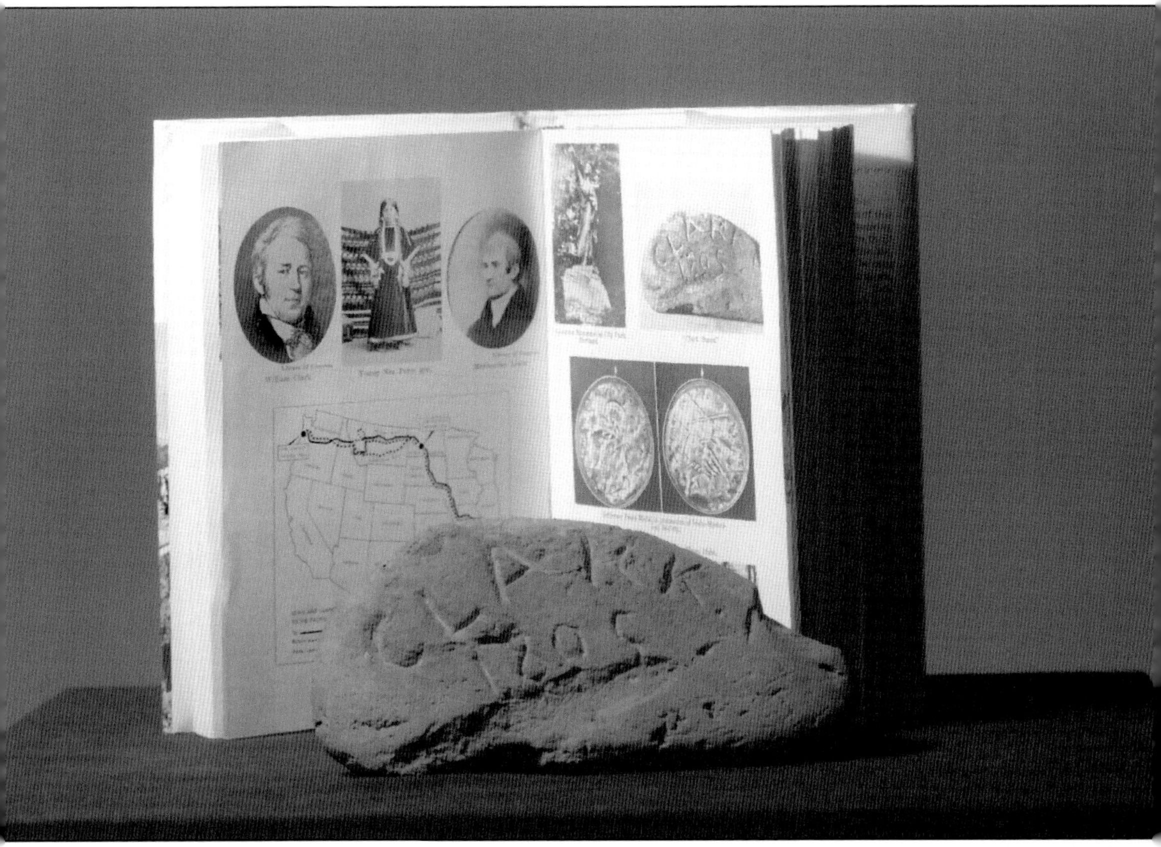

While plowing a field near Irwin east of Idaho Falls in 1912, M. D. Yeaman's son Cyrus unearthed this rock, inscribed with "Clark 1805." The Idaho *Register* declared the rock an artifact of Lewis and Clark's Corps of Discovery expedition of 1804–1806 and offered it for public viewing. The *Register* noted there was "little doubt, if any, but that the words were left by the explorer Clark," but also noted "there was some critical comment . . . to the effect that Clark did not travel down the south fork of the Snake River." Yeaman donated the Clark Stone to the Idaho State Historical Museum in March 1912.

Five

Two Newspapermen Depart

In 1910, the Sumner brothers severed their ownership in the *Post*. Henry Gabbe kept control for only a few years before selling out to banker Frank Butsoe. Butsoe then sold out to C. C. Wilson, who struggled along before selling out to two young, energetic professionals, Ben and Cliff Read.

Starting in an old wooden building at the corner of Shoup Avenue and Broadway, the Read brothers made a go of it, and by 1919 the *Daily Post* moved into a newly constructed building at A Street and Capital Avenue, with a new high-speed cylinder press.

On May 17, 1919, the courtly Wheeler was crossing Broadway at Park Avenue on his evening constitutional when he was struck by a laundry truck. He died two days later. All three newspapers remembered Wheeler fondly, the *Times* remarking that "an exceptionally long line of cars followed the remains to Rose Hill cemetery." His old competitor, Sam Dennis, called Wheeler "an honest and courageous man who never forgot that he was a gentleman."

"He printed columns and columns of booster articles in this paper and he never . . . failed to join in any and every effort made to induce new settlers to come in. . . . In short, practically all the matter which has been used in advertising this country either emanated from his office or was a rehash or enlargement of something that had previously been originated by him," Dennis said.

Dennis credited Wheeler as a leader in establishing a county fair association when "the people were few, settlements were scattered and everybody was poor. But it started Idaho Falls as the center of attraction in this part of the state and she has held the lead ever since." Despite Wheeler's lengthy battles with labor over the years, "few employers have more cause to be regretted and mourned . . . by their former employees than W. E. Wheeler," Dennis said. "He was always personally interested in his help, always a loyal friend, and he always went a little further than most in looking out for the welfare of those who worked for him. . . . No one knows how far the influence of an honest, upright, duty-doing gentleman may extend, but there are many of his former employees now living who know exceedingly well that much of good in their lives came to them through his influence and example."

96 PEACE AND PROSPERITY EDITION

—THE—

New Daily Post

Will Be Issued in a Short Time

The new Post will have

—One more Column
—All of the Associated Press news possible to obtain
—More Home News
—More Snake River Valley News
—More State News

It will be printed on this modern newspaper press which will be installed soon in the new quarters being erected for us by the Colonial Investment Co.

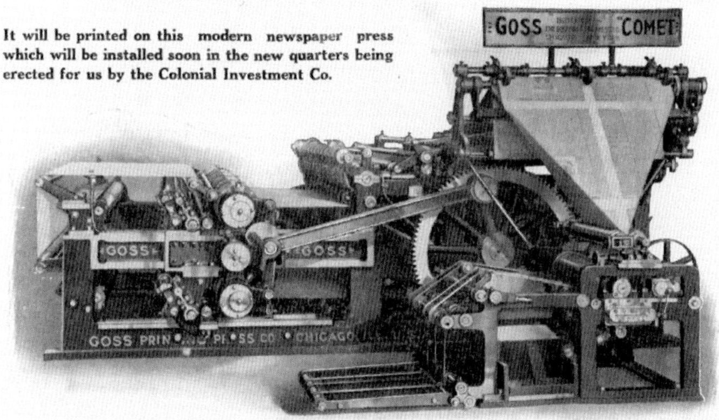

A Powerful Member of the Fourth Estate—A Real Press.

If you are not a Subscriber now, mail your Subscription in immediately, so you will not miss one issue of your Home Newspaper.

At the end of World War I, the *Post* announced a move to Capital Avenue, promising "the new *Daily Post*," with one more column, more local, area, and state news, and "all of the Associated Press news possible to obtain." The move was preceded by installation of a "modern newspaper press," a Goss Comet. "A powerful Member of the Fourth Estate—A Real Press," the advertisement claimed.

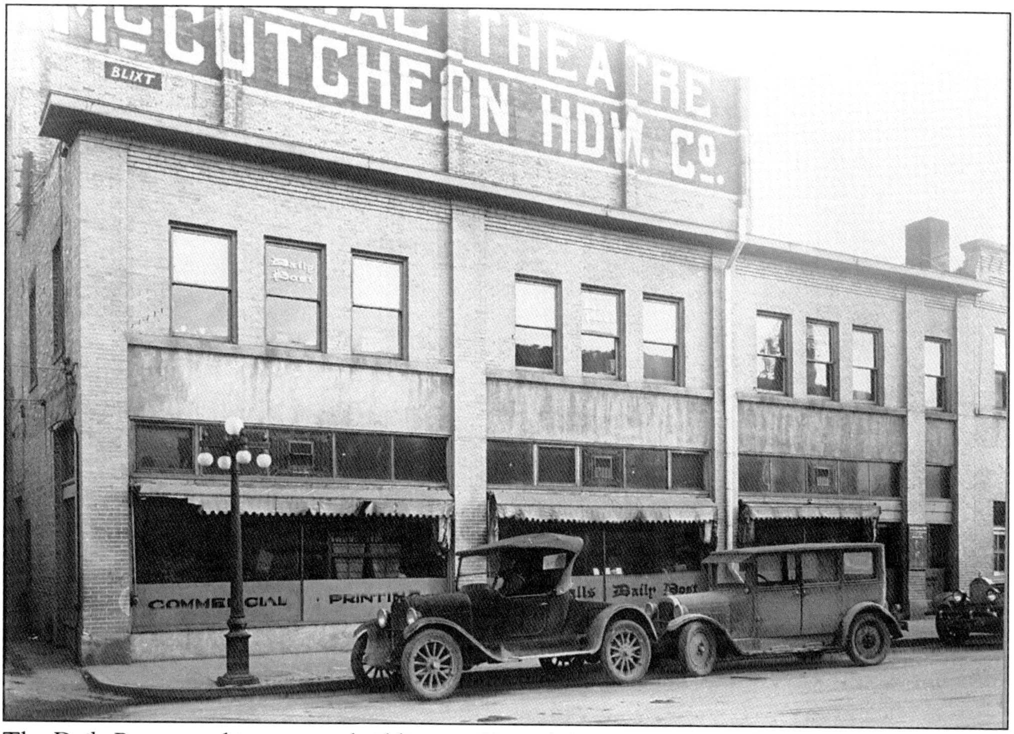

The *Daily Post* moved into a new building on Capital Avenue in 1919. The building, constructed by the Colonial Investment Company, of which Dr. C. M. Cline was the majority stockholder, included the Colonial Theater and McCutcheon Hardware and was later to be occupied by C. C. Anderson's department store.

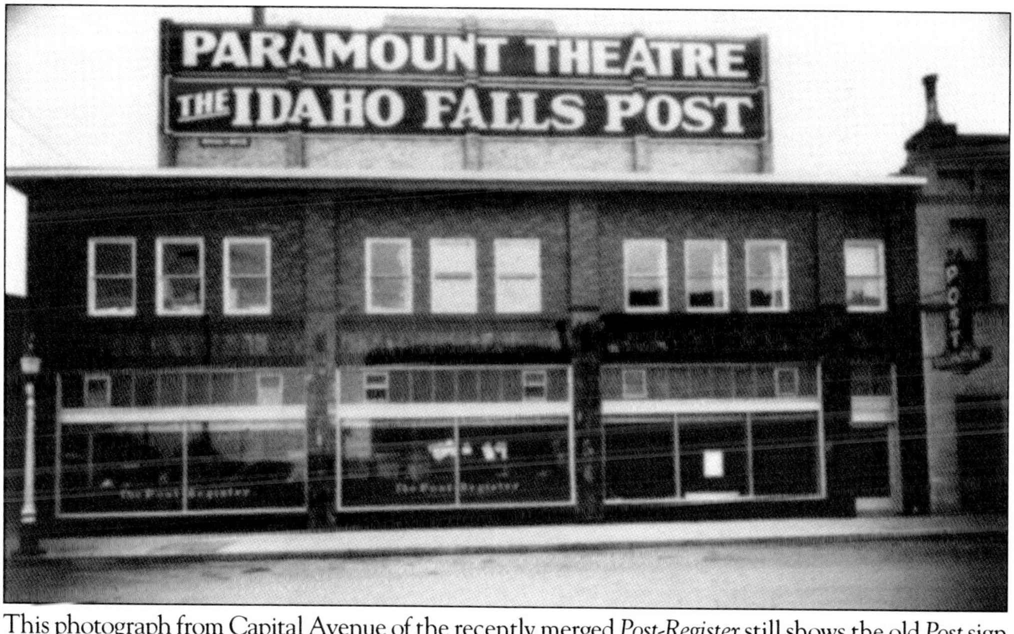

This photograph from Capital Avenue of the recently merged *Post-Register* still shows the old *Post* sign on the theater wall above. At various times, the sign over the newspaper proclaimed it as the home of the *Post*, the *Times-Register*, the *Post-Register*, and the Paramount (now Colonial) Theatre.

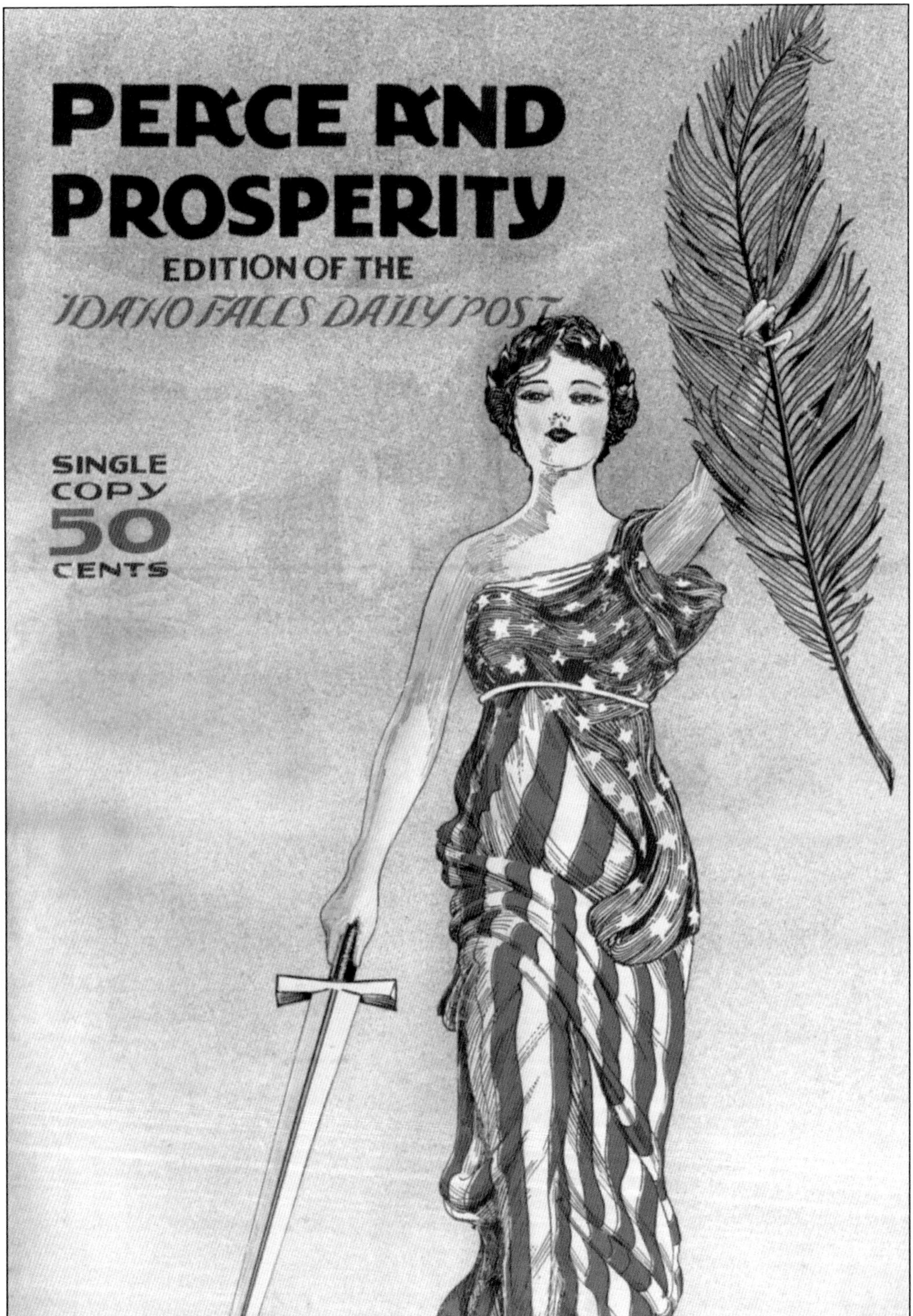

The *Post*'s 1919 "Peace and Prosperity Edition" presented stories about local heroes of World War I, including several advertisements listing those from each town in the area who died in the war.

Six

The Downtown Years

Following the end of World War I, a period of prosperity in Idaho Falls resulted in rapid expansion of downtown businesses. Stately department stores representing distinct architectural styles appeared along Shoup and Park Avenues and Broadway: F. W. Woolworth and Sears and Roebuck (1919), Montgomery Ward (1928–1929), and S. H. Kress (1930).

As tourism grew up around the passenger station at the end of C Street, hotels to accommodate travelers appeared: the Eleanore (1914), Idaho (1917), Underwood (1918), and the Bonneville (1926–1927). As quickly as the town grew, so did the three newspapers who served it, each reliant on the advertising that drew customers to downtown.

But competition was increasing, with each paper fighting to "go daily" so they could become preeminent. On September 14, 1920, the partners of the *Times* bought the *Register* from M. B. Yeaman, who continued as editor. Snyder and Dennis had changed the political leanings of the *Times* back to the Democratic party in 1915, merging its readers with the traditionally Republican *Register* while competing with the daily *Post*. The *Times-Register* established a daily publication schedule on January 1, 1921, but returned to a semiweekly by May 1. They tried again in 1930, but the Depression had begun and stores were closing.

The *Times-Register* wound up selling to the *Post* on October 31, 1931. Snyder joined the new *Post-Register* staff for a time. Snyder was appointed to the Farm Credit Association, serving on the local draft board. In 1946, he joined former Republican state legislator Aden Hyde in publication of the *Eastern Idaho Farmer*, a small, politically conservative agricultural weekly with headquarters next door to the *Post* on Capital Avenue. The *Farmer* was a continuation of the *Idaho Commoner* and was later purchased from Hyde by the *Post-Register* and the Porter family, owners of the *Rexburg Standard-Journal*. Dennis died on May 31, 1949, in Idaho Falls. At the time of his death, he was a probate judge.

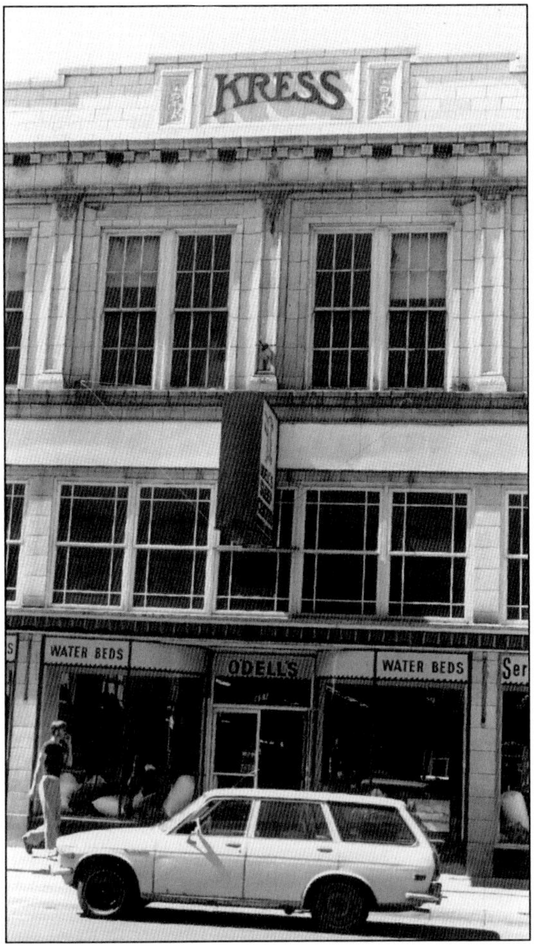

The S. H. Kress and Company Building at 451 Park Avenue is one of 15 downtown buildings on the National Register of Historic Places. It was built between 1930 and 1932. The Kress chain, operating from 1896 to 1981, was known for its fine architecture; a number of Kress stores, now put to other uses, are ranked as national landmarks. Noted builder Seymour Burrell was the company's corporate architect.

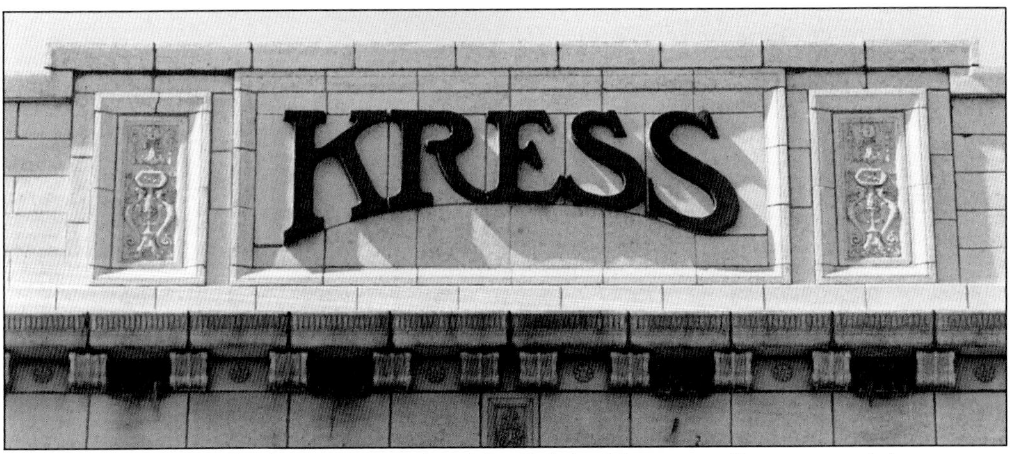

Historic Kress insets like this, crowning the Idaho Falls building, are still seen around the country, including New York City, Los Angeles, and Canal Street in New Orleans. The Idaho Falls store was built on the site of the city's first fire department; when the site was sold to Kress, the money was used to finance construction of the new city hall. The Kress Foundation, an arts supporter, survives the company that founded it.

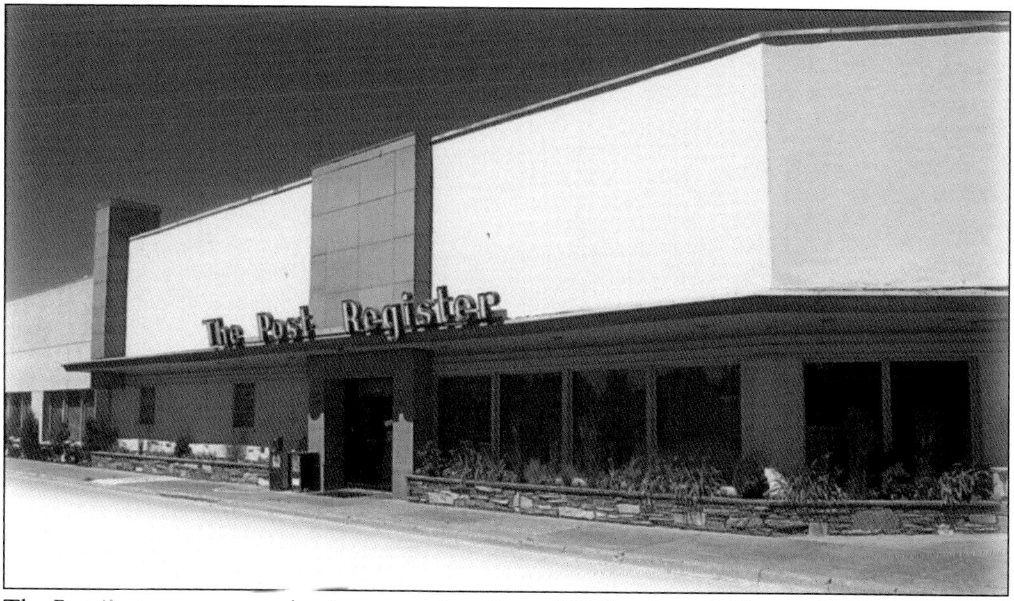

The *Post-Register* was moved to its present location at 333 Northgate Mile in 1959, outgrowing the downtown location. It had a circulation o 18,500. A new, 24-page Goss press capable of printing 25,000 papers an hour had been been installed in advance, and May 1, a Saturday, was designated as moving day. Eight giant Linotype machines, all the heavy equipment, and office furniture was loaded up as the Saturday edition was finished. The moving job was completed in six hours, and the paper was ready to print Monday morning's edition.

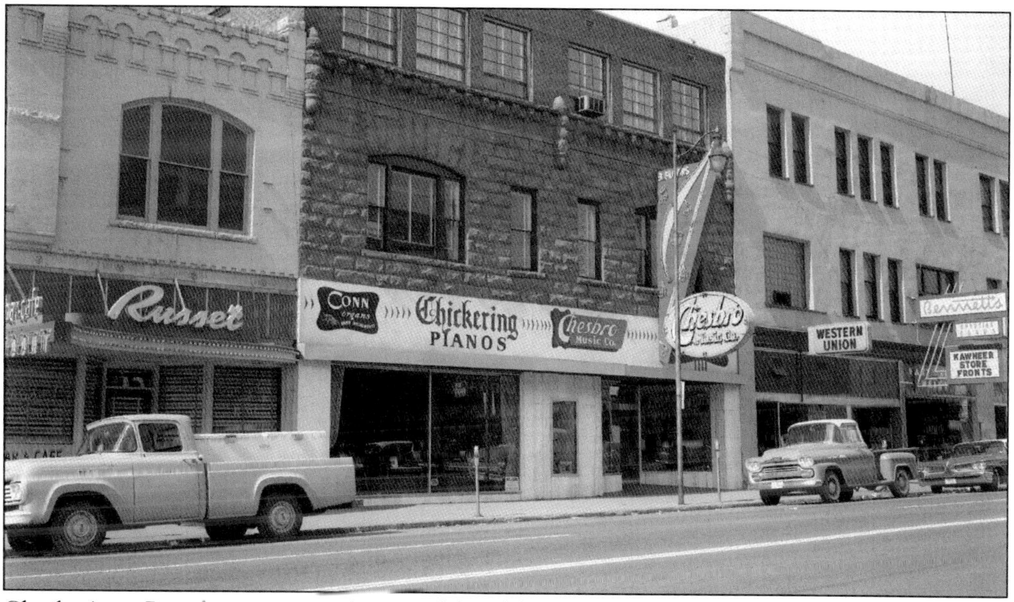

Chesbro's on Broadway is not only one of the oldest surviving businesses in Idaho Falls but the largest distributor of sheet music in the western United States. Horace and Ella Chesbro built their first store in 1918 with living quarters on the second floor, then moved to the present location on Broadway in the mid-1920s. In 1925, there were no bands in Idaho Falls area schools, so Chesbro hired band teachers to establish school music programs in several towns, including Rexburg and Idaho Falls.

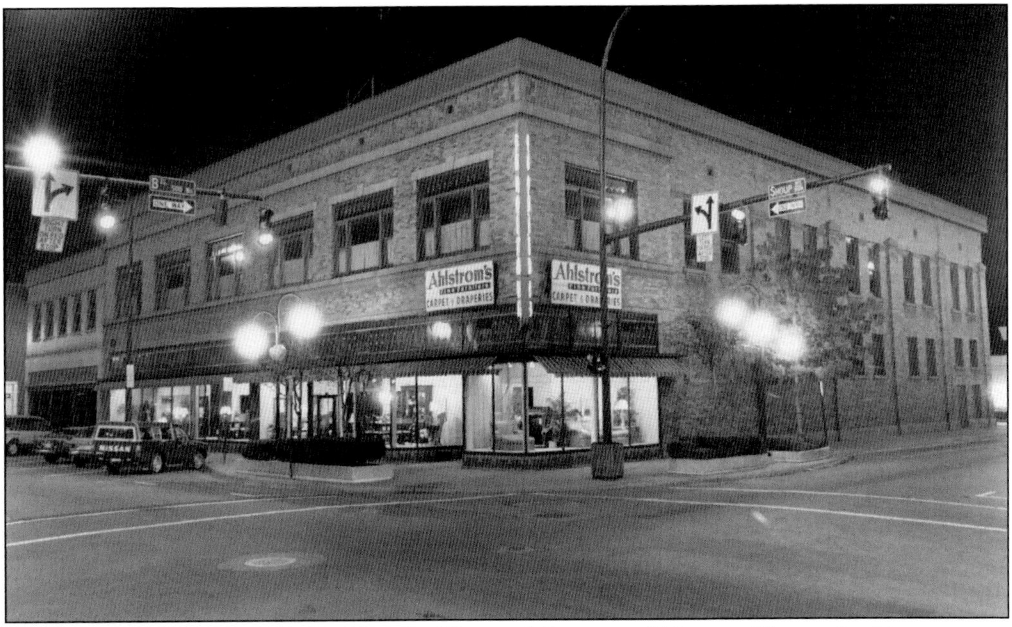

Another former department store on the National Register of Historic Places, the Montgomery Ward Building was constructed in 1928–1929 at 504 Shoup Avenue. The downtown department stores fueled economic development in the early part of the 20th century but began dying out in the 1960s and 1970s as Idaho Falls pushed out into suburbs and shopping centers.

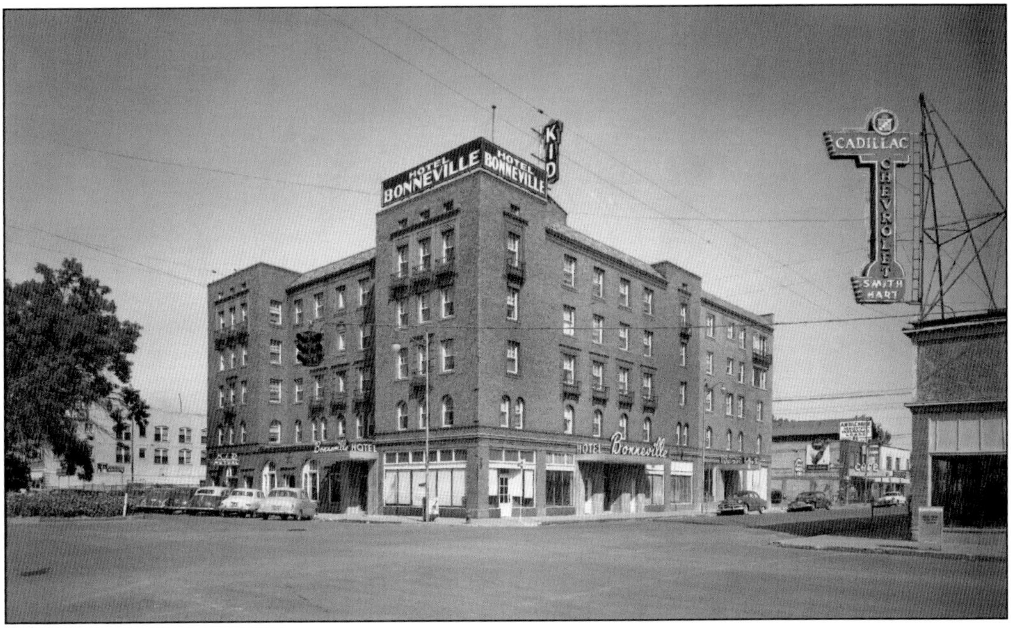

The Hotel Bonneville on C Street (now Constitution Avenue) was built by the Idaho Falls Community Hotel Corporation, a group of 421 local citizens under the direction of Idaho Falls attorney O. A. Johannsen and the chamber of commerce. It was built to bring a first-class hotel with convention facilities downtown and boasted a large central lobby, two dining rooms, and a ballroom. The five-story Italian Renaissance–style building boasted the state's first "fireproof" construction. (Perk's Photo collection.)

Another publicity still taken around 1920 uses movie stars Lillian Russell and Ben Turpin to emphasize the Idaho baker. The photograph was distributed by Northern Pacific Railroad to promote "the Route of the Great Baked Potato."

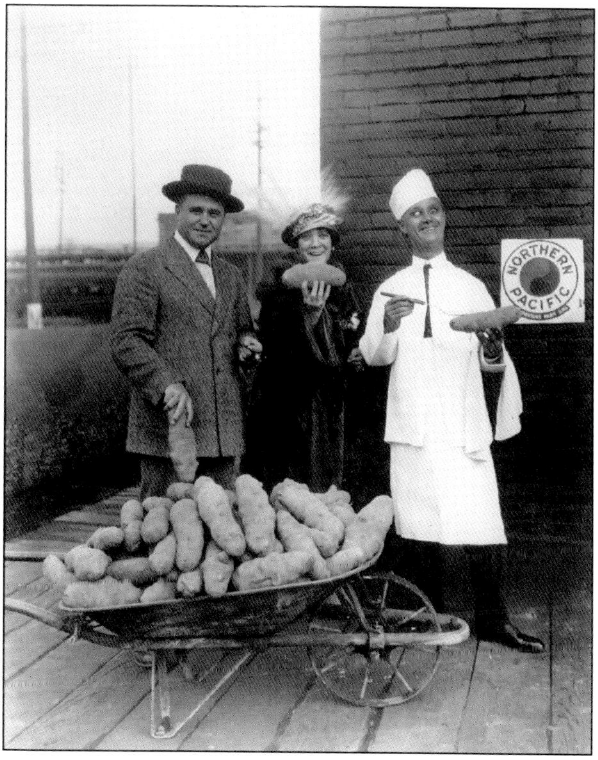

Idaho Falls west of the railroad tracks was a series of tree-lined residential streets just north of the downtown area, but there were few residences east of Holmes Avenue prior to the atomic energy test site's arrival in the early 1950s. This photograph looking west toward the Arco desert shows the stockyards with railroad tracks and sparsely settled North Yellowstone Highway traversing eastward, and was taken about the time the *Post Register* moved its offices from downtown to 333 North Yellowstone Highway. (Perk's Photo collection.)

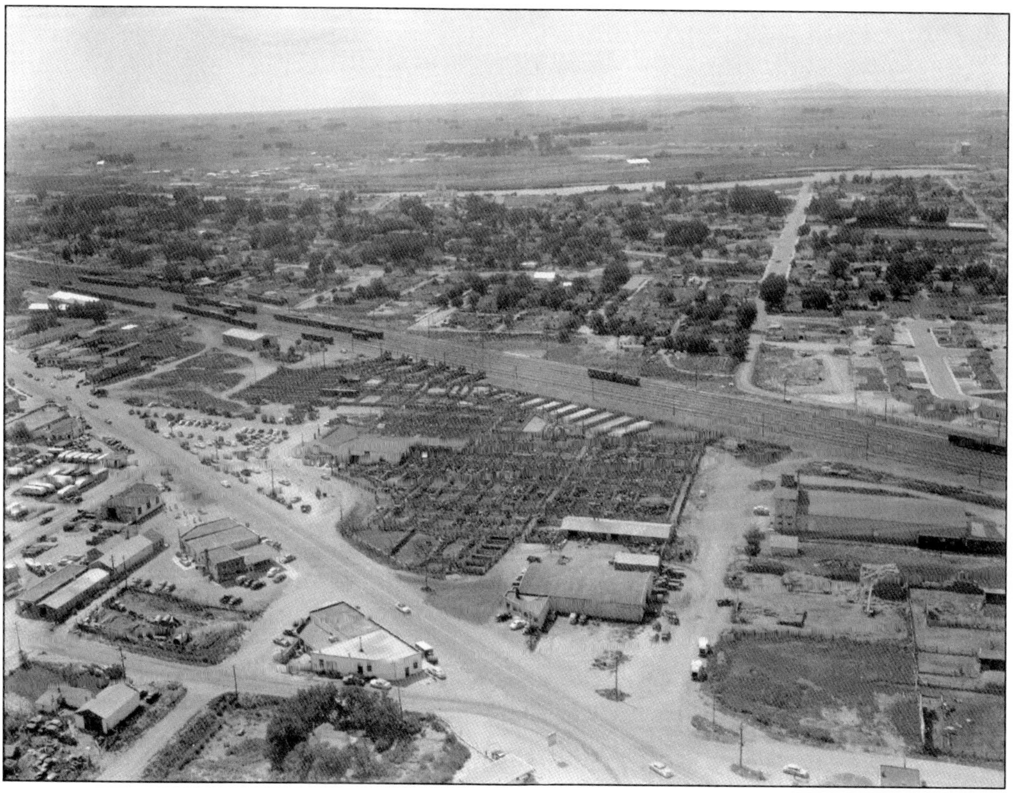

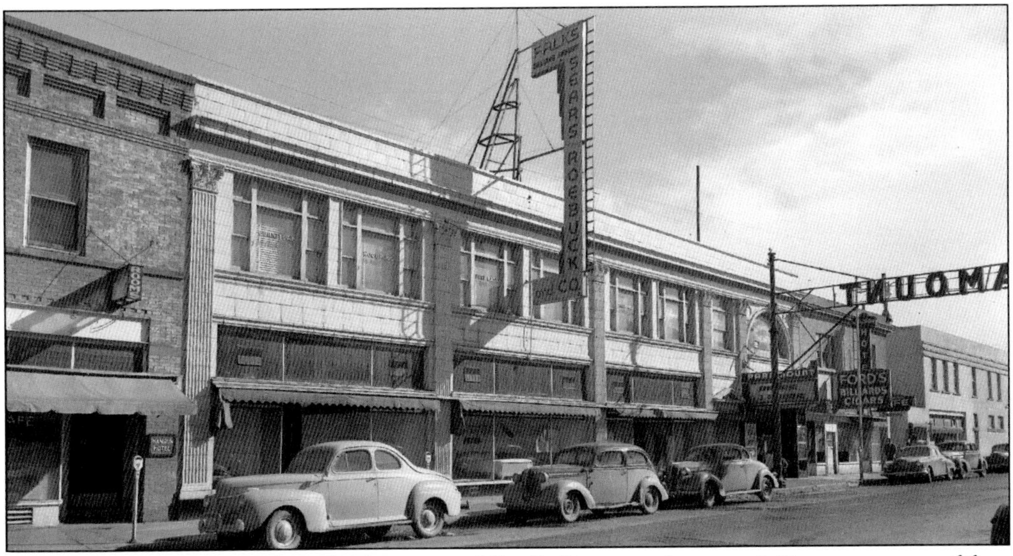

The Paramount (now Colonial) Theatre and Ford's Bar next door on A Street are two of four landmarks still in operation for their original intended use, according to Jan Blickenstaff of the city's planning department. The others are all nearby: the Independent Order of Odd Fellows Hall at the corner of Park Avenue and A Street; and the Center Theater on Park, formerly the Rex Theater. The Colonial Theater on A Street is now home of the Idaho Falls Arts Council and the Willard Arts Center. (Perk's Photo collection.)

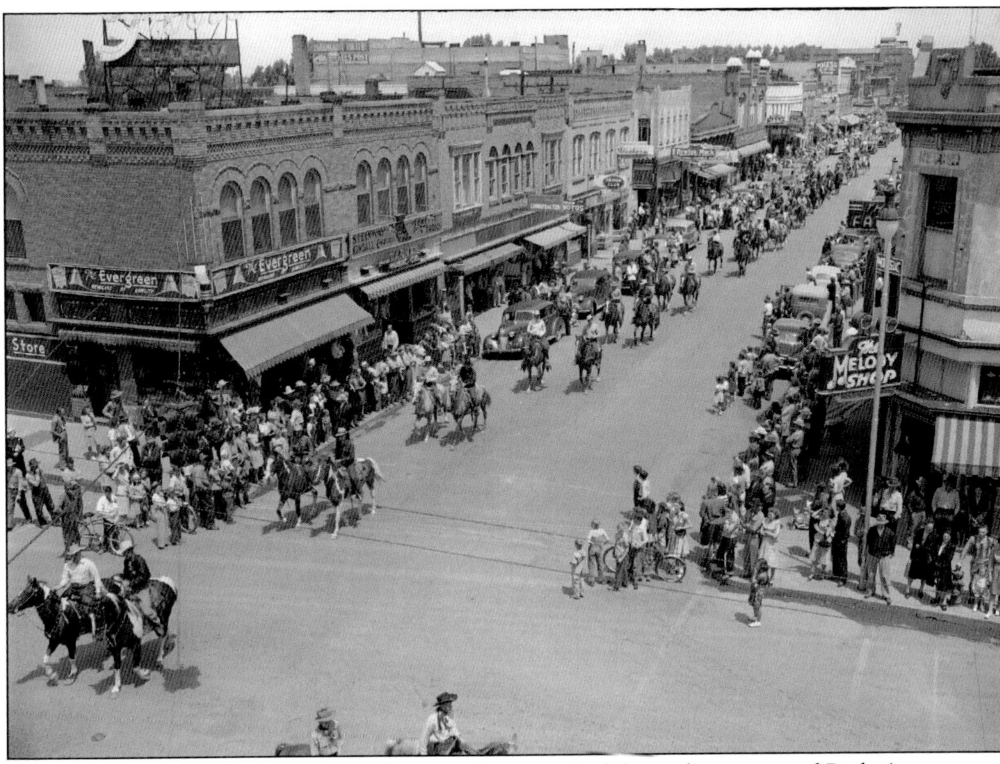

This parade in downtown Idaho Falls was photographed from the corner of Park Avenue and Broadway. The outdated "*Idaho Falls Post*" sign looms in the background.

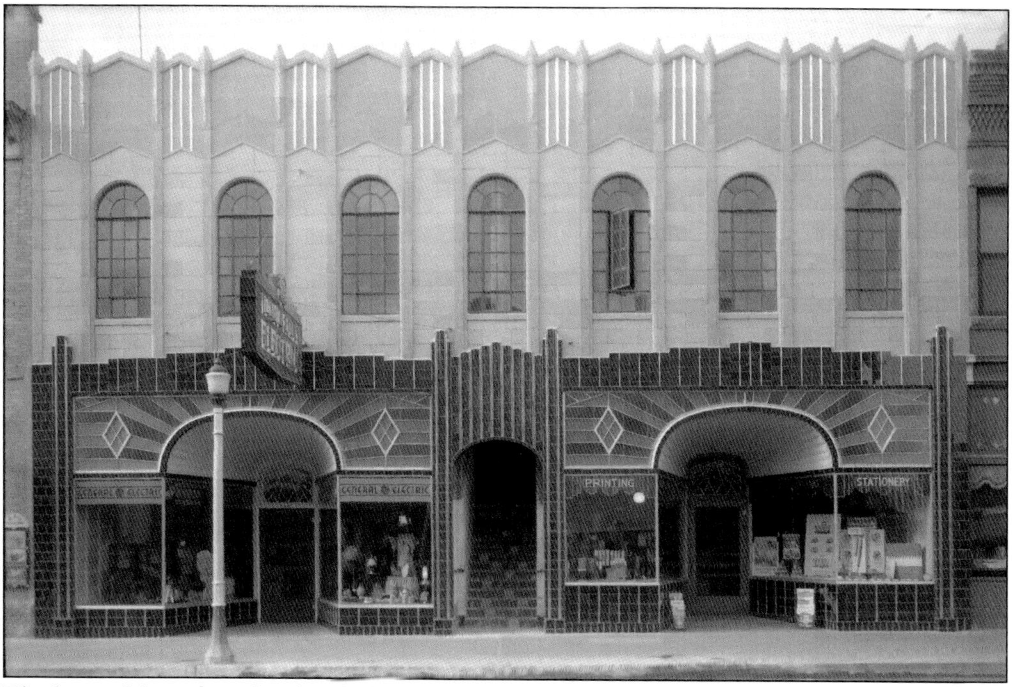

The beautiful art deco facade of Idaho Falls Electric (left) and Scott's bookstore and stationery (right) was one of only a few exhibiting that architectural style in downtown Idaho Falls. Covered now by more modern materials, the building on the south side of Broadway was originally the Scenic Theater, built around 1910. (Perk's Photo collection.)

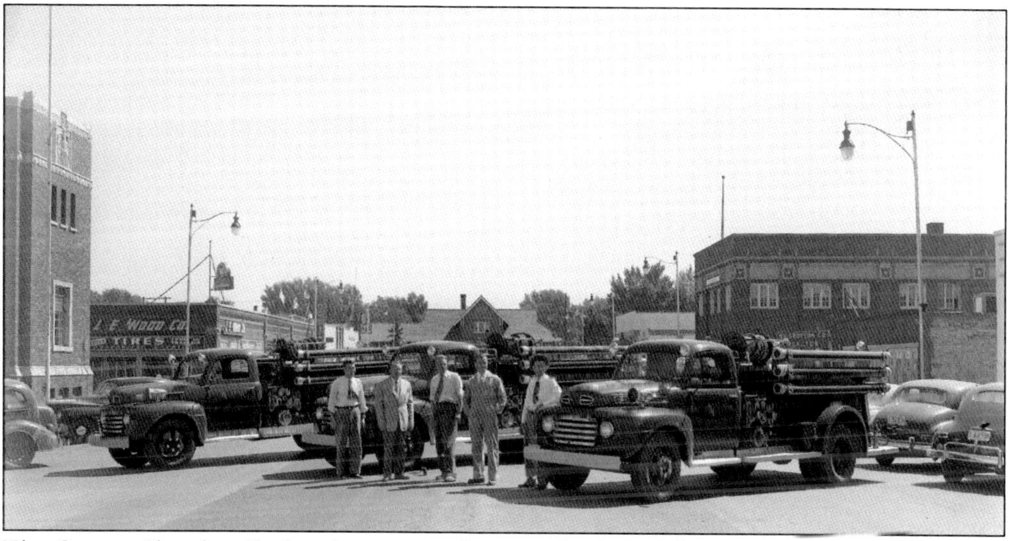

The Oregon Shortline Railroad passenger depot at the foot of C Street is just visible behind a display of fire engines spread out in front of city hall. The depot was torn down in the 1960s to make room for Yellowstone Highway, but during the heyday of passenger trains, the hotels along C Street (now Constitution Way) catered to rail travelers. The Underwood (347 Constitution Way), the five-story Bonneville Hotel, and the former Hotel Idaho (482 Constitution Way) are on the National Register of Historic Places, as is the Idaho Falls City Building, just visible on the left, built in 1929–1930. (Perk's Photo collection.)

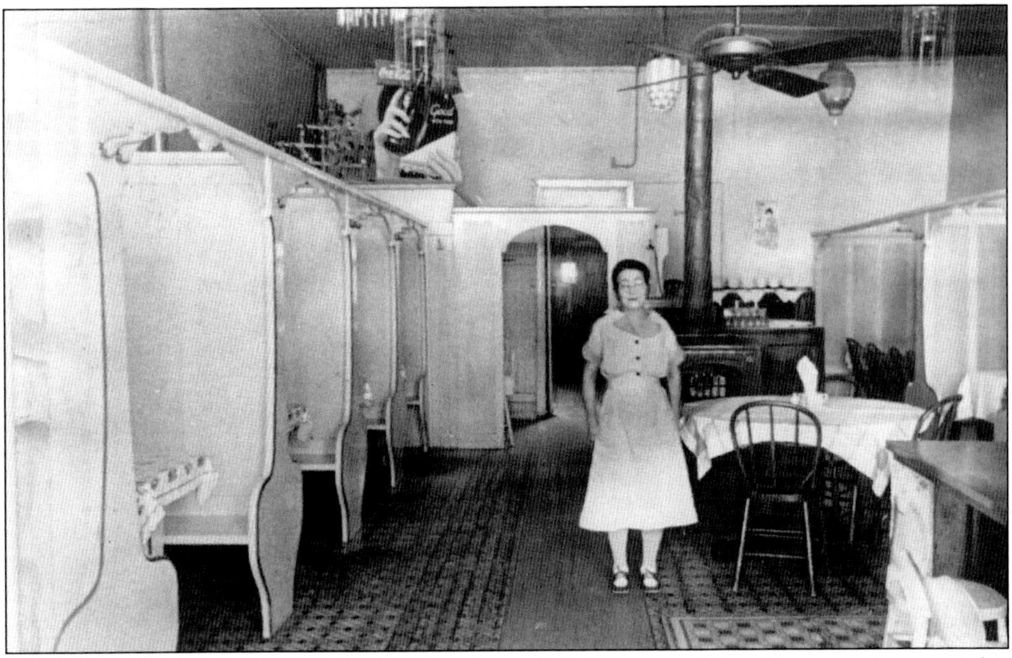

Several downtown restaurants were landmarks in their day; one of the oldest eateries was Ada's Café at 376 Shoup Avenue. It was established in 1930 as the Idaho Noodle Parlor by Mrs. Kane Mori, shown in the restaurant's interior. She was the mother of Ada Kishiyama, who took over the restaurant and ran it for more than 40 years with her husband, Bill, and sons Dan and Spencer. The Idaho Noodle Parlor menu, below, offers pork noodles for 30¢ and a T-bone steak for 50¢. Ada's closed its doors in 1988 after 58 years.

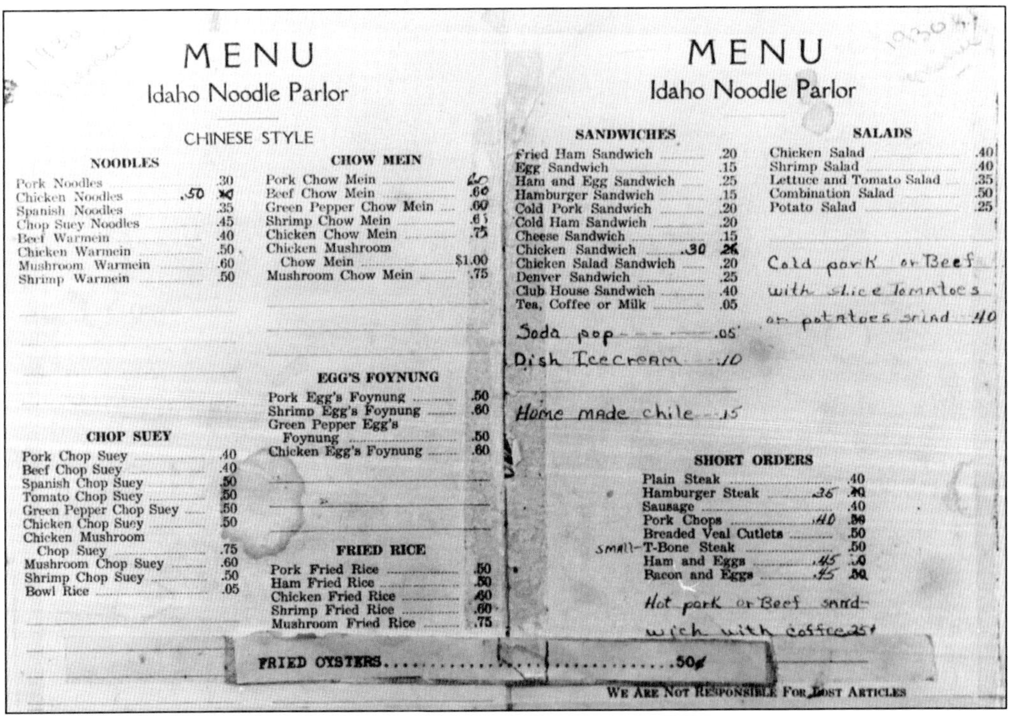

MENU

Idaho Noodle Parlor

CHINESE STYLE

NOODLES

Pork Noodles	.30
Chicken Noodles	.50 .40
Spanish Noodles	.35
Chop Suey Noodles	.45
Beef Warmein	.40
Chicken Warmein	.50
Mushroom Warmein	.60
Shrimp Warmein	.50

CHOW MEIN

Pork Chow Mein	.60
Beef Chow Mein	.60
Green Pepper Chow Mein	.60
Shrimp Chow Mein	.65
Chicken Chow Mein	.75
Chicken Mushroom Chow Mein	$1.00
Mushroom Chow Mein	.75

EGG'S FOYNUNG

Pork Egg's Foynung	.50
Shrimp Egg's Foynung	.60
Green Pepper Egg's Foynung	.50
Chicken Egg's Foynung	.60

CHOP SUEY

Pork Chop Suey	.40
Beef Chop Suey	.40
Spanish Chop Suey	.50
Tomato Chop Suey	.50
Green Pepper Chop Suey	.50
Chicken Chop Suey	.50
Chicken Mushroom Chop Suey	.75
Mushroom Chop Suey	.60
Shrimp Chop Suey	.50
Bowl Rice	.05

FRIED RICE

Pork Fried Rice	.50
Ham Fried Rice	.50
Chicken Fried Rice	.60
Shrimp Fried Rice	.60
Mushroom Fried Rice	.75

FRIED OYSTERS..........................50¢

MENU

Idaho Noodle Parlor

SANDWICHES

Fried Ham Sandwich	.20
Egg Sandwich	.15
Ham and Egg Sandwich	.25
Hamburger Sandwich	.15
Cold Pork Sandwich	.20
Cold Ham Sandwich	.20
Cheese Sandwich	.15
Chicken Sandwich	.30 .25
Chicken Salad Sandwich	.20
Denver Sandwich	.25
Club House Sandwich	.40
Tea, Coffee or Milk	.05
Soda pop	.05
Dish Icecream	.10
Home made chile	.15

SALADS

Chicken Salad	.40
Shrimp Salad	.40
Lettuce and Tomato Salad	.35
Combination Salad	.50
Potato Salad	.25

Cold pork or Beef with slice Tomatoes or potatoes salad .40

SHORT ORDERS

Plain Steak	.40
Hamburger Steak	.35 .40
Sausage	.40
Pork Chops	.40 .50
Breaded Veal Cutlets	.50
small-T-Bone Steak	.50
Ham and Eggs	.45 [illegible]
Bacon and Eggs	.45 .50

Hot pork or Beef sand-wich with coffee 25¢

WE ARE NOT RESPONSIBLE FOR LOST ARTICLES

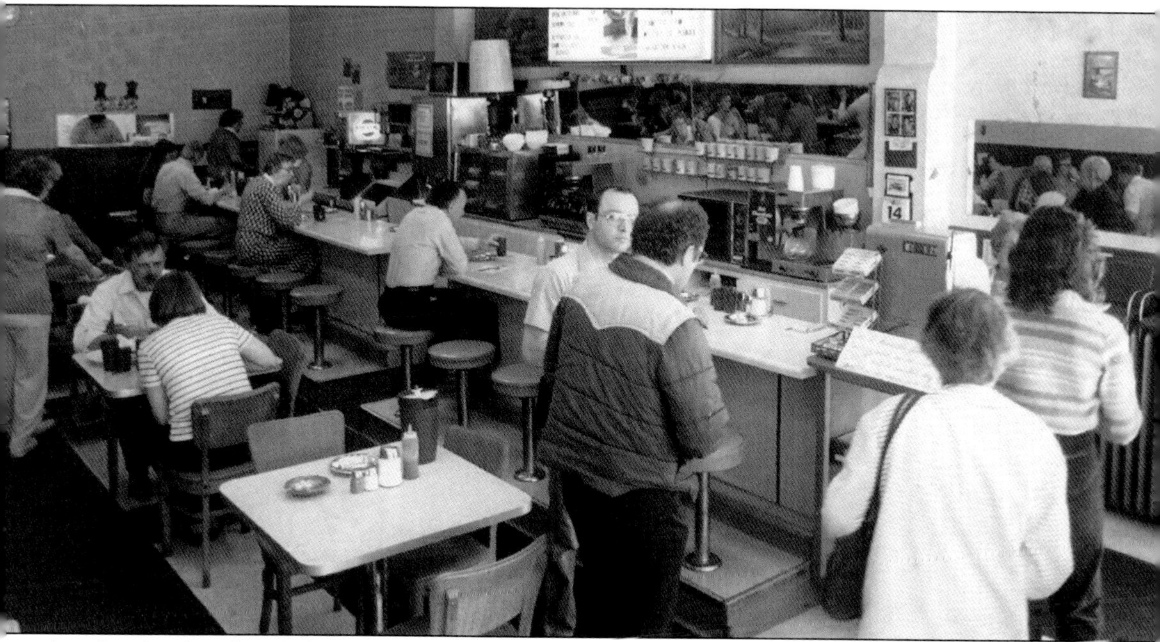

Another landmark café from Idaho Falls' downtown heyday was Hudson's at 549 Park Avenue. Waitresses sported name tags proclaiming "30 years of the same old lousy service" in 1982, when owners Ruth and Ray Hudson closed rather than submit to the building owner's plans to remodel.

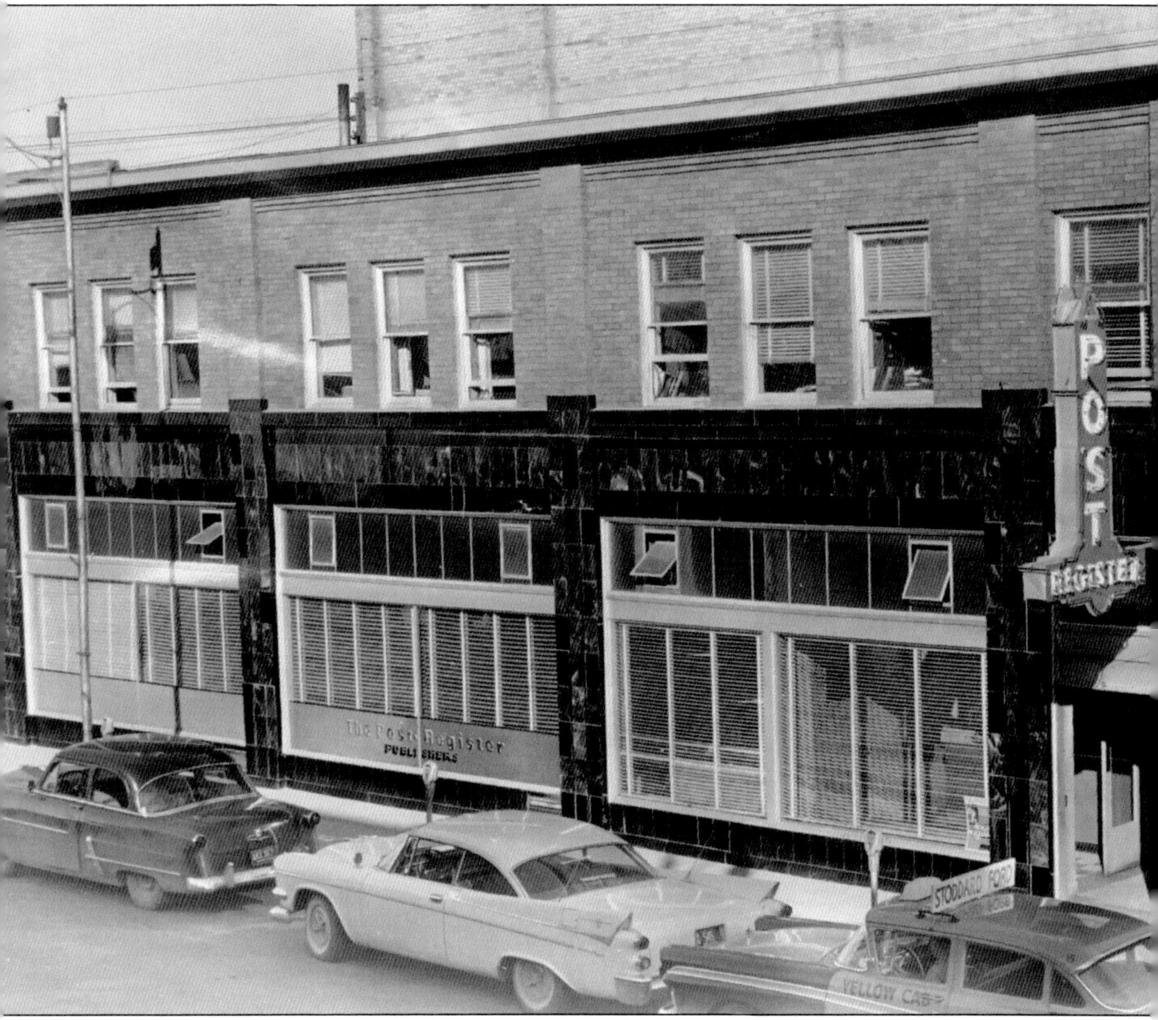

Following its merger with the *Times-Register*, the paper erected a neon "*Post Register*" sign over its door on Capital Avenue. By the time this picture was taken in the 1950s, its 40-year lifespan at its downtown location was nearing its end.

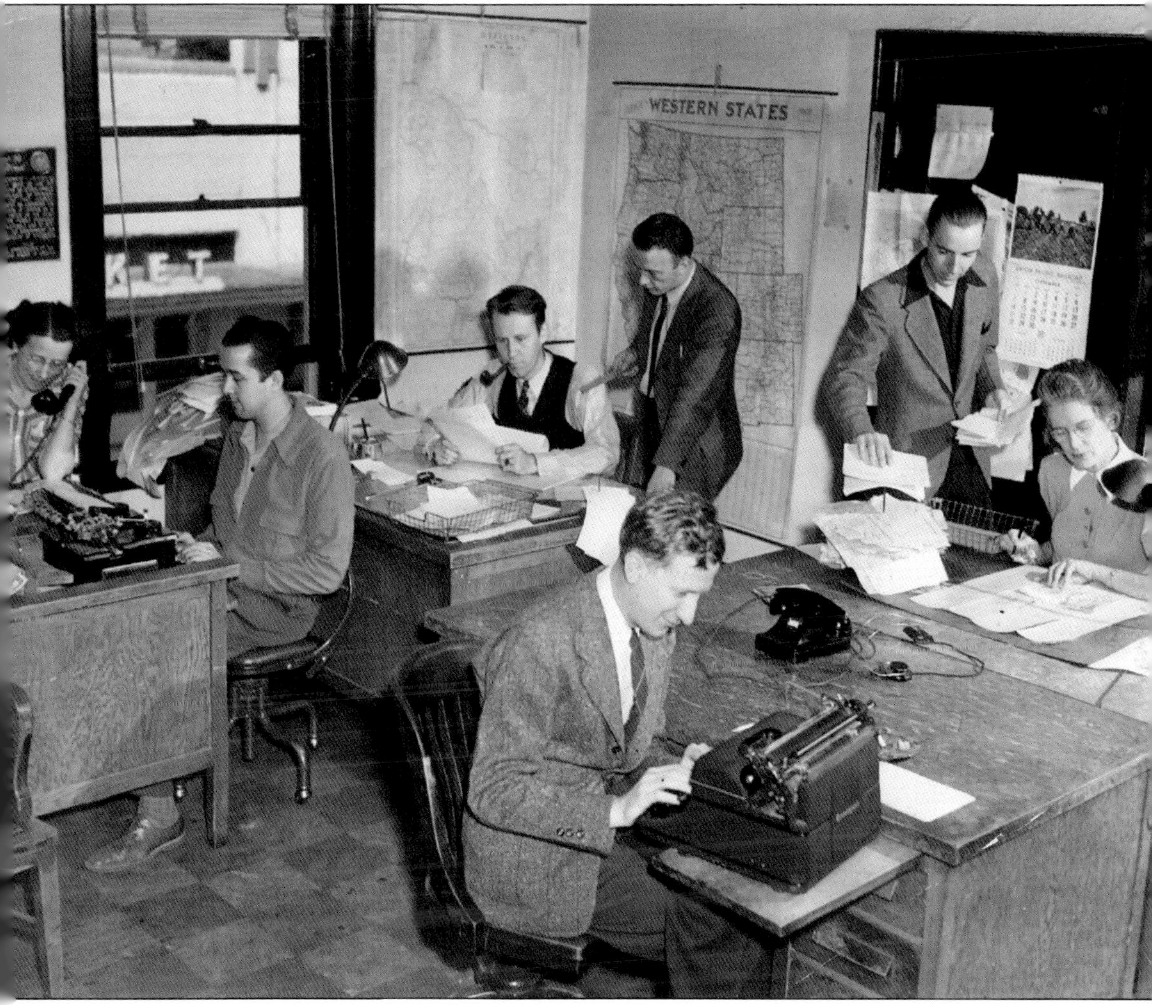

The *Post-Register* newsroom overlooked Capital Avenue from 1919 to 1959. While reporters took dictation or typed stories on manual typewriters, editors checked page layouts and spiked copy for a proofreader to make corrections prior to publication.

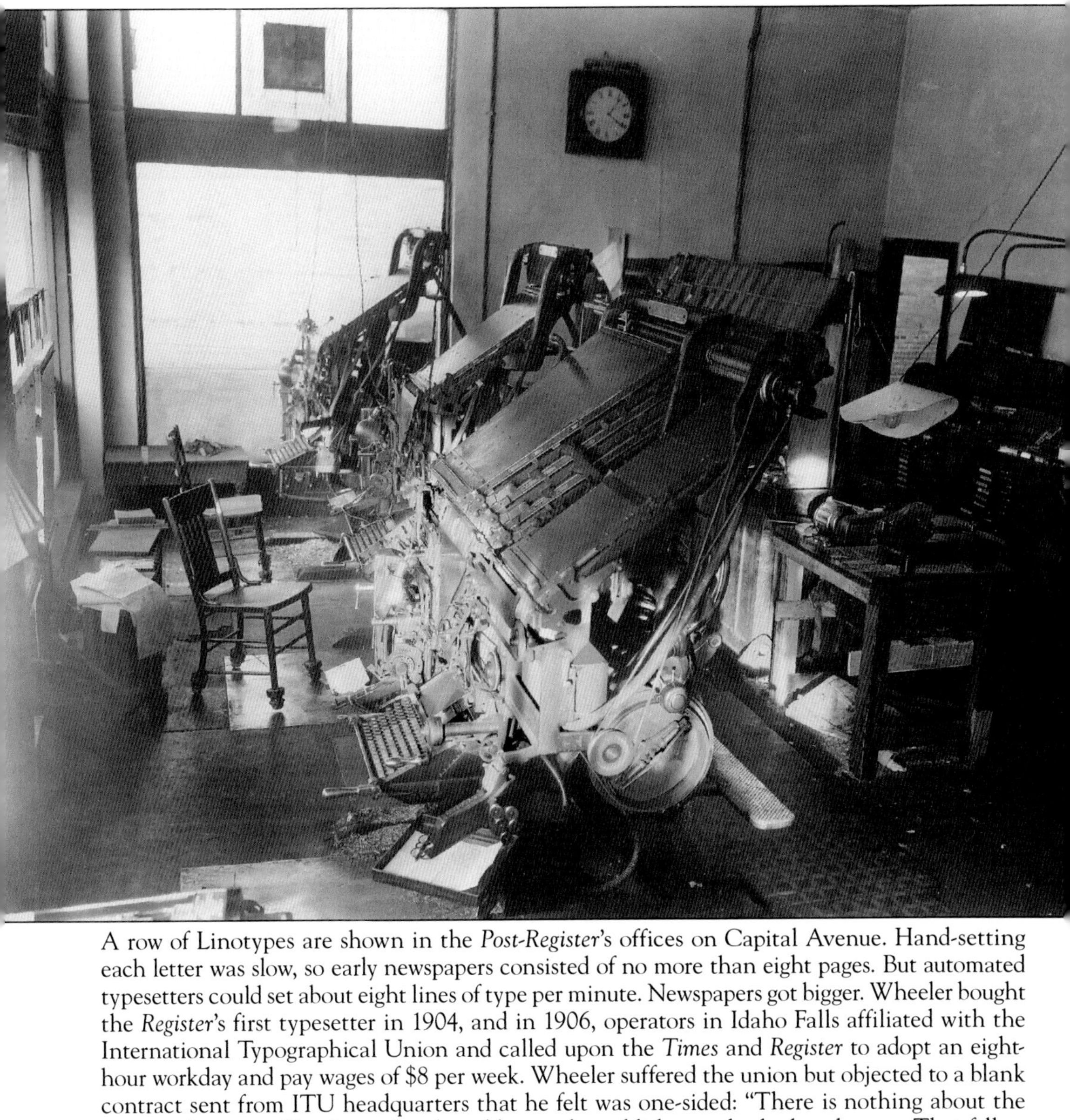

A row of Linotypes are shown in the *Post-Register*'s offices on Capital Avenue. Hand-setting each letter was slow, so early newspapers consisted of no more than eight pages. But automated typesetters could set about eight lines of type per minute. Newspapers got bigger. Wheeler bought the *Register*'s first typesetter in 1904, and in 1906, operators in Idaho Falls affiliated with the International Typographical Union and called upon the *Times* and *Register* to adopt an eight-hour workday and pay wages of $8 per week. Wheeler suffered the union but objected to a blank contract sent from ITU headquarters that he felt was one-sided: "There is nothing about the printer who goes off and gets drunk and leaves the publisher to do the best he can. That fellow is a shining light in the union."

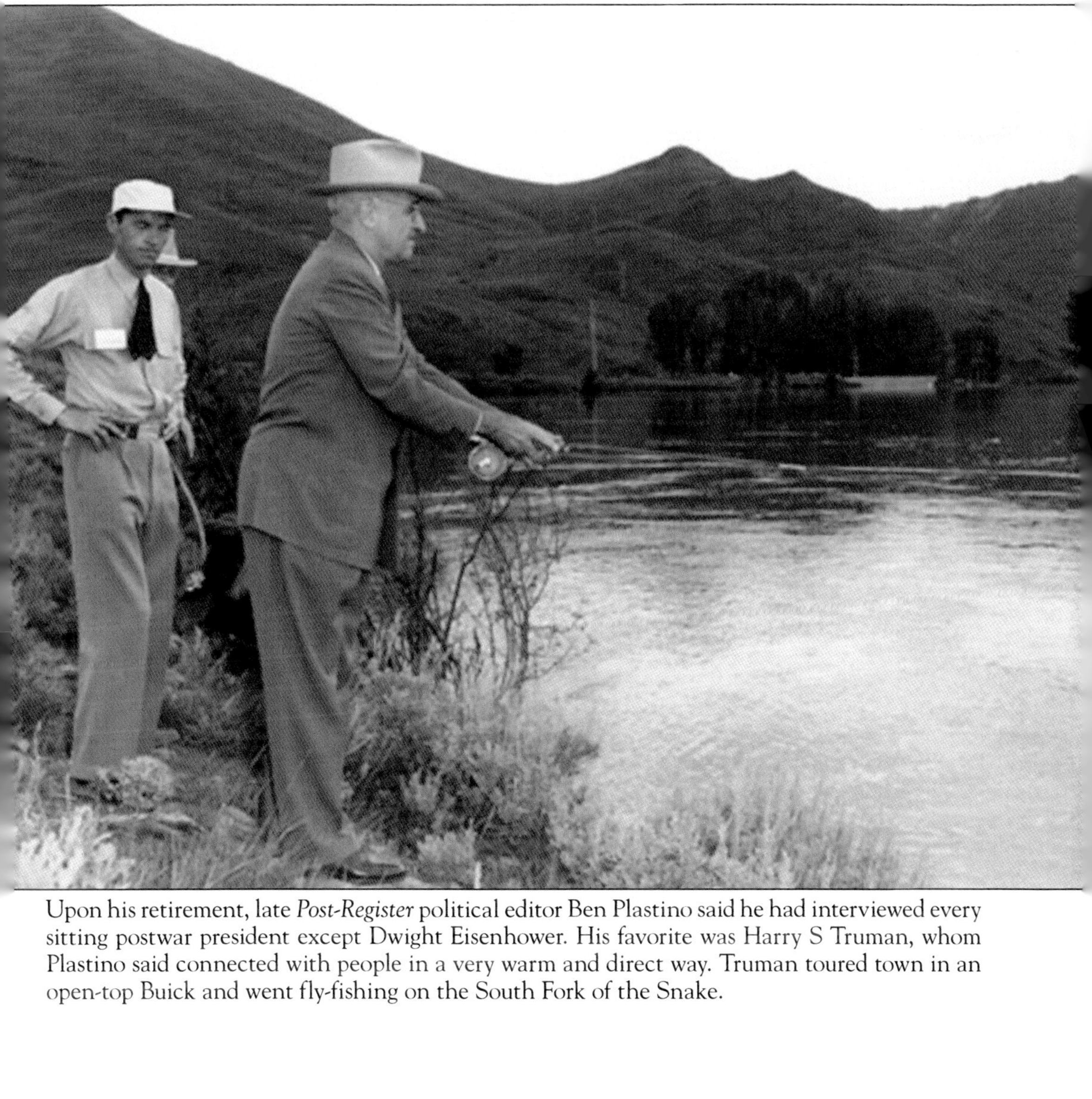

Upon his retirement, late *Post-Register* political editor Ben Plastino said he had interviewed every sitting postwar president except Dwight Eisenhower. His favorite was Harry S Truman, whom Plastino said connected with people in a very warm and direct way. Truman toured town in an open-top Buick and went fly-fishing on the South Fork of the Snake.

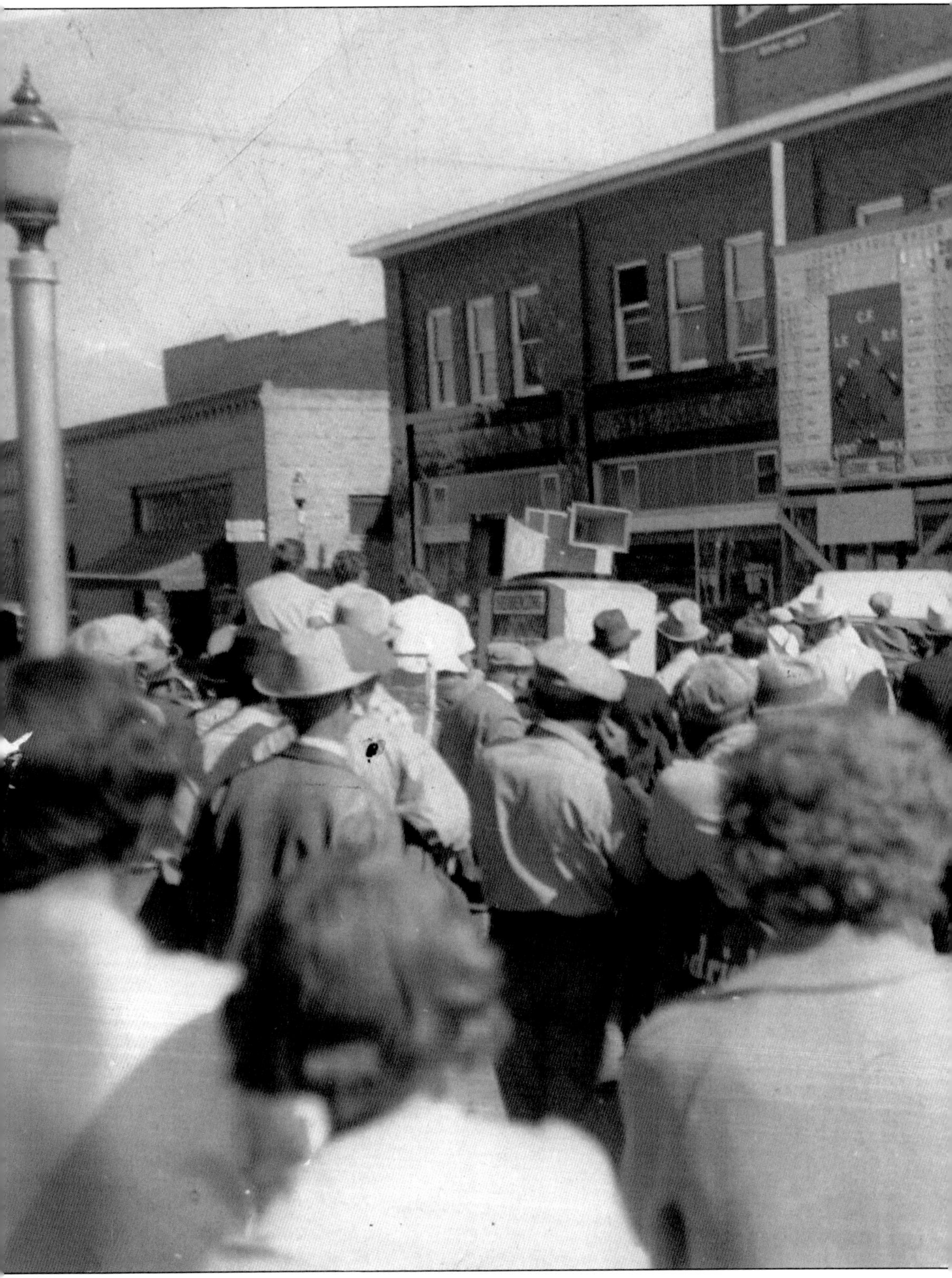

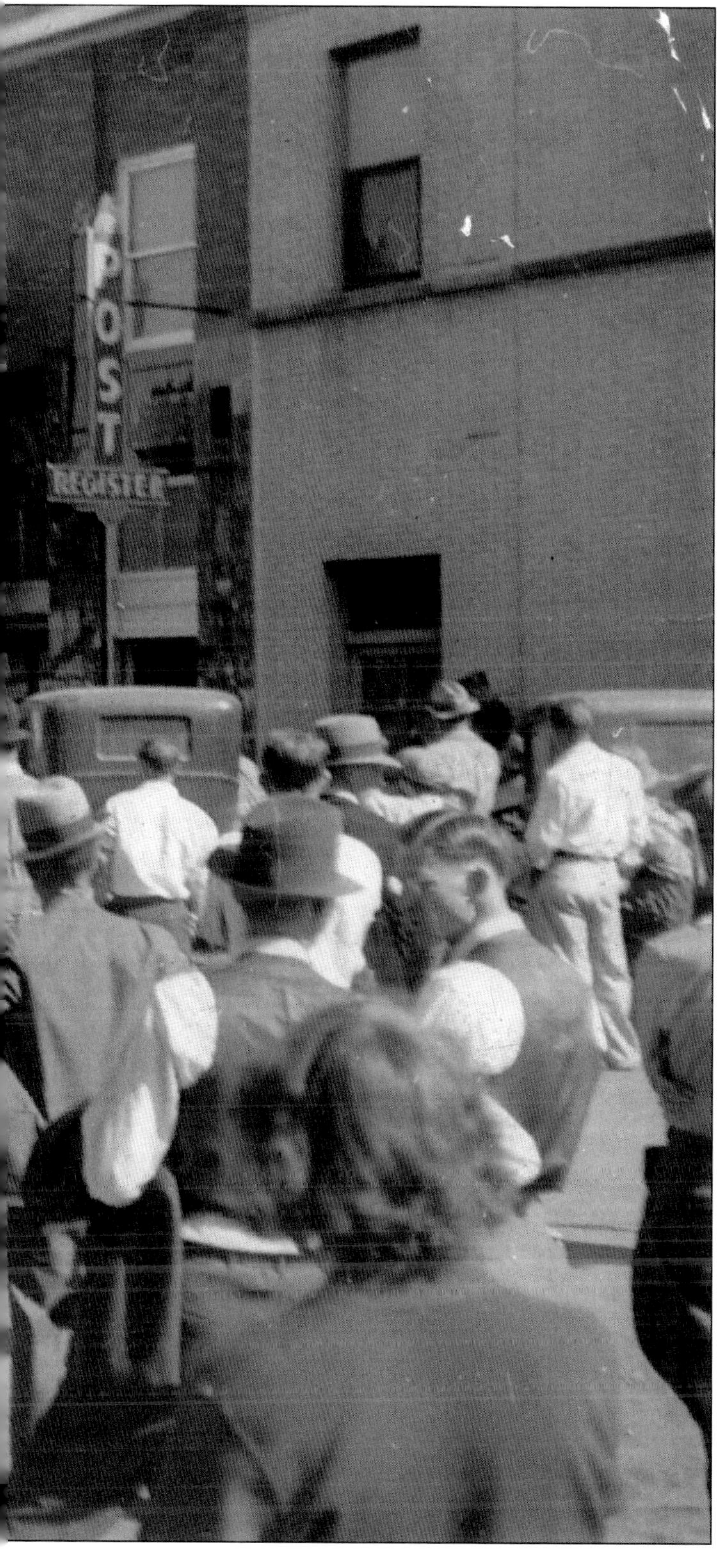

During the 1930s and 1940s, Capital Avenue in front of the *Post-Register* building would be blocked to traffic for the World Series. A 10-foot-square scoreboard was hung from a second-story window and, as the play-by-play came in over the leased telegraph wire, an announcer with a megaphone or sound system (center left) broadcast the results to the crowd standing out front. Mechanical runners would help baseball fans visualize the plays around a baseball diamond, manipulated by *Post-Register* circulation directors Joe Flora or Ernie Shononey. The board emitted chalk dust from a hole at home plate to indicate the ball's flight and direction, at a time when radio broadcasts were in their infancy and televised games were still a long way in the future.

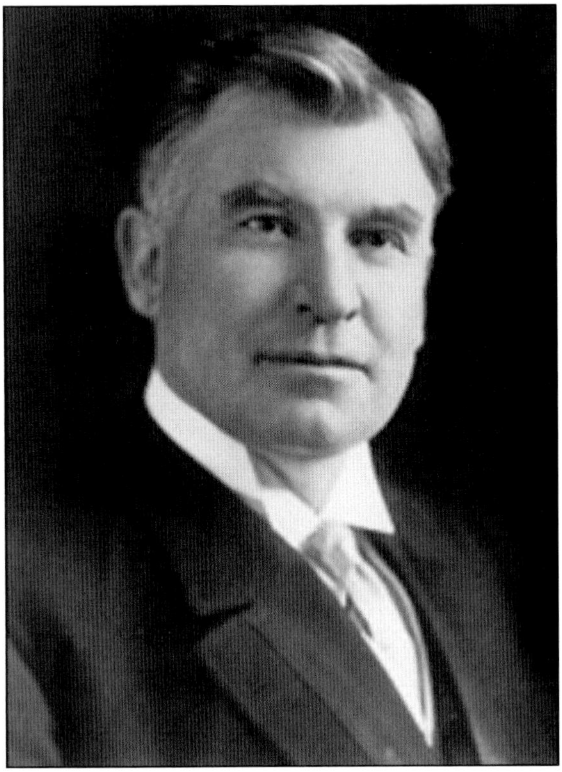

One family has controlled the state's second-largest newspaper for nearly 100 years, all descended from U.S. senator James H. Brady, seen here. Brady came to Idaho in 1895 after operating a small weekly newspaper in Kansas. He built a real estate empire and served one term as governor of Idaho and in the U.S. Senate from 1913 to 1918.

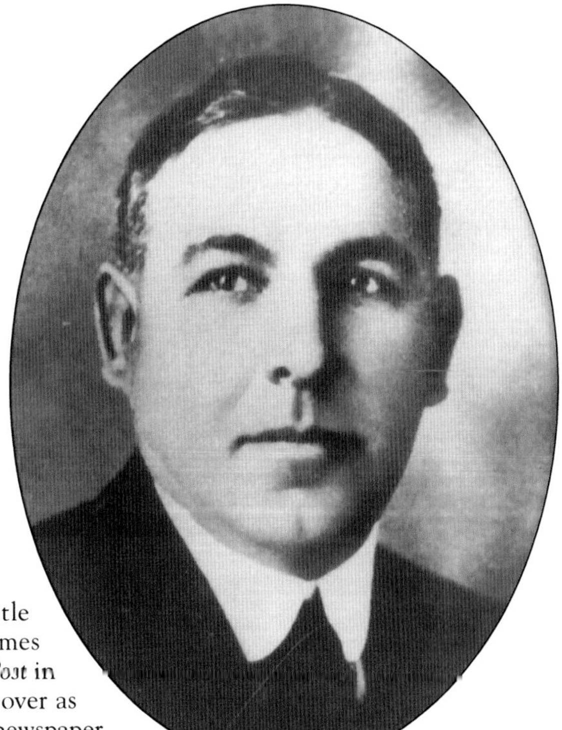

J. Robb Brady Sr. came to Idaho to settle the estate of his father, U.S. senator James H. Brady, but stayed on and bought the *Post* in 1925. A grandson, Jerry M. Brady, took over as publisher in 1999 and still serves as the newspaper corporation's head.

Seven

THE *POST-REGISTER*

After Sen. James H. Brady's death in 1918, his sons came to Idaho to settle his estate and were surprised at how extensive his holdings were, including land and irrigation projects and the Bannock Hotel in Pocatello.

J. Robb Brady Sr. had started in newspapers as a printer's devil at age six and was one of the founders of the *Tulsa (Oklahoma) World*. In 1925, Brady bought the *Idaho Falls Daily Post* and commuted from Pocatello on the train to run it. One of Brady's first decisions was to hire the Boise newspaper's young managing editor, E. F. McDermott. McDermott had an extraordinarily long and productive tenure at the paper, taking over when J. Robb Brady Sr. died in 1926, just a year after the purchase.

By 1931, it became apparent that the agricultural area in the grip of the Great Depression could not support two daily newspapers, and McDermott engineered the merger of the *Post* and the *Times-Register*. The last remnant of the feisty old *Times* was dropped from the masthead, and the newspaper became the *Post-Register*, combined circulation 4,550. M. B. Yeaman continued, again, as editor of the merged newspaper. Curiously, in the front-page announcement of the merger, no Brady was listed as an owner. Local stockholders were McDermott, Yeaman, Snyder, J. D. Ellis, J. H. Beasley, the Edith Read estate, and Mrs. M. T. Clark.

The new consolidated newspaper was continued from the plant facing Capital Avenue. In the Capital Avenue building, the presses were in the basement, the composing room on the street-level floor and the editorial offices upstairs on the second floor. It was home for the *Post-Register* for 28 years until the move to North Yellowstone Highway. McDermott ran the new paper as publisher for more than 50 years and steered the newspaper through a development program that won it national commendations for both typographical excellence and news content.

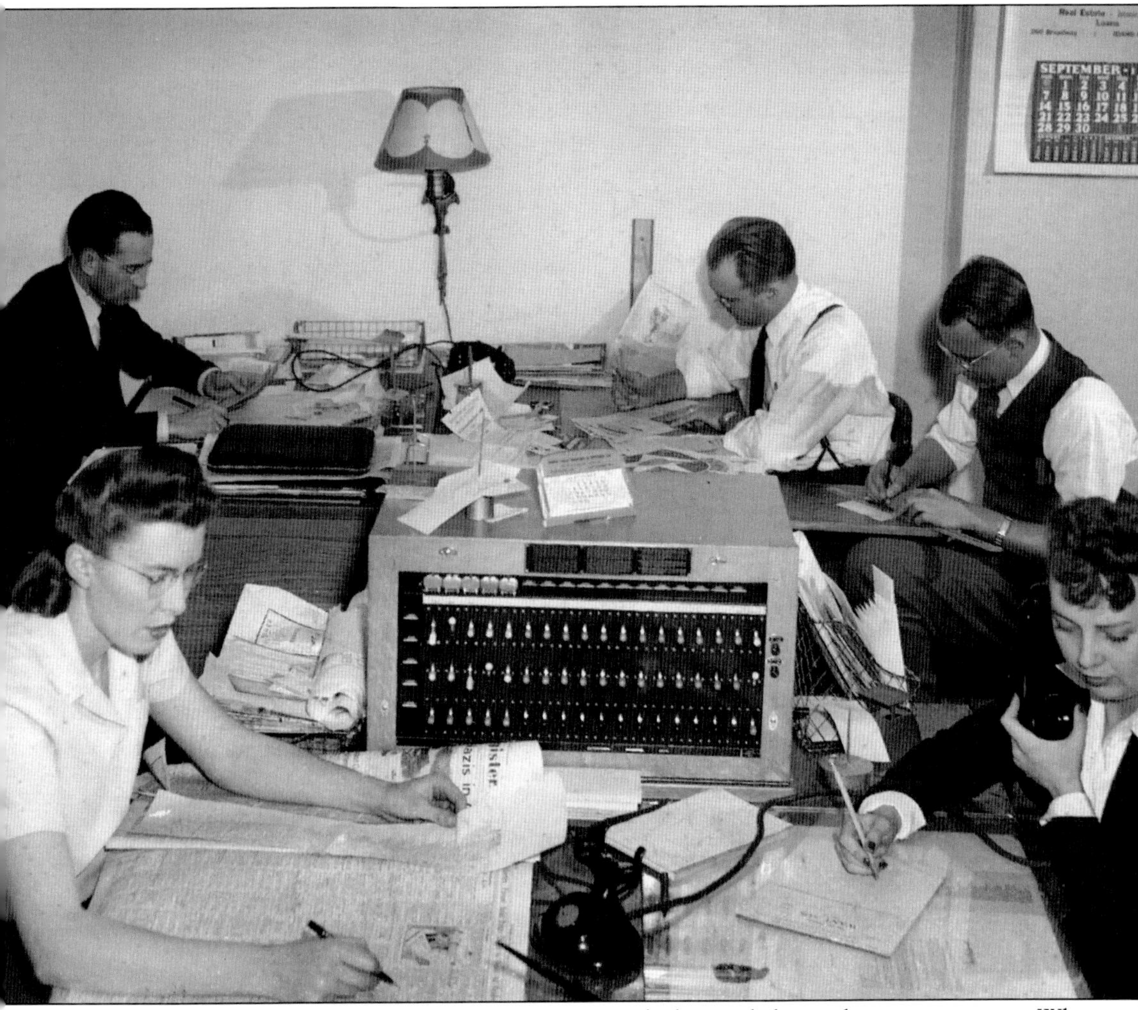

The *Post-Register* advertising department in 1941 was a little crowded in its downtown quarters. When the newspaper moved to its new home on Northgate Mile in 1959, available space quadrupled.

Idaho's most controversial literary figure was author Vardis Fisher, shown in this 1941 photograph. Fisher was born and raised near Ririe and became Idaho's most prolific author. In between writing 38 novels and pursuing a career as a college professor, he was also a weekly newspaper columnist from 1941 to 1968. At the time of his death, he was still writing a weekly column for the *Eastern Idaho Farmer*, whose editorial offices were next door to the *Post-Register*'s on Capital Avenue. The *Farmer* was operated for a time by Aden Hyde and former *Times* publisher William Snyder. The *Farmer* faded from the scene in about 1979.

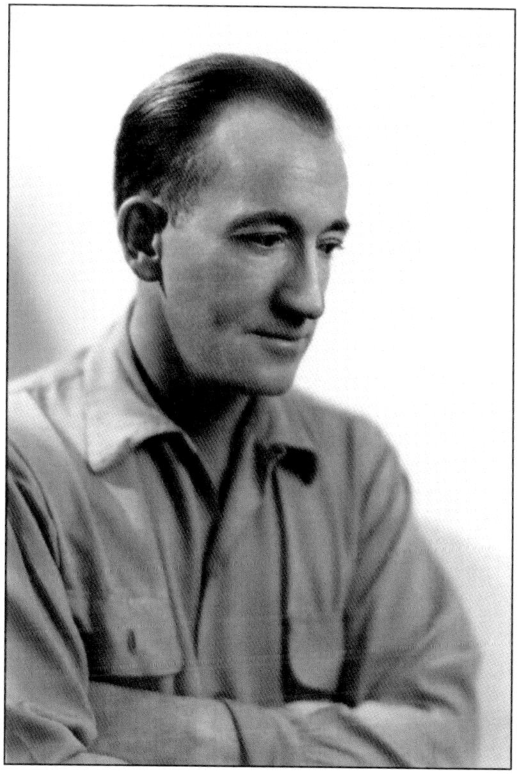

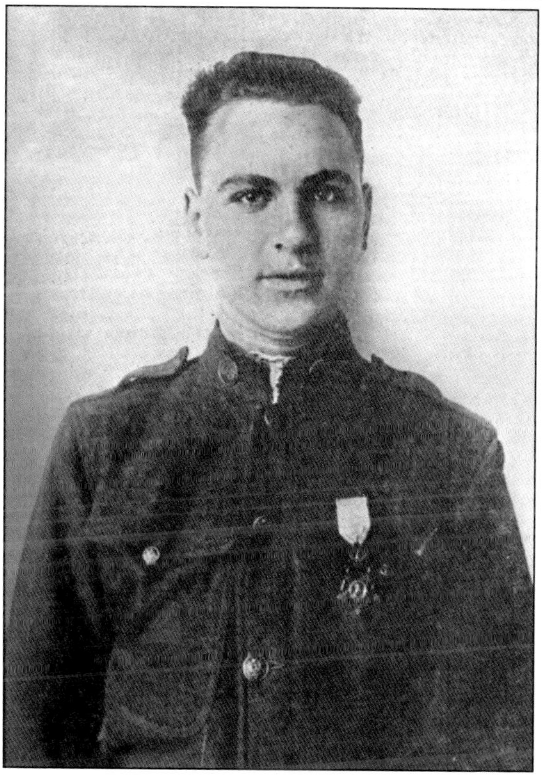

Army private Thomas C. Neibaur of Sugar City was Idaho's only World War I Medal of Honor recipient. After Neibaur died in poverty in 1942, his children in a foster home, columnist Vardis Fisher wrote a moving tribute in a newspaper column and demonstrated once again why his bluntness sometimes made him difficult to take. "When I read of Tom's death my mind went back first to the last time I saw him. It was early in 1938 and he came into my office in Boise, a dirty and starved and ragged man. . . . It is our shame that your native state turned the head of a boy with empty flattery and then completely forgot him. You once fought heroically to save the world for democracy; the lights will go on again but for you. Your light will shine brightly sometime in the future when a history of this state is written that will sift the worthy from the worthless and place the headstones where they belong."

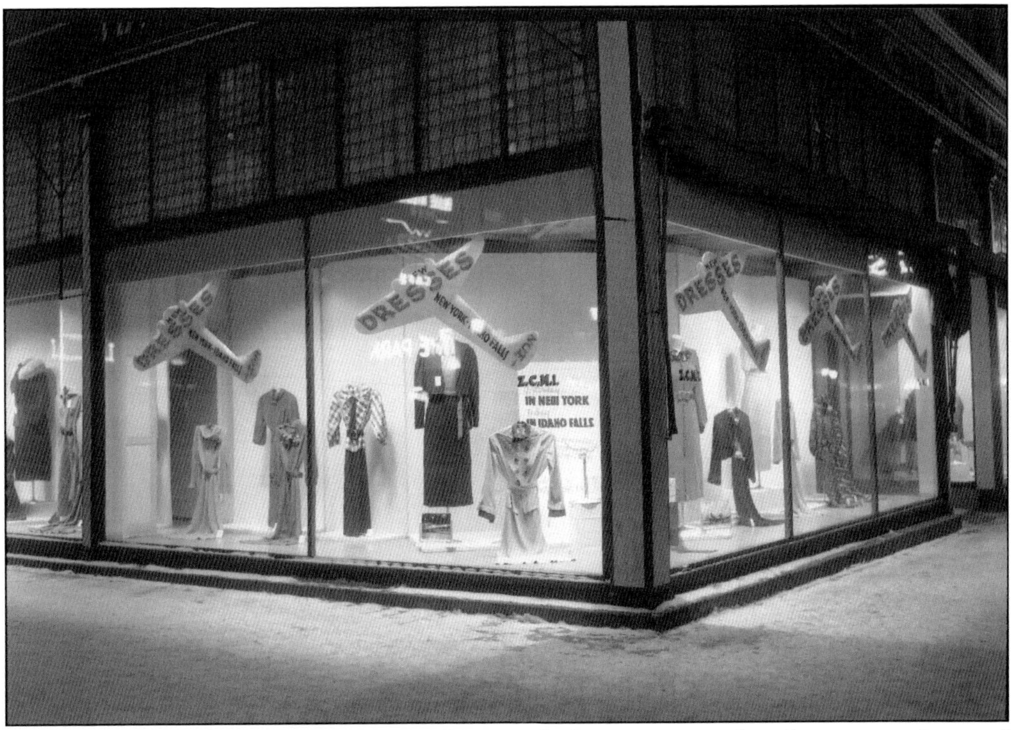

Dresses on sale at the Zion's Cooperative Mercantile Institution window downtown advertised the latest fashions: "Yesterday in New York, Today in Idaho Falls." ZCMI, founded in 1868, was the first department store in the United States. The Church of Jesus Christ of Latter-day Saints was a significant influence in the chain, retaining a majority interest until its sale in 1999 to the May Department Stores Company. By 2002, ZCMI had moved into the Grand Teton Mall when it and three other stores in Utah and Idaho were sold to Dillard's.

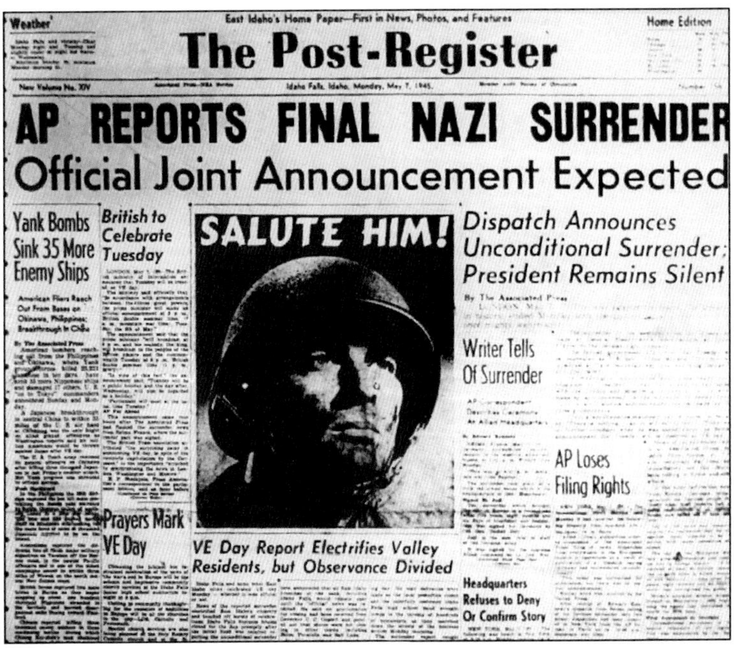
East Idaho's Home Paper—First in News, Photos, and Features

Home Edition

The Post-Register

Idaho Falls, Idaho, Monday, May 7, 1945.

AP REPORTS FINAL NAZI SURRENDER

Official Joint Announcement Expected

Yank Bombs Sink 35 More Enemy Ships

British to Celebrate Tuesday

SALUTE HIM!

Dispatch Announces Unconditional Surrender; President Remains Silent

Writer Tells Of Surrender

AP Loses Filing Rights

Prayers Mark VE Day

VE Day Report Electrifies Valley Residents, but Observance Divided

Headquarters Refuses to Deny Or Confirm Story

The 1945 *Post-Register*'s "circus"-style layout featured stacked banner headlines with lesser stories getting smaller headlines as the reader progressed down the page, often in three or more "decks." The style lent an air of urgency on even a mundane news day, in an era when newspapers simply did not have color options.

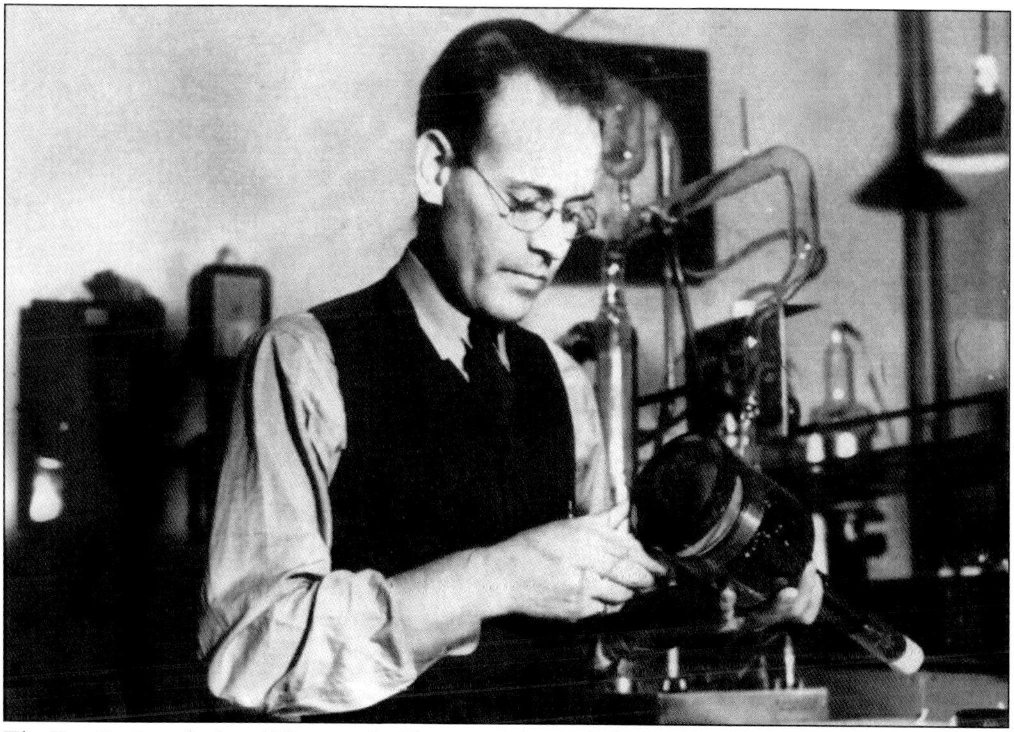

The *Post-Register* declared "Success for Hometown boy" Philo T. Farnsworth in a story announcing Farnsworth's return to eastern Idaho to help open the first eastern Idaho television station, KID-TV. The television station went on the air from its first studios on Ammon Road on December 20, 1953. If any state deserves credit as the place where television was invented, it is here, where Rigby High School student Farnsworth first sketched an electronic system and image dissector for chemistry teacher Justin Tolman. But Farnsworth spent most of his life elsewhere, producing several patents including one for television. The Utah native, an elder in the LDS Church, was honored by Utah with a place in Statuary Hall in Washington, D.C., and a 20¢ stamp was issued to honor him in 1983. Farnsworth is also honored at the Farnsworth TV Museum in Rigby, where Marie Taylor and her grandchildren were visiting in 1989 when the lower photograph was taken by *Post Register* photographer Robert Bower.

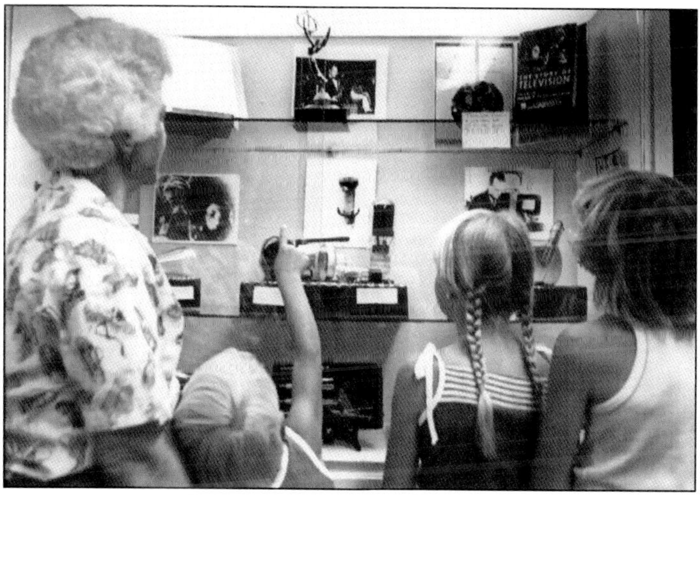

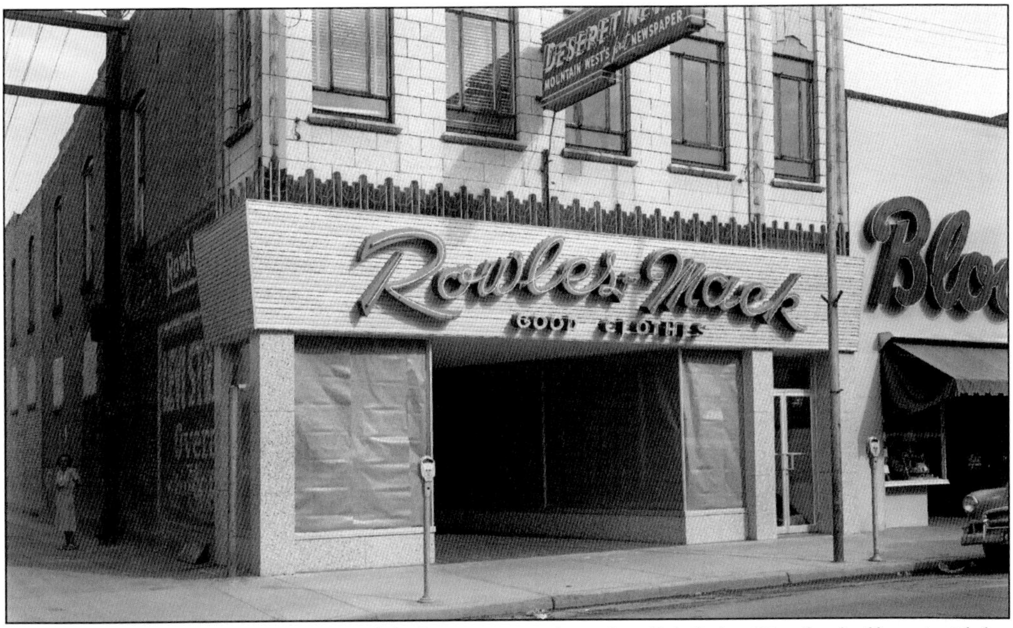

The *Deseret News*, a Mormon-owned daily newspaper based in Salt Lake City, had offices in Idaho Falls until a newsprint shortage in the 1970s forced the paper to retrench its circulation routes. The *News* offices were upstairs over a clothing store on Park Avenue, just around the corner from the *Post-Register* a block away.

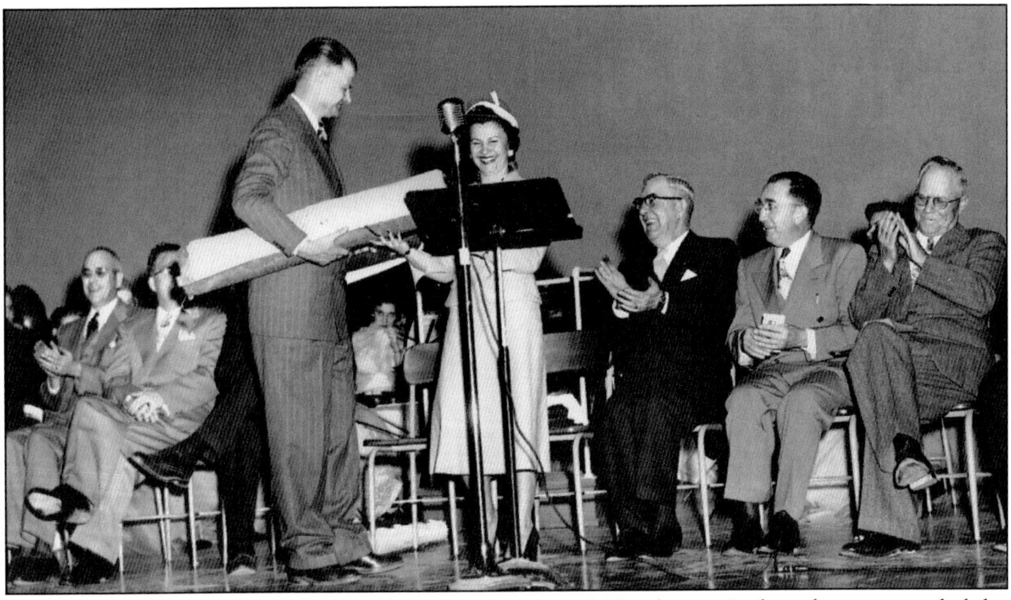

A 1987 news article described Ida Holden as an "energetic I. F. volunteer" when she was awarded the Alexis de Tocqueville medallion at the Kennedy Center for the Performing Arts in Washington, D.C. The medal has been given by the United Way since 1973 to honor volunteers. Holden is shown in this photograph at the dedication of the Civic Auditorium on March 13, 1953, with, from left to right, schools superintendent Clair E. Gale, former superintendent W. W. Christensen, and former mayors Thomas L. Sutton and Ed Fanning. The Holden family was linked to the newspaper since the town's earliest days. (Photograph by Melville's Studio, Idaho Falls.)

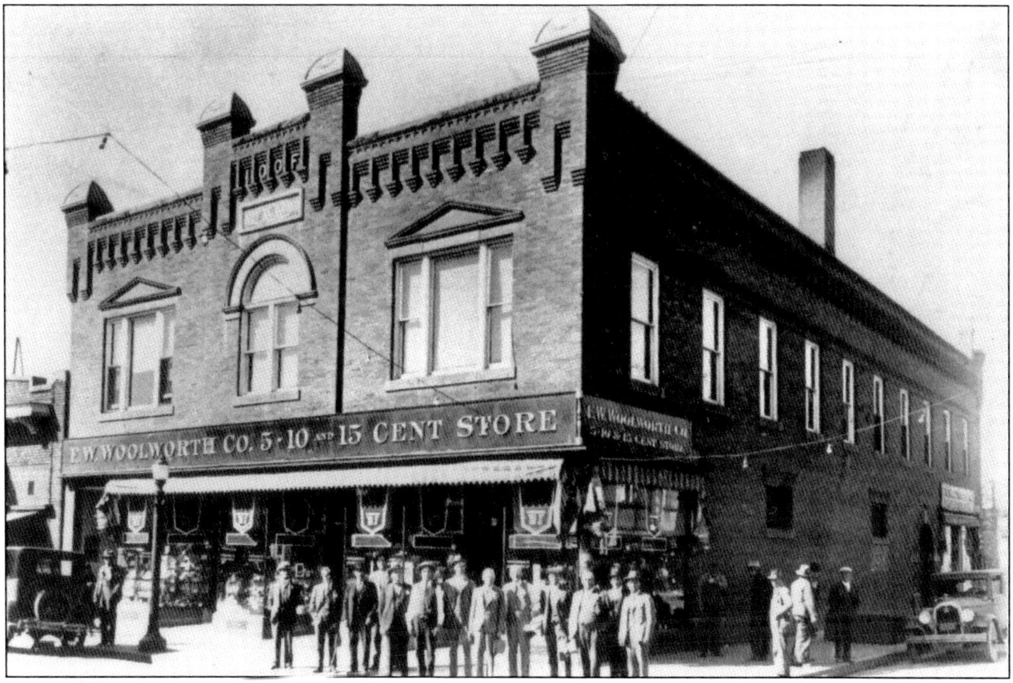

The F. W. Woolworth Company closed its doors at Park Avenue and A Street in 1970 after 51 years in the same location, another downtown department store that was a victim of shopping malls drawing new business to the outskirts of town.

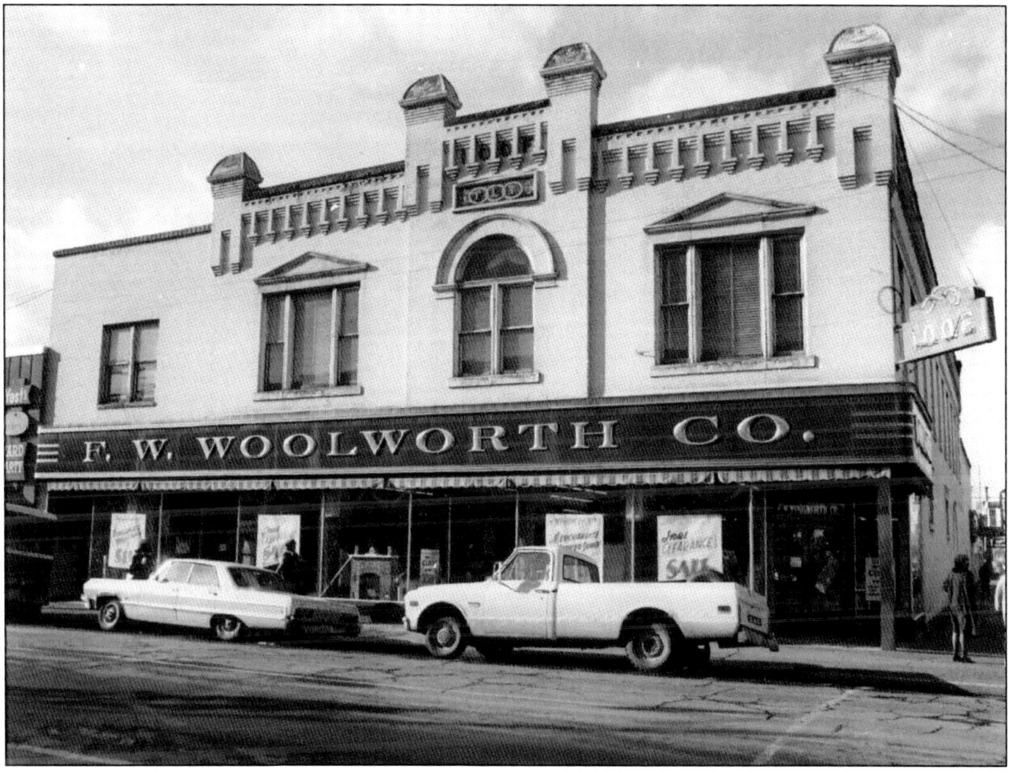

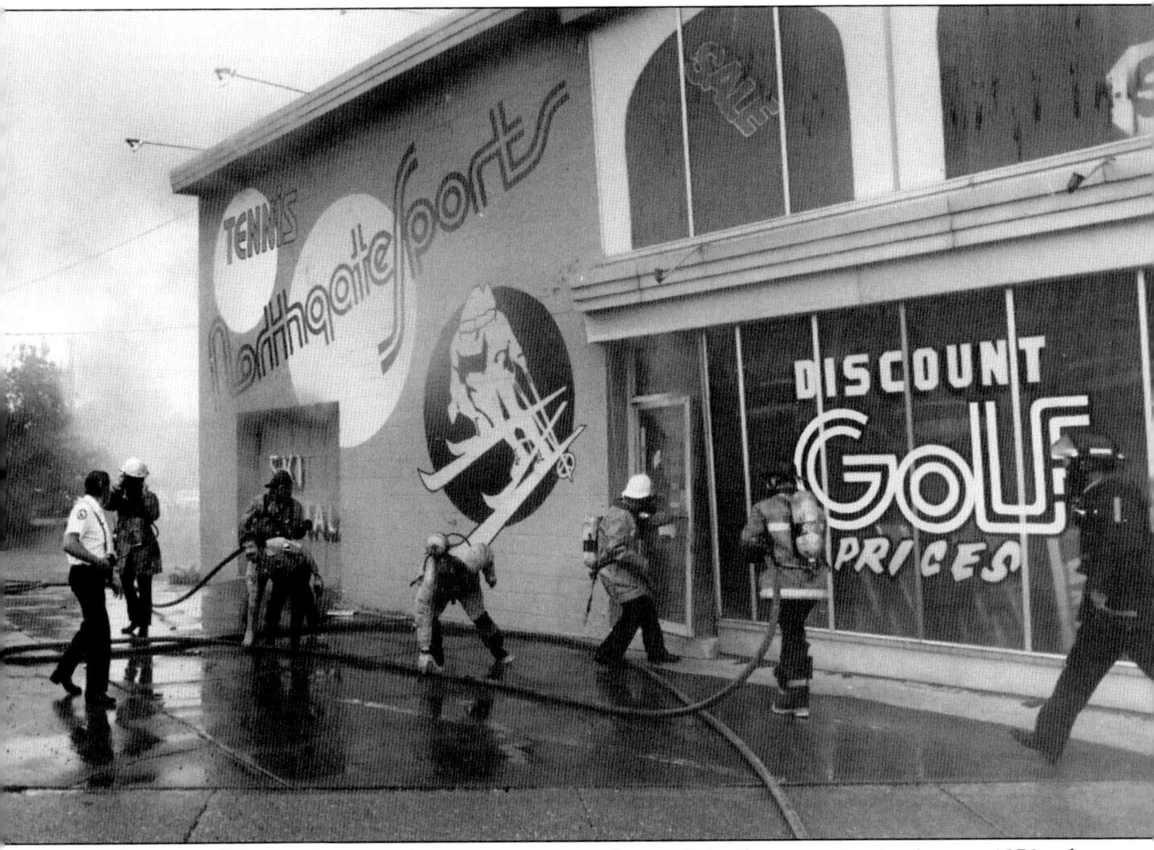

The second fire to threaten the newspaper struck on a Monday morning in August 1979, when the Northgate Sports Center next door was gutted by flames. A double fire wall between the two buildings prevented any damage to the newspaper's pressroom. The store suffered about $250,000 damage to merchandise alone. The building is now owned by the *Post Register* and houses its circulation and business departments.

Eight

E. F. McDermott's Visionary Era

The 50-year string of E. F. McDermott's business accomplishments began in hard times and continued through a period of unparalleled prosperity. In the depth of the Depression era, he created the Goodfellow Fund, a two-week Christmas fund drive that continues to this day. He is also credited with helping to launch the Community Chest, which became the United Way, eastern Idaho's biggest non-sectarian charity. For the newspaper's 50th birthday in 1934, he organized a three-day diamond jubilee celebration.

As one of the lay leaders of Holy Rosary Parish, he was instrumental in the construction of Sacred Heart Hospital. McDermott had a hand in founding the Idaho Falls Country Club and then, in 1940, brought semiprofessional baseball to Idaho Falls. He even managed the local team and went on to run the Pioneer League. In December 1937, the *Post-Register* rolled out its "Morning Rural Edition," the afternoon paper's first attempt at an early-morning publication. The edition was delivered by mail to rural subscribers and by train to outlying areas.

The end of World War II heralded a period of growth and prosperity for the region and the paper. The Snake River Valley fulfilled its earlier promise and became a major producer of farm products and a world center for potato production.

In 1949, McDermott spotted the opportunity to put a broader base under eastern Idaho's economy. He helped spearhead the drive to bring the Atomic Energy Commission's reactor research station here. He wrote front-page editorials and served as a member of a lobbying delegation to Washington. The paper made no pretense at objectivity on the matter.

McDermott had also been a cheerleader for construction of the Palisades Dam, a $70-million project that started in 1951. Those were boom times in Idaho Falls. The value of the nuclear research lab project exceeded the assessed valuations of the surrounding counties. All that construction work on the desert and up the South Fork brought new workers, and homebuilding activity set records in the 1950s, with more than 600 building permits per year. More than 1,600 homes were built in Idaho Falls between 1949 and 1951.

McDermott laid the strong foundation that has allowed it to resist the national trend toward chain ownership of newspapers and competition from new media, first radio and then television in 1953. McDermott was "Mr. Newspaper" in Idaho Falls until his death in 1977.

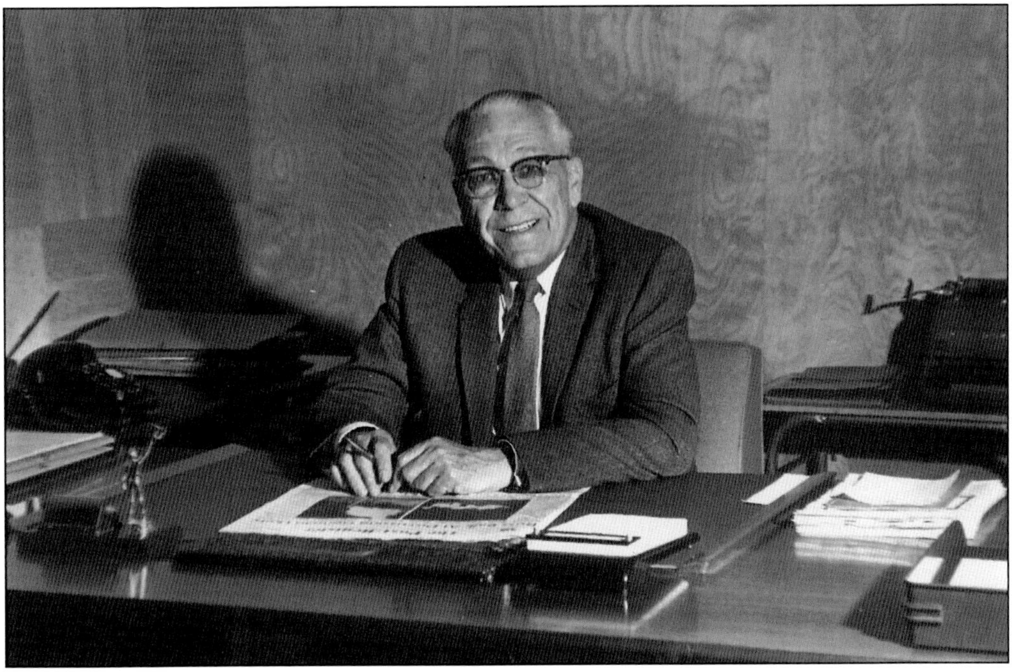

E. F. McDermott ran the *Post-Register* for 50 years. He celebrated the newspaper's 50th birthday in 1934 with a three-day diamond jubilee at the height of the Depression.

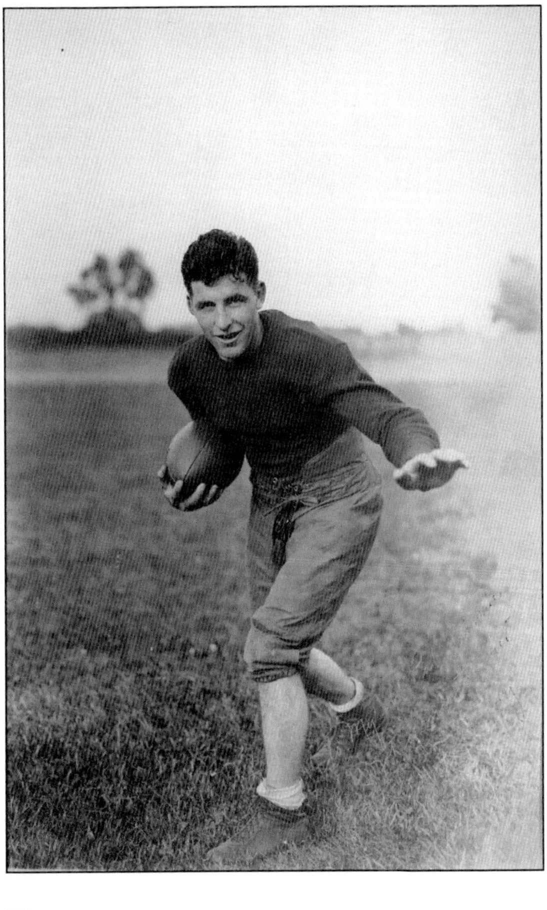

During the beginning of McDermott's tenure, Jim Brady was the quarterback of Knute Rockne's Notre Dame team that "won one for the Gipper" in 1928 against Army, then returned to eastern Idaho in 1933 to help run the family newspaper business. In 1946, he started KIFI radio and ran the *Post* corporation as president until his death in 1984. (University of Notre Dame.)

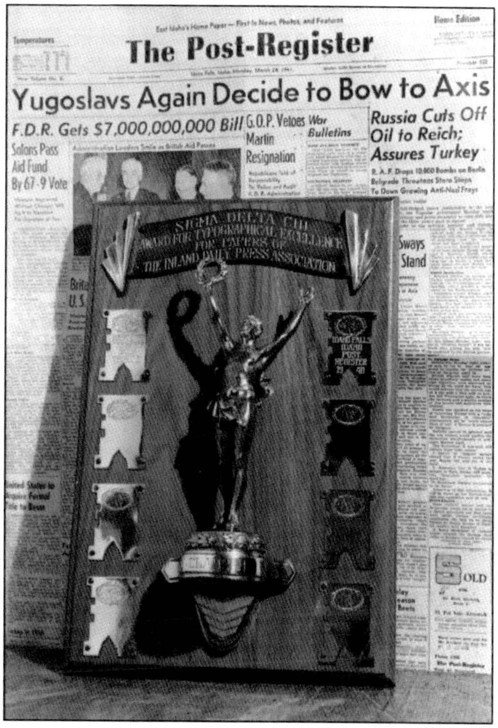

The *Post-Register* won a national award for typographic excellence in 1941 for members of the Inland Daily Press Association.

A team photograph shows the Idaho Falls Russets when they were affiliated with the Detroit Tigers. Since about 1926, Idaho Falls has had a professional baseball team. For many years, *Post-Register* publisher E. F. McDermott was instrumental in the team's survival. In 1948, the *Post-Register*'s owners, with H. C. "Bud" Frew, Arch Wackerli, and Robert Rust, bought the club and McDermott directed the operation. The partnership sold the club in 1955, offering club stock to fund the continued operation. McDermott remained as club director then and for many years thereafter, representing the team at the league level until his death in 1977. The Russets began to adopt the nickname of their parent major league team in the 1950s. More recently, it has been a rookie classification circuit; the team was renamed the Idaho Falls Chukars and affiliated with the Kansas City Royals.

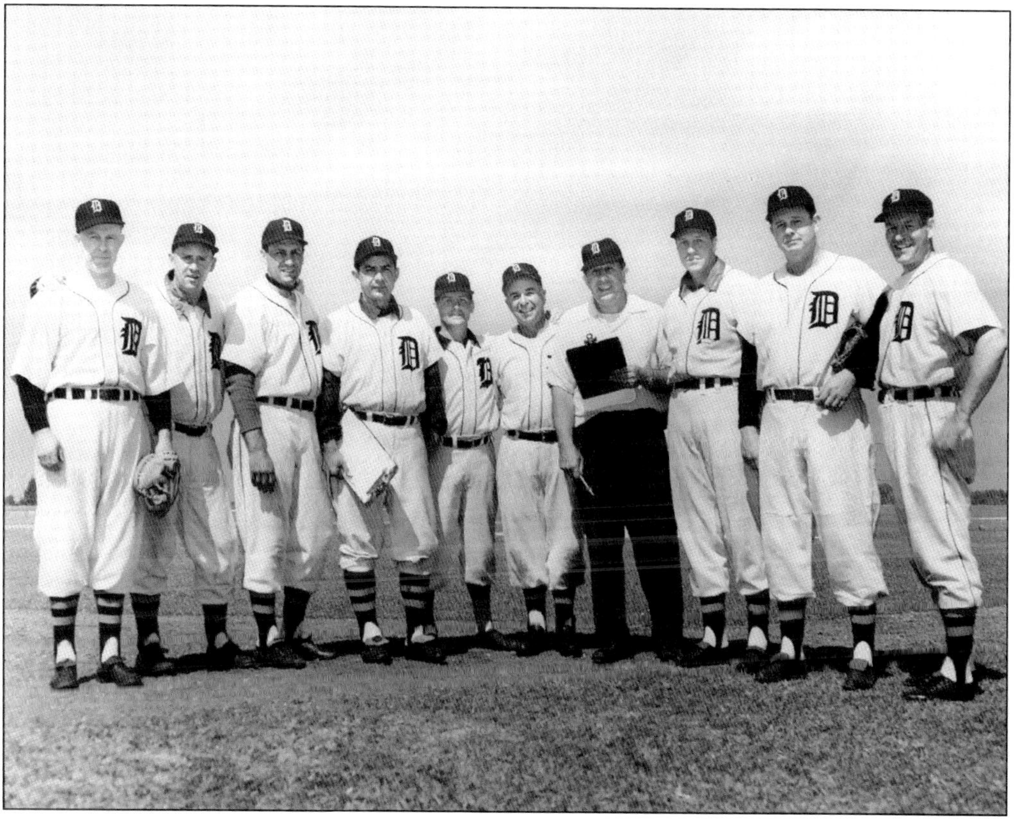

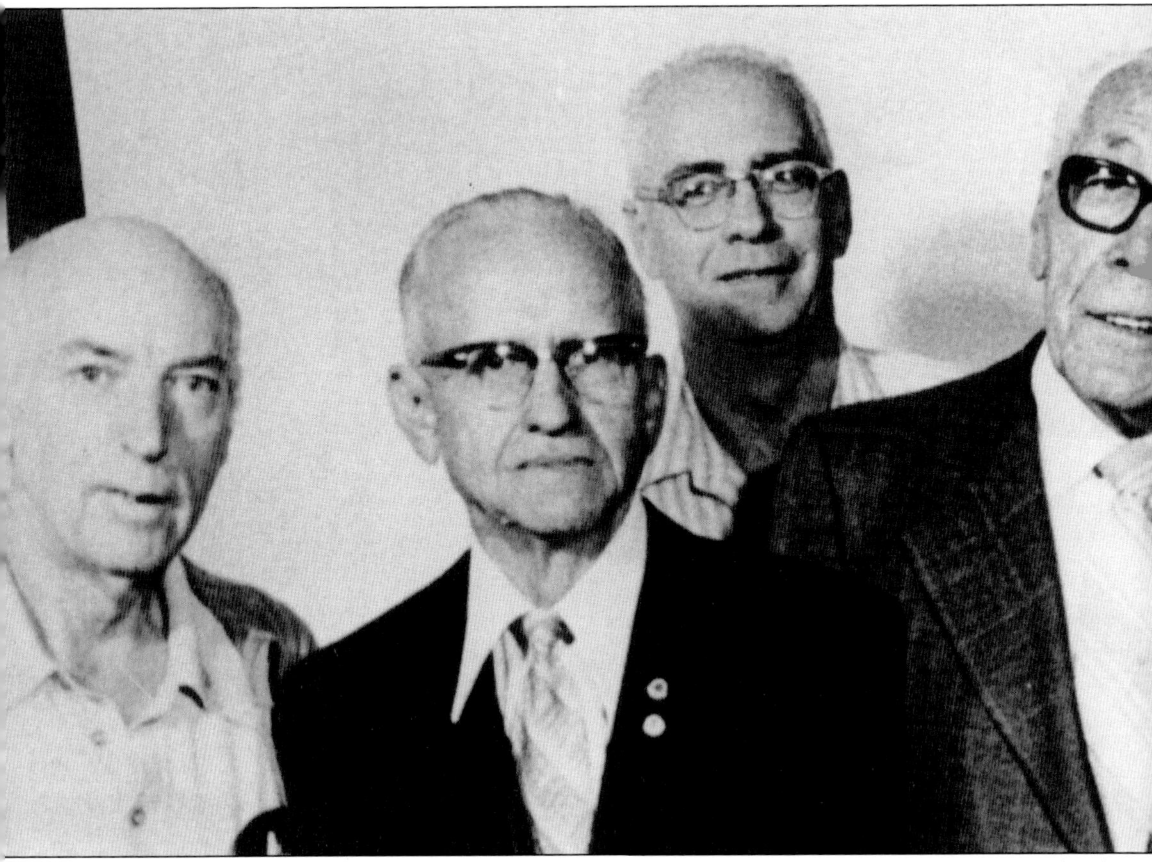

This photograph of E. F. McDermott with several charter members of the International Typographical Union was taken shortly before he died in 1977. From left to right are Sam Baugh, Lafe Baker,

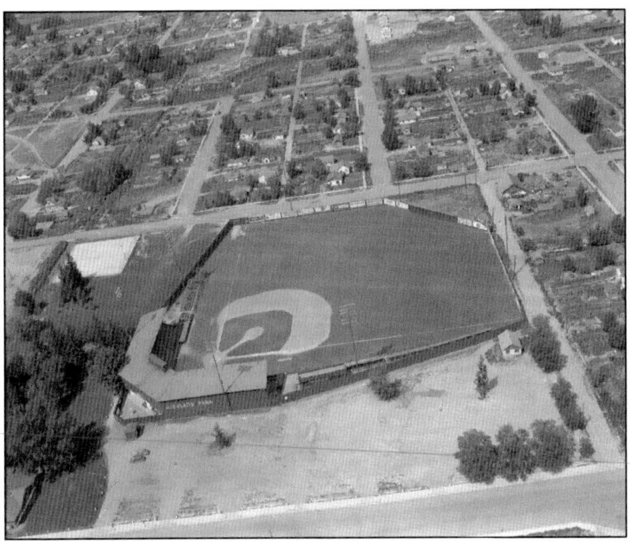

E. F. McDermott was also involved in the original construction of the field at the city's Highland Park (left), built in 1939 for the 1940 season. After the old wooden structure burned in the fall of 1975, an all-concrete structure was dedicated and named for him in ceremonies on July 6, 1977. The stadium was renamed Melaleuca Field following a $5.6-million renovation in 2007 that raised its capacity to 3,400. Several professional baseball stars played in front of Idaho Falls fans over the years. One of the first was Billy Martin in 1946.

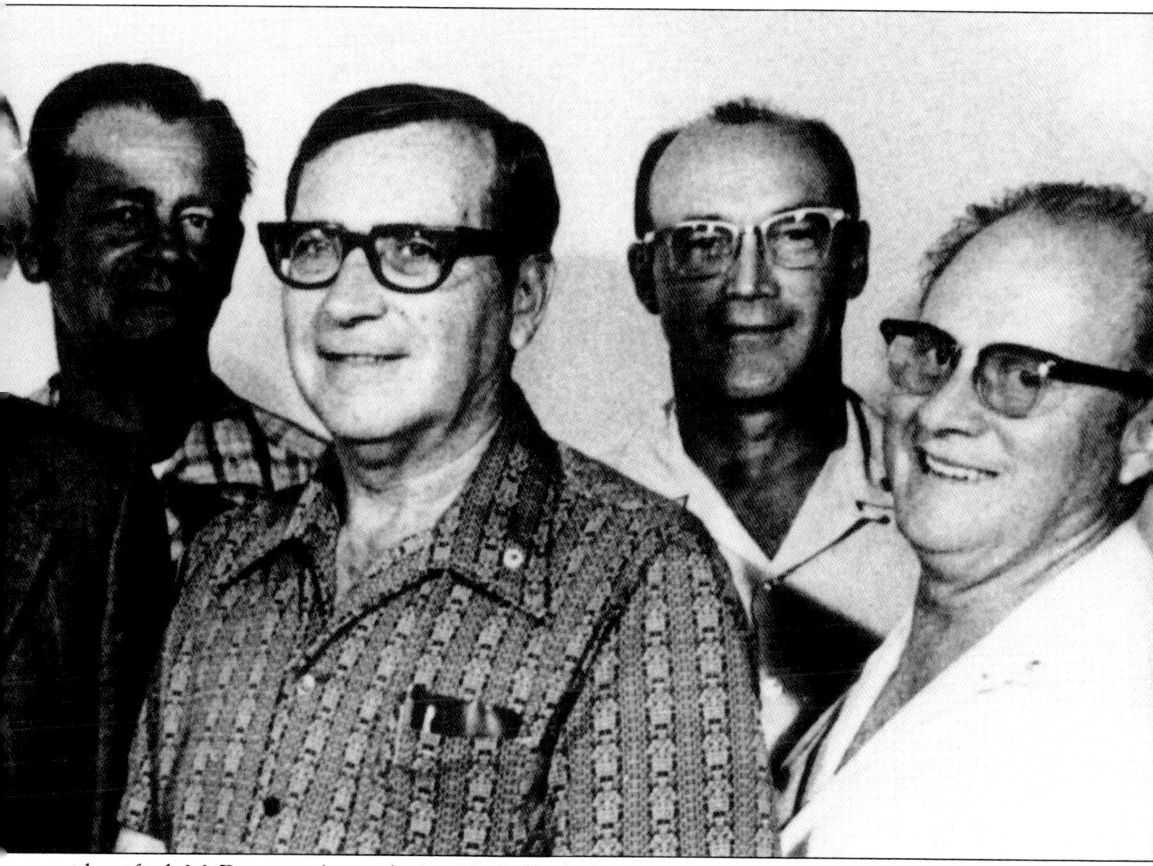

unidentified, McDermott (center), Art McCulloch, LaVar Peterson, Bill Oler, and unidentified. (Keith Gardner.)

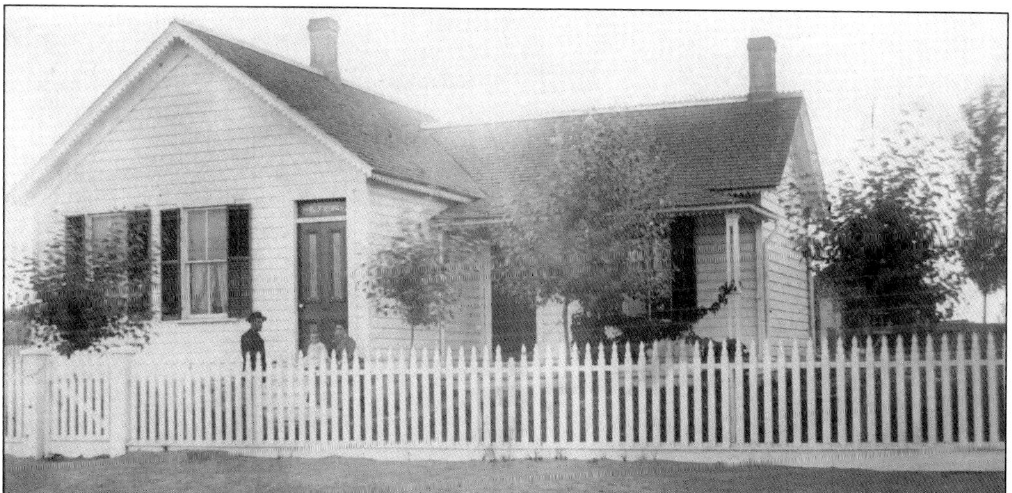

The Goodfellow tradition was started by longtime publisher Edwin F. McDermott, but another E. F., Ed F. Winn, was the fund's largest contributor. For decades, Winn's estate contributed the single largest amount to the fund each year.

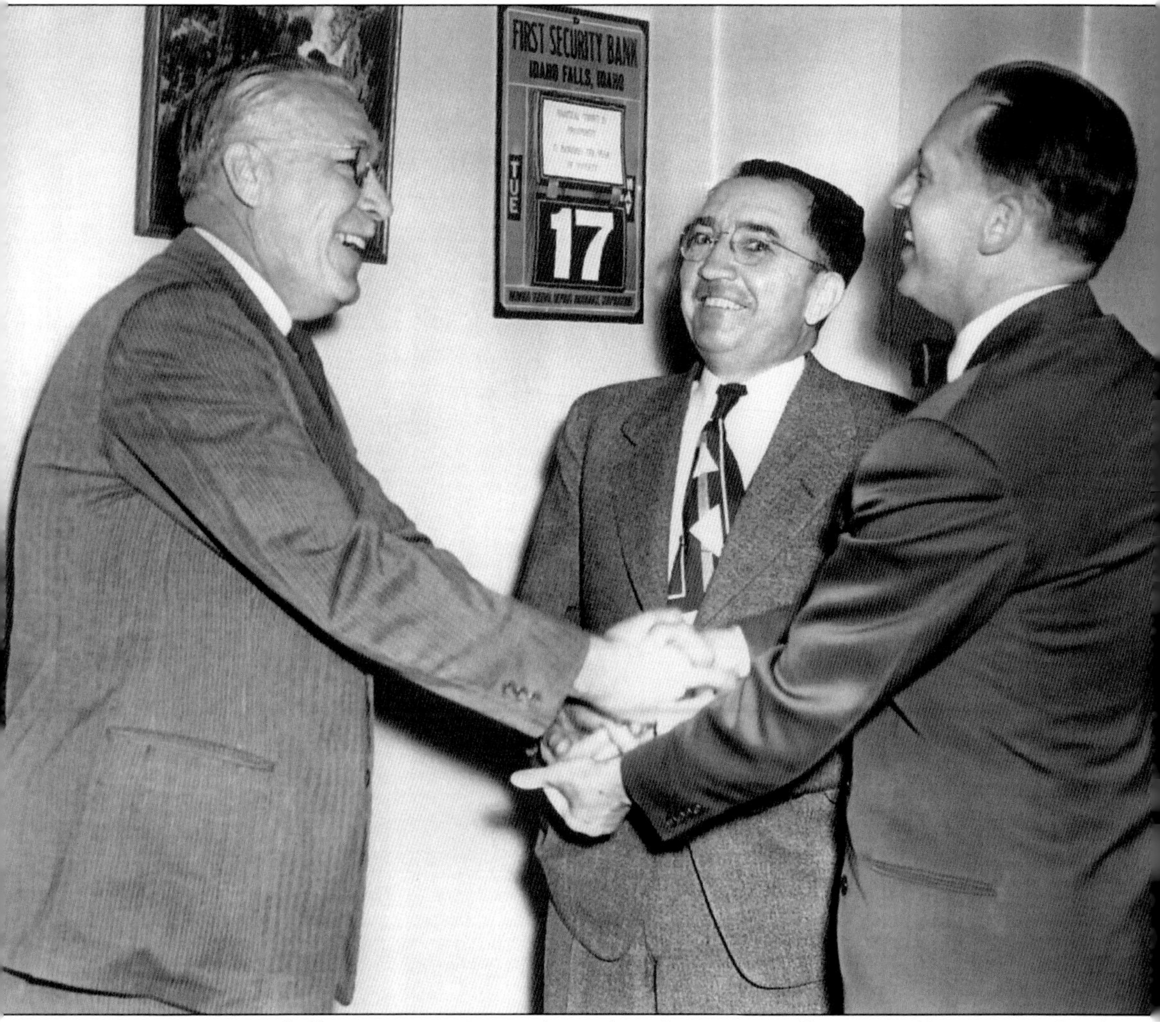

E. F. McDermott (left), Mayor Tom Sutton (center), and attorney William S. Holden congratulated each other after the Atomic Energy Commission chose Idaho Falls as headquarters city for the National Reactor Testing Station over Pocatello, Blackfoot, and Arco. When it came time to choose, "The leaders of the Idaho Falls Chamber of Commerce, particularly Bill Holden, an attorney, and E. F. McDermott, the publisher of the *Idaho Falls Post-Register*, were equally quick to react," winning the contest simply by outworking the other towns, according to a 50th anniversary history of the site by Susan M. Stacy. (William T. Holden.)

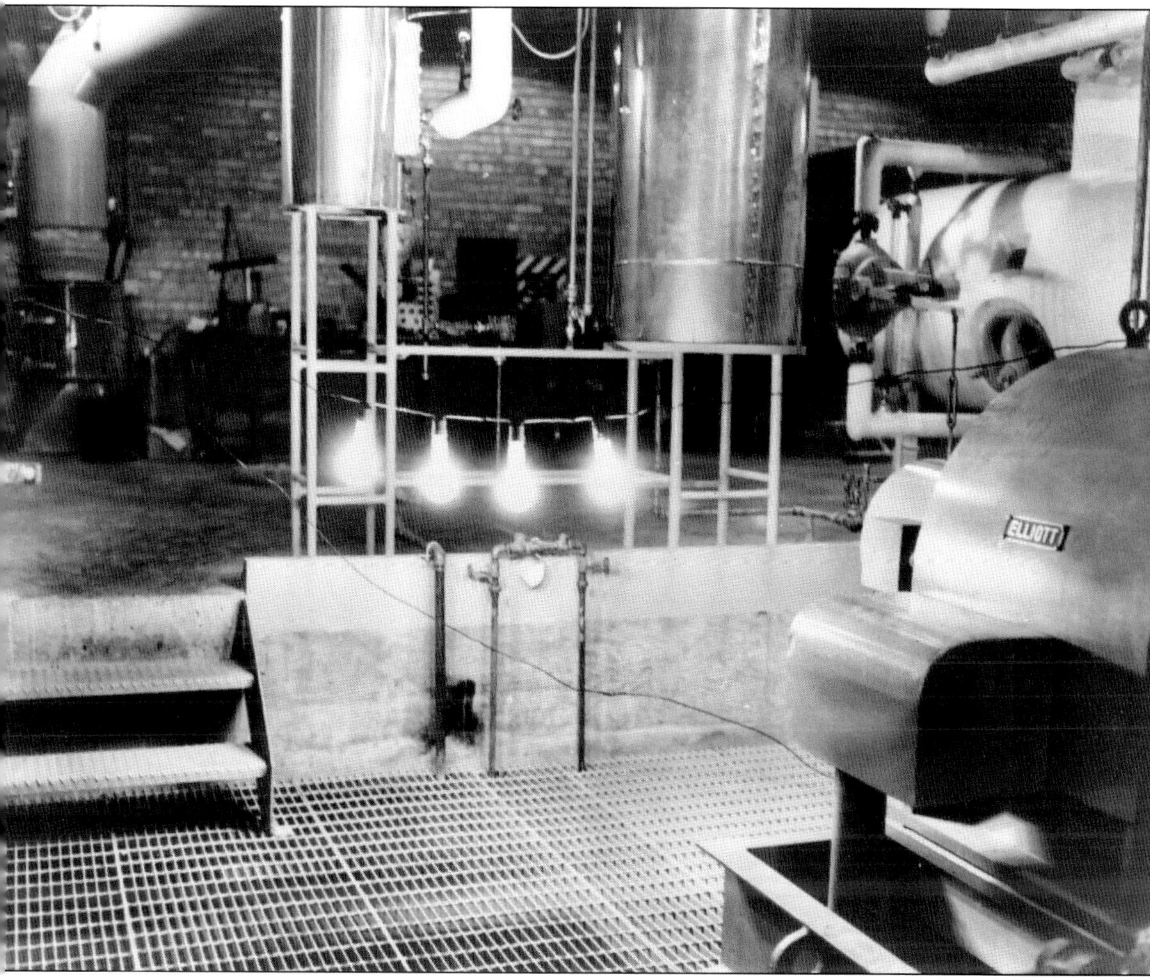

A string of lights is illuminated by electricity from the world's first nuclear power plant, Experimental Breeder Reactor No. 1, on December 20, 1951. EBR-1 was the first reactor built at the nuclear development and testing site west of Idaho Falls.

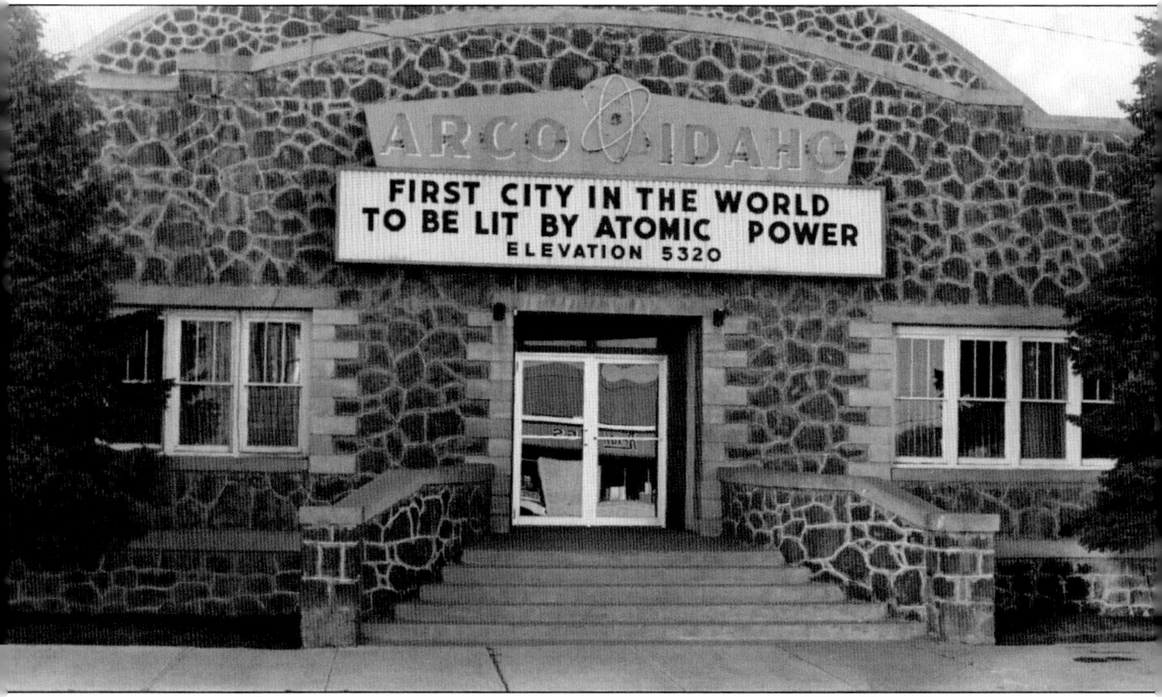

Arco, 60 miles west of Idaho Falls, is proud of being the first city in the world to be lit by atomic power on July 17, 1955.

This chalkboard recorded the names of the scientists present on December 20, 1951, when usable electric energy was first produced from a nuclear reactor, EBR-1. Ten years later, some of the scientists present that day gathered in front of the board in this anniversary photograph. The site was designated a National Historic Landmark in 1966.

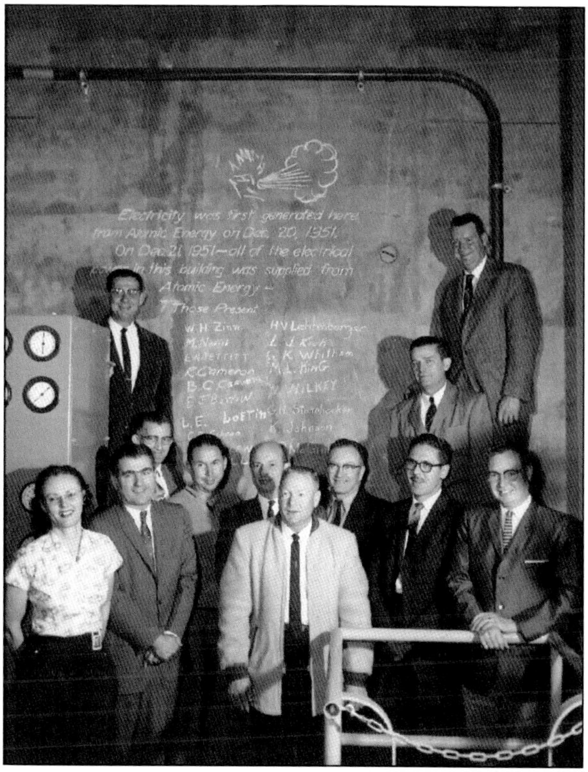

A steam explosion at the BORAX reactor sends up an Old Faithful–like eruption on the Arco Desert during one of numerous accident tests during the early days of the Idaho National Laboratory. Tests like these helped scientists make reactors safer, but later the tests were moved indoors.

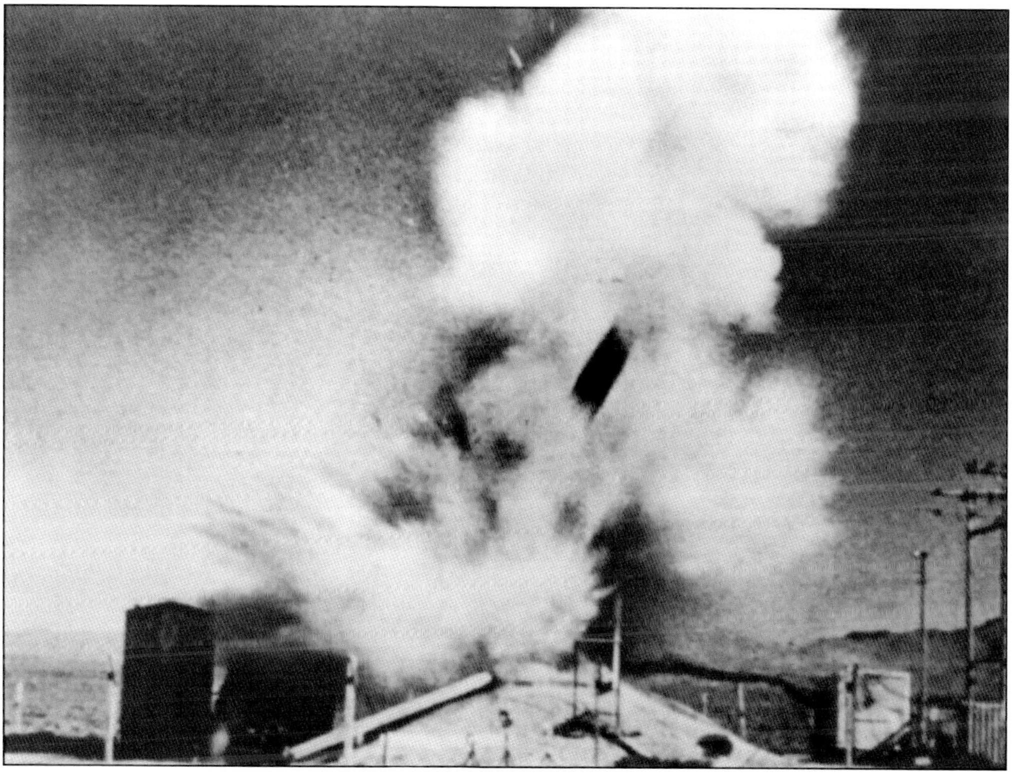

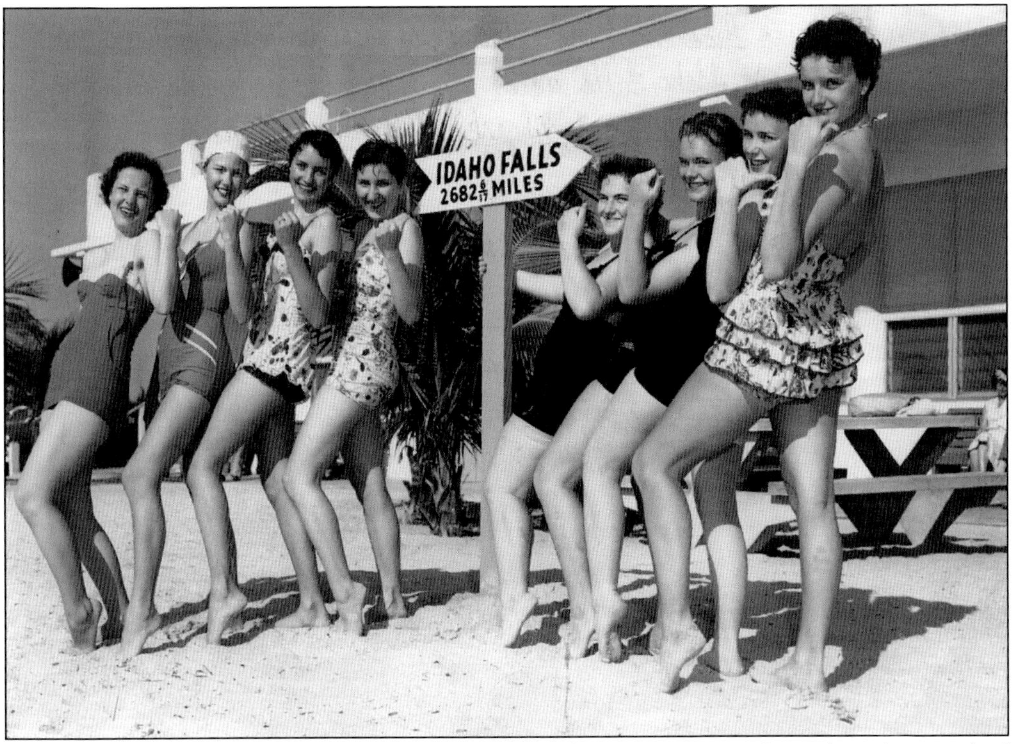

Publicizing the allure of its hometown was part of the newspaper's job, and it often worked hand-in-hand with the local chamber of commerce. A chamber-sponsored exchange program for Idaho Falls High School students in 1955 produced this publicity still from Bradenton, Florida. Clowning in their bathing suits with a sign pointing toward Idaho Falls were Marilyn McBirney, Sandy Nichols, Karel Lourie, Barbara Ovard, Caol Kuharski, Nannette Burkhart, Sally Braithwaite, and Shirley Reed.

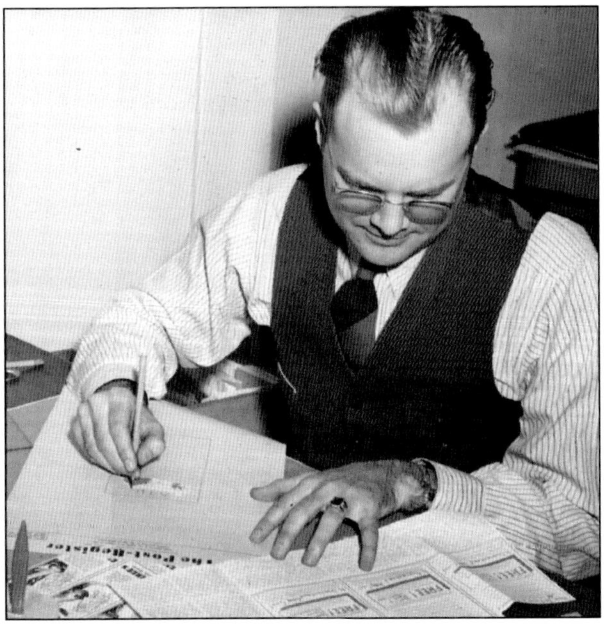

A close-up of the ad writer's task of layout and word composition shows Hayden Stites translating a rough draft into a finished advertisement ready for the printers. The photograph was taken in 1941.

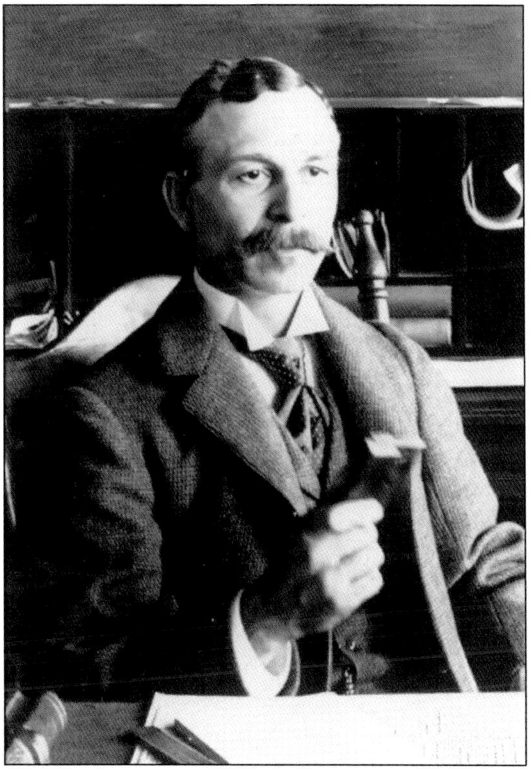

The Goss Printing Press Company of Chicago, Illinois, started in 1885, about the time the *Register* began printing in Eagle Rock. Founded by Sam (right) and Fred Goss in the tradition of many turn-of-the-20th-century American manufacturers, it sold a Goss Comet to the *Post*. More Goss presses followed, and the *Post Register* announced it would replace its 13-unit Goss Urbanite press with a Goss Magnum 4 "flexi" full-color press in 2009.

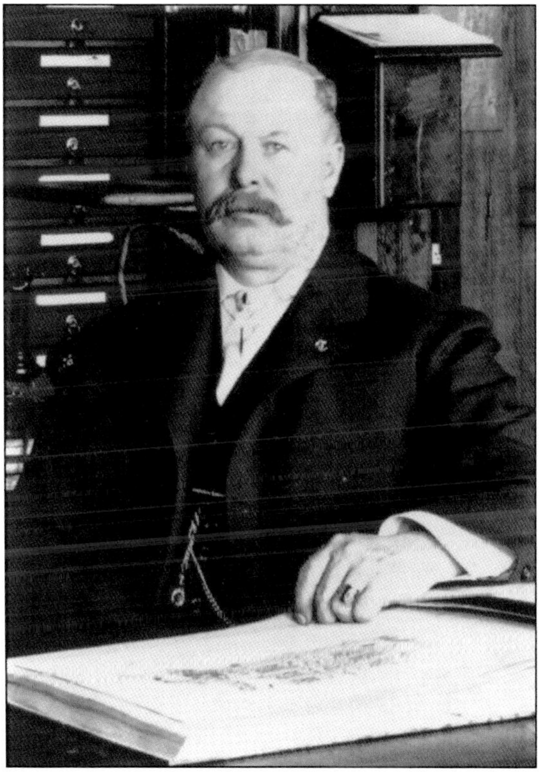

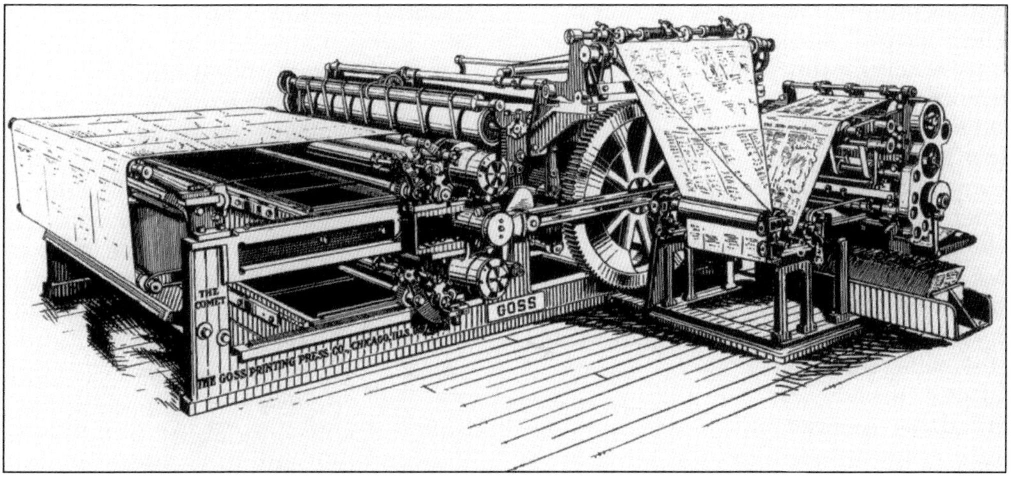

The *Idaho Falls Post* installed its first "real" newspaper press, a Goss Comet, in 1919 as part of a move into a newly constructed building on Capital Avenue.

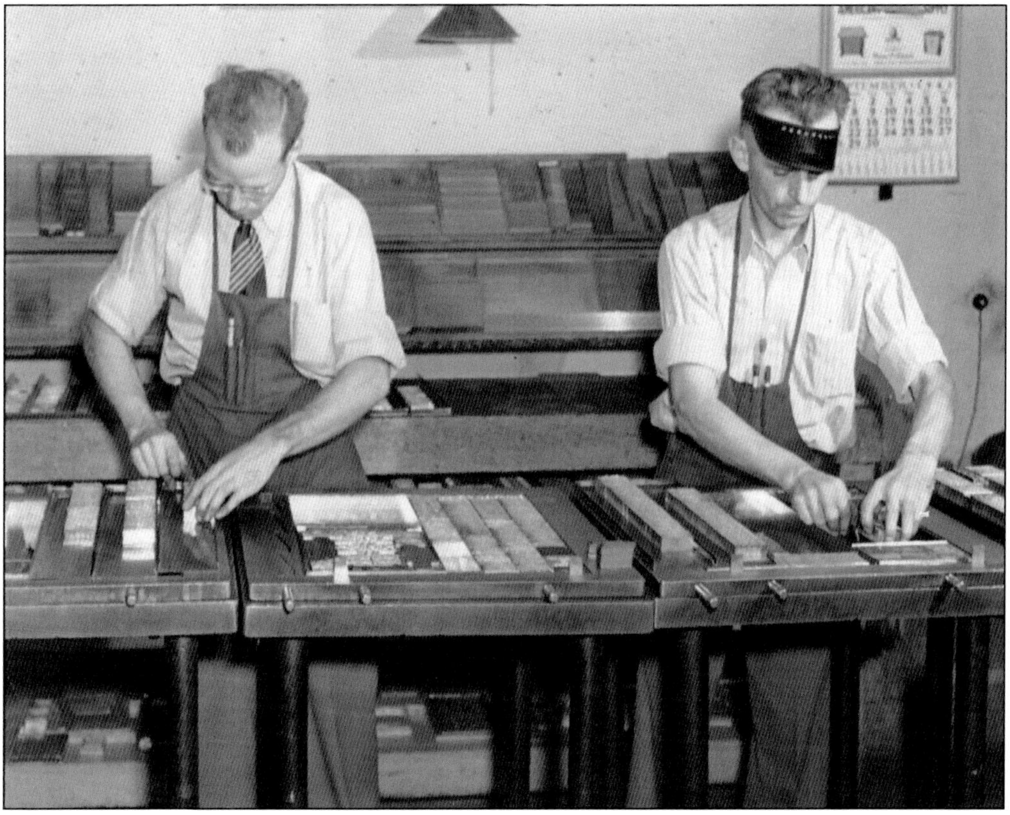

Even with innovations in letterpress printing technology in the 1940s and 1950s, there was some assembly required. At the makeup table, Tom Greer (left) and composing room foreman Wallace Merman (right) are shown fitting cast-lead galleys of news and advertisements together in September 1941. Heavy steel tables on casters called turtles held the galleys, which were locked tightly into a metal frame called a chase and rolled around for proofing and casting.

The process of proofing a newspaper page in lead was as follows: The heavy form was lifted off the rolling table and positioned on the proof press, the roller was inked, and the image was transferred onto a sheet of proof paper.

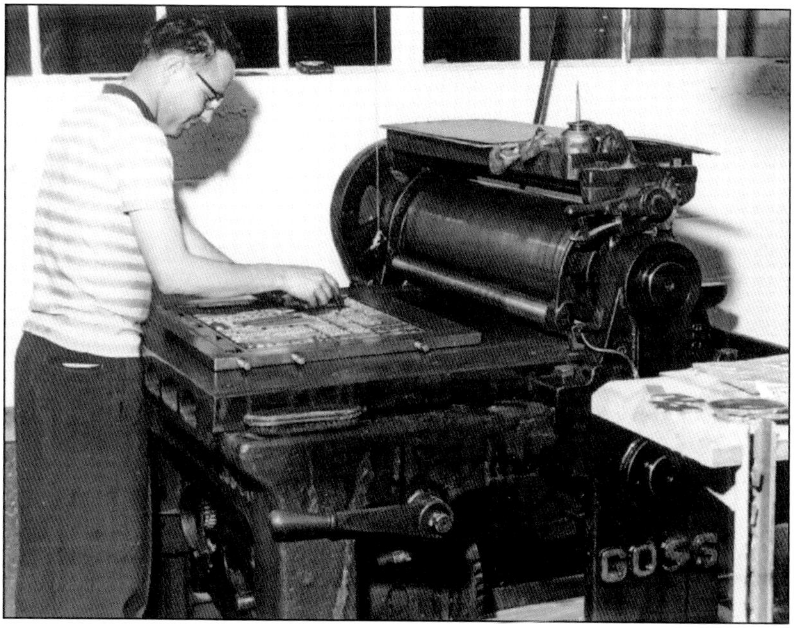

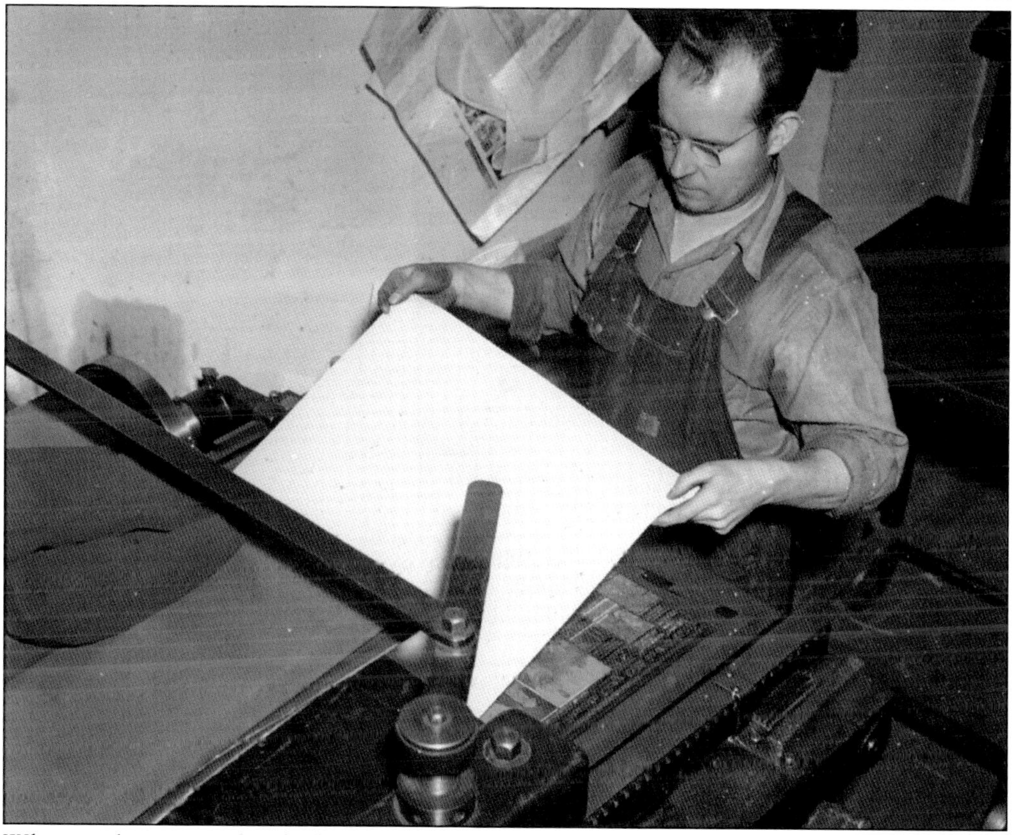

When makeup men finished with the page forms, they were trundled to the stereotyping department's mat press. Lloyd Schofield is shown placing a sheet of moist cardboard over a page of type. Exerting tons of pressure, the steel roller made a mold of the page.

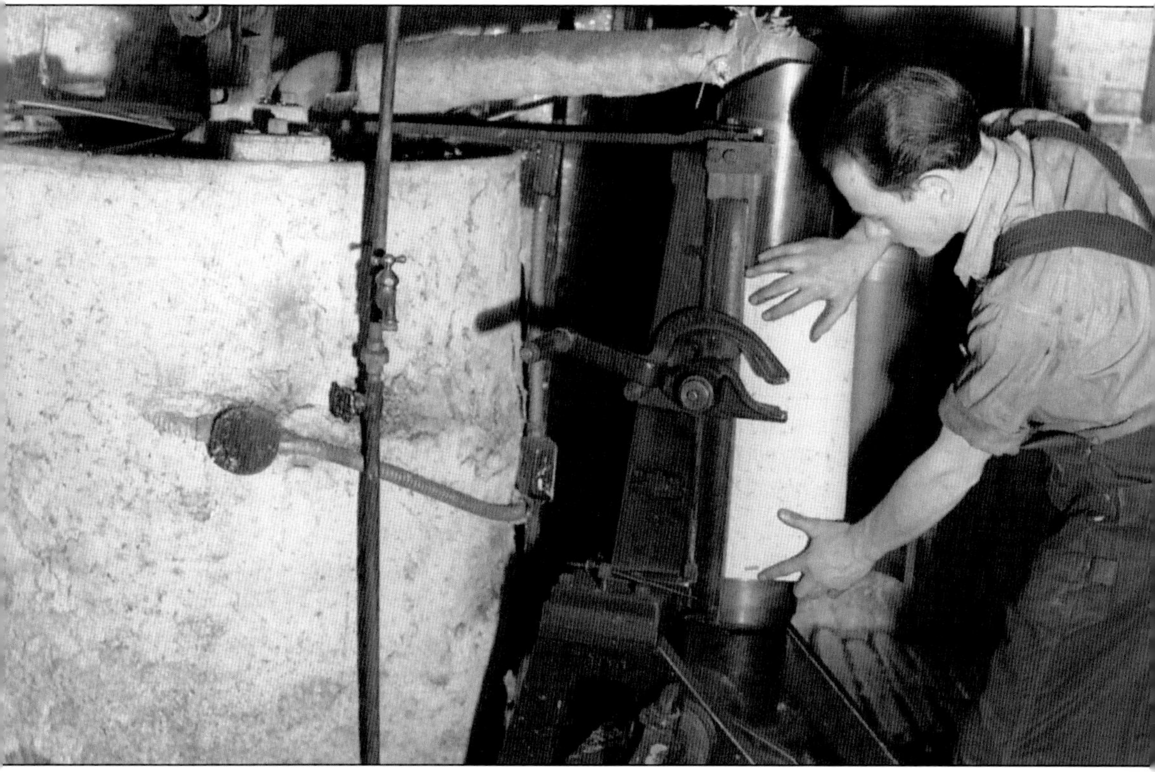

The cardboard matrix was placed in a box that shaped it into a tubular form (hence the term "Dek-A-Tube"). Pressman Dean Ingram is pumping molten type metal from a furnace through a conduit and into a mold formed by the matrix.

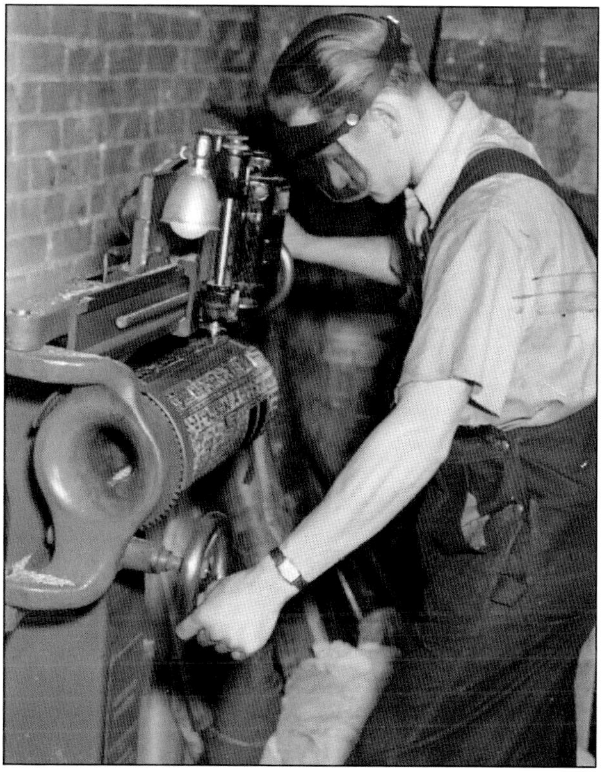

After being cast into a metal tube, a plate router was used to remove excess lead and fix casting imperfections. The Rout-O-Plate, below, was a fancier, safer version that replaced a plastic mask with a glass window.

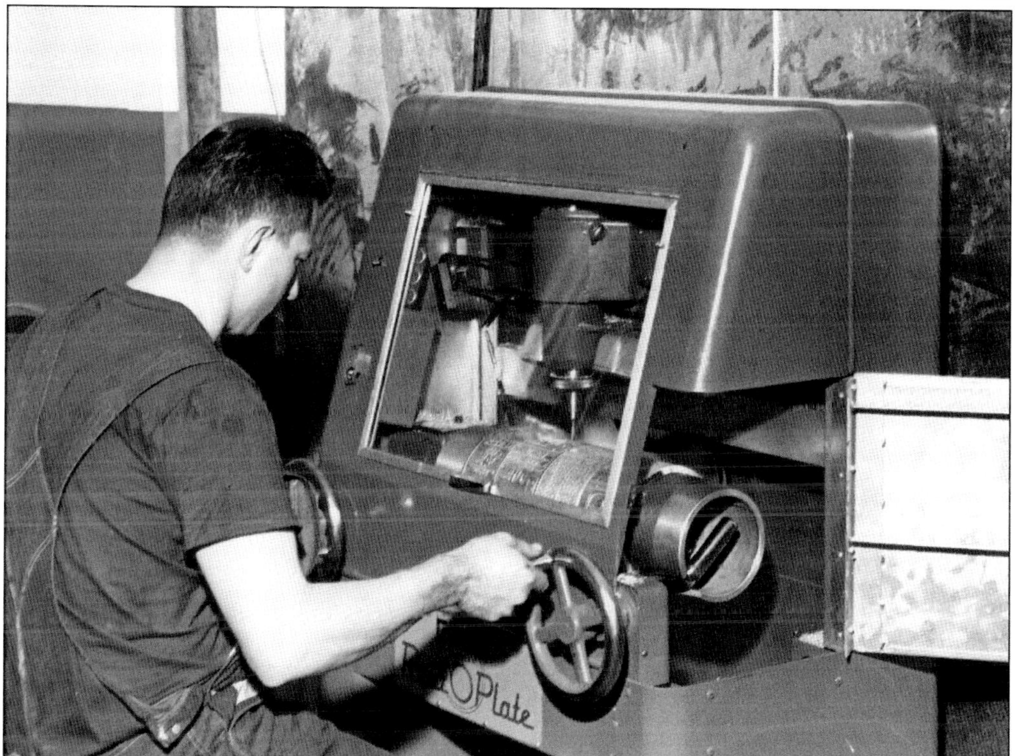

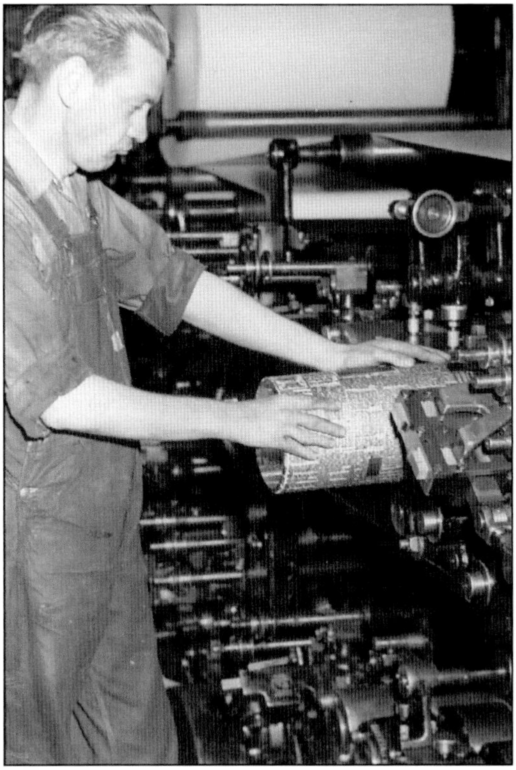

The final step in the letterpress page preparation process was this: A pressman inserted the tubular page form over a press unit's roller. Then rolls of newsprint passed through the press units in a web. The raised letters on the metal plates collected a film of ink that was transferred onto newsprint. Beginning in 1977, a new process, offset printing, replaced letterpress technology. Today all these steps are done electronically on a computer screen.

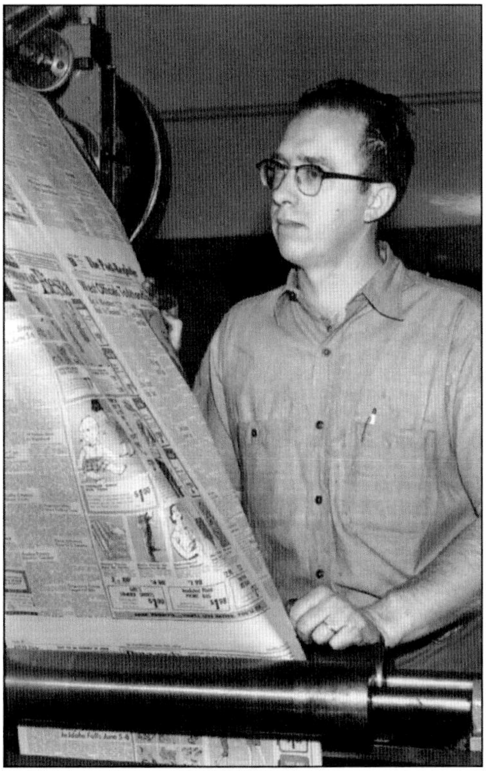

Pressroom foreman Don Kirby checks inking on the *Post-Register*'s 24-page Goss Dek-a-Tube letterpress on June 3, 1959. The new press turned out 25,000 papers an hour for three daily editions. The Dek-A-Tube letterpress was replaced in the late 1960s after only a few years of service by a 44-page, twin-line Unitubular press—still letterpress, but using heavy plastic plates instead of lead tubes.

Letterpress printing was a marvel of technology—19th-century style. The process was part blacksmithing and part precision engineering. This view of the composing room captures the experience: hours standing on concrete floors under low-hanging fluorescent lights assembling a 24-page daily newspaper from hot lead ingots. The Linotypes in the center of the room were clanking, noisy behemoths, often squirting streams of molten lead on the forearms of their operators.

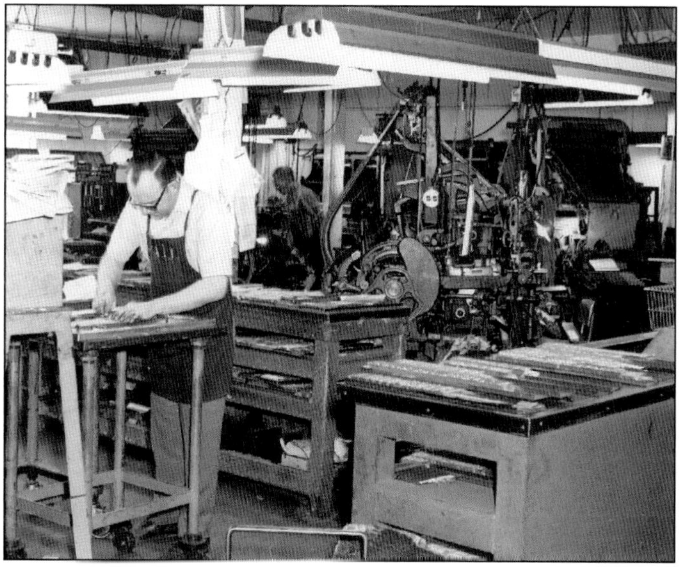

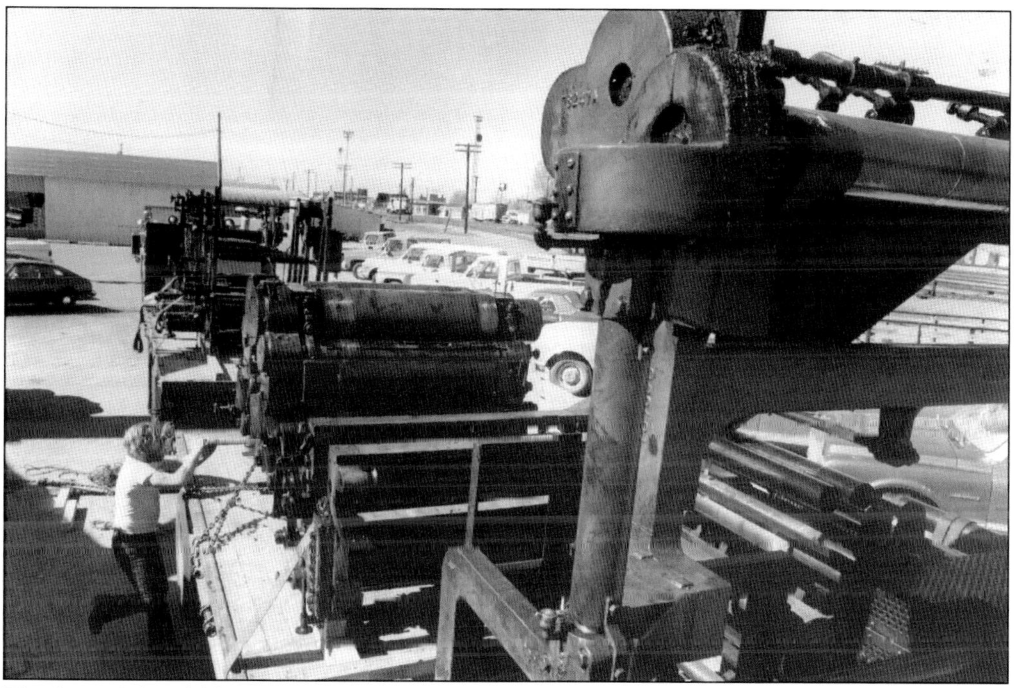

The last of the old letterpress printing units was taken out of service following installation of its new Goss offset press in April 1977. The units were sold to printers in Salem, Oregon, and Santa Fe Springs, California. The new offset press changed the printing process from the front door back and required intensive staff-wide training.

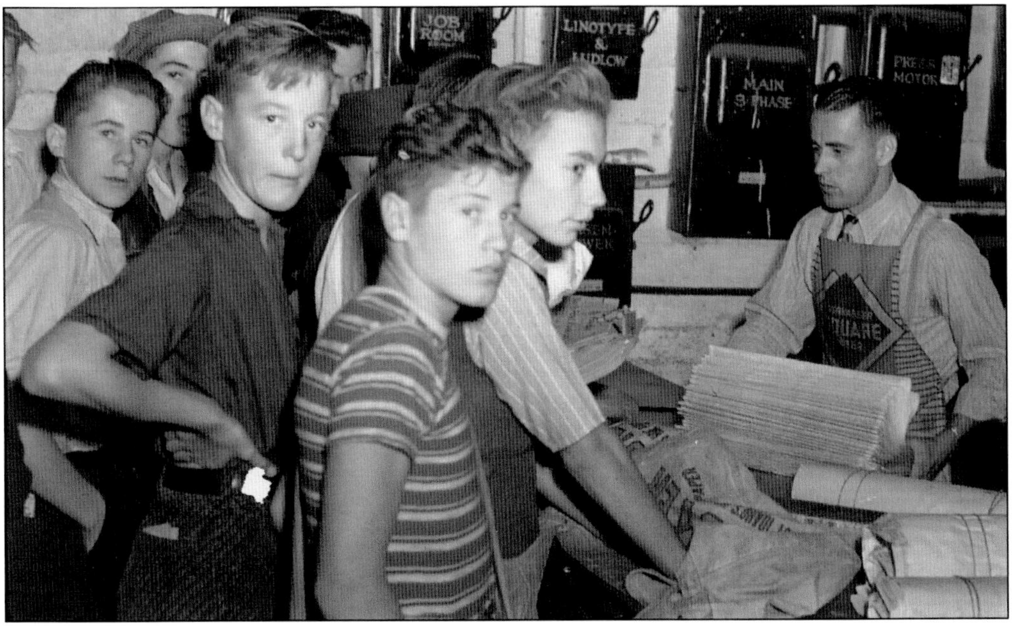

As the papers came off the press, they were stacked and counted into bundles for delivery. Here circulation manager W. E. "Ernie" Shononey distributes papers to delivery boys for door-to-door delivery. Other bundles were addressed and mailed or were placed on trucks, buses, and trains. This photograph was taken in 1941.

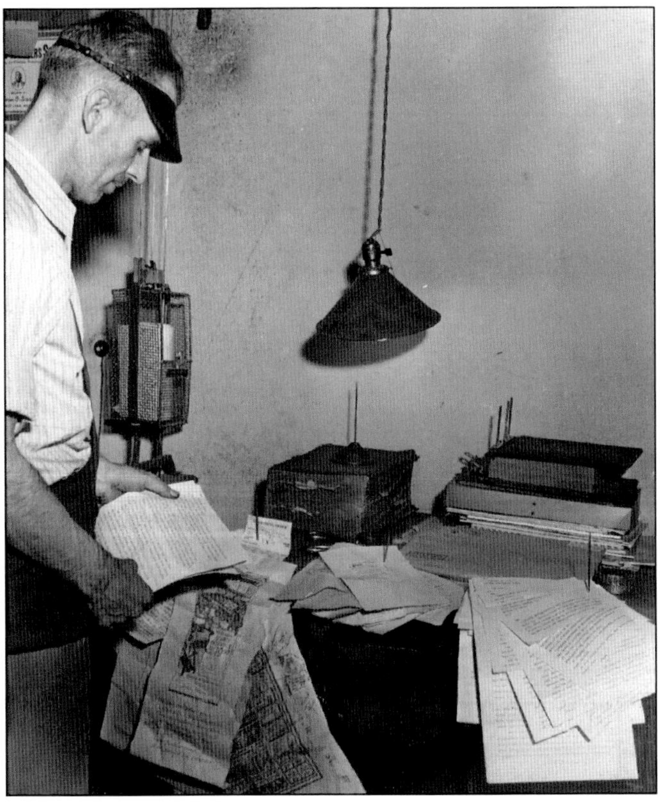

The front end of the newspaper process was glamorized in the 1940s by such movies as *The Front Page*, but in reality it involved a lot of wire-stripping, copy-reading, and fact-checking. This view of the wire room shows a copy editor wearing the ubiquitous green eyeshade while sorting copy onto spikes next to a tattered and well-used dictionary, grubby with ink rub-off from the hands of editors.

An intriguing story about a series of dynamitings in Idaho Falls resulted in the awarding of an Associated Press Managing Editor's Association national citation and a Pulitzer Prize nomination in 1958. John McDermott wrote the series of news articles. He became the newspaper's general manager and worked at the newspaper for 36 years.

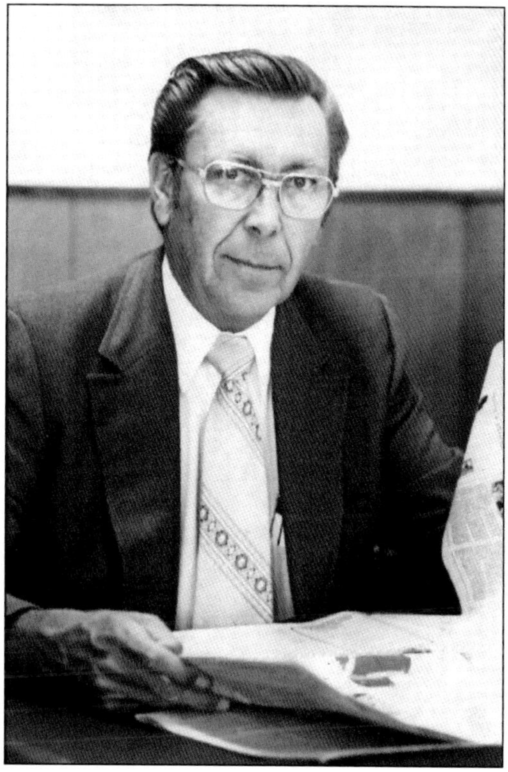

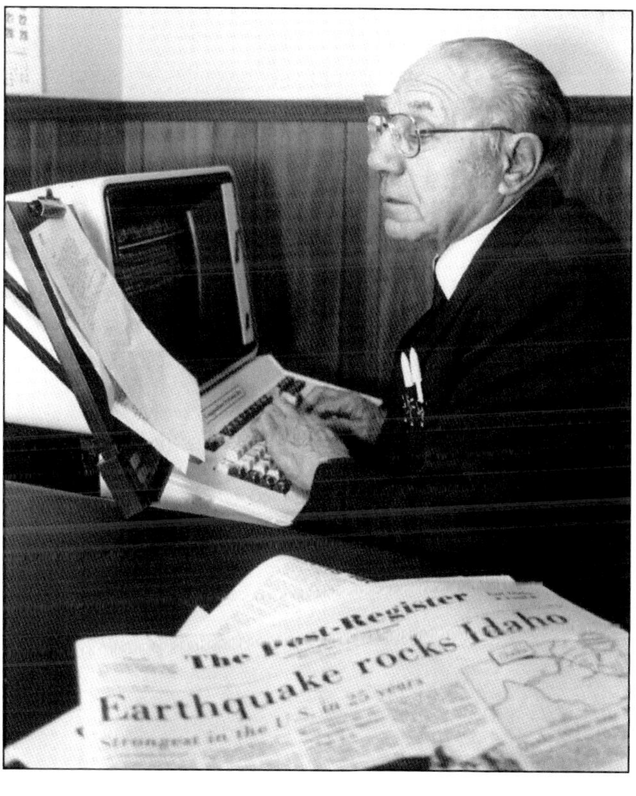

Post Register executive editor Ben Plastino covered or supervised many of the newspaper's biggest stories over a 50-year career, including the Yellowstone earthquake of 1959 and the Teton Dam controversy. Plastino was part of the first ground party to reach the earthquake area. He was political editor when the fight over building the Teton Dam ignited local passions nearly two decades later. Under Plastino's leadership, the *Post-Register* supported the dam's construction; to be fair, most of the newspaper's readers did as well. The dam collapsed in 1976 as it was filling for the first time. Plastino's last day at the newspaper was punctuated by an earthquake in central Idaho in 1983.

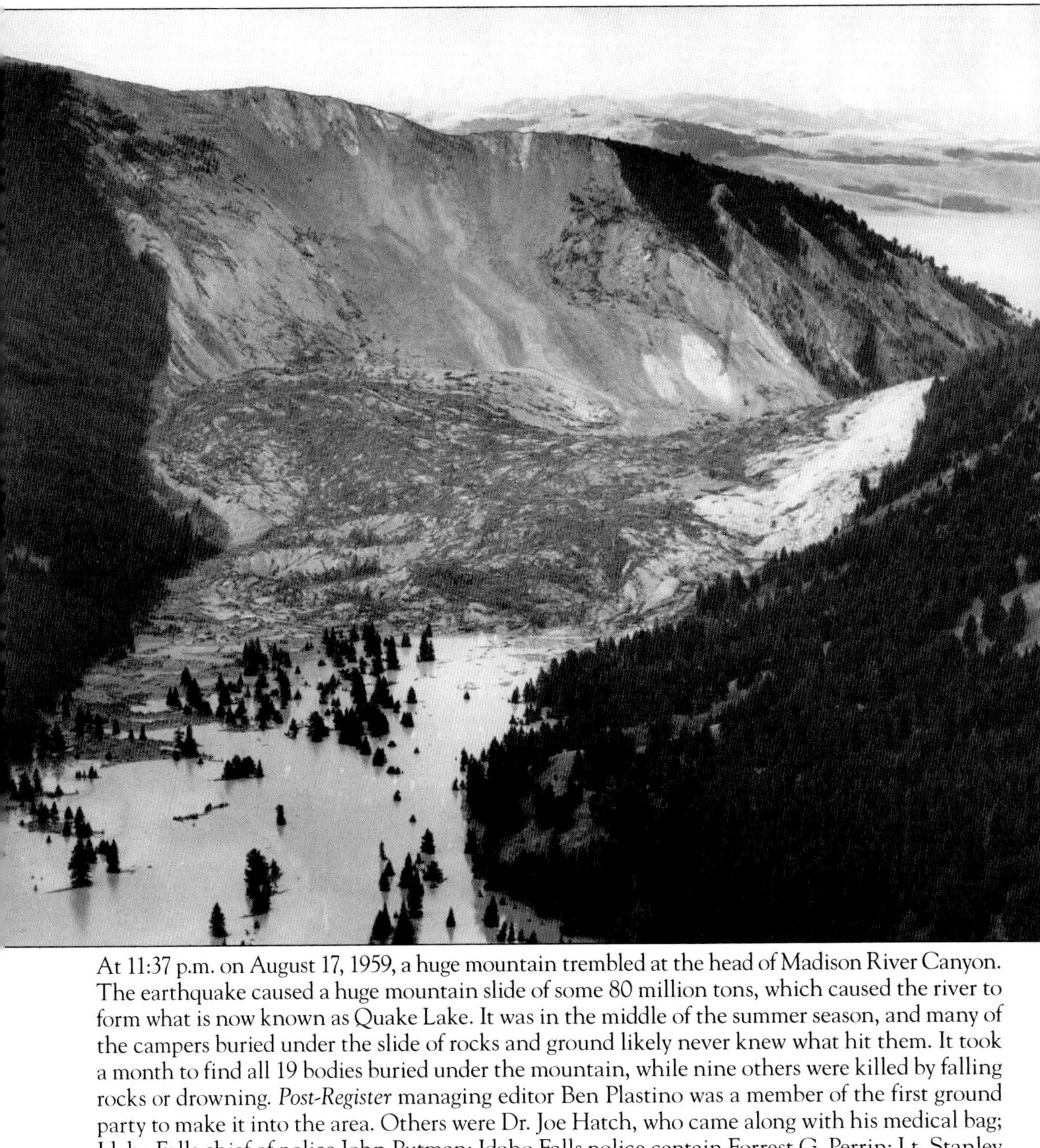

At 11:37 p.m. on August 17, 1959, a huge mountain trembled at the head of Madison River Canyon. The earthquake caused a huge mountain slide of some 80 million tons, which caused the river to form what is now known as Quake Lake. It was in the middle of the summer season, and many of the campers buried under the slide of rocks and ground likely never knew what hit them. It took a month to find all 19 bodies buried under the mountain, while nine others were killed by falling rocks or drowning. *Post-Register* managing editor Ben Plastino was a member of the first ground party to make it into the area. Others were Dr. Joe Hatch, who came along with his medical bag; Idaho Falls chief of police John Putman; Idaho Falls police captain Forrest G. Perrin; Lt. Stanley Ward; Sgt. Bud Hathaway; Idaho Falls patrolmen Wayde Scott and Hyrum Whittaker; Bonneville sheriff A. E. Heslop; and Bonneville Civil Defense director Lewis C. Ross. The *Post-Register* staff received special commendation from the Associated Press for its round-the-clock efforts to get information and photographs of the devastating natural disaster.

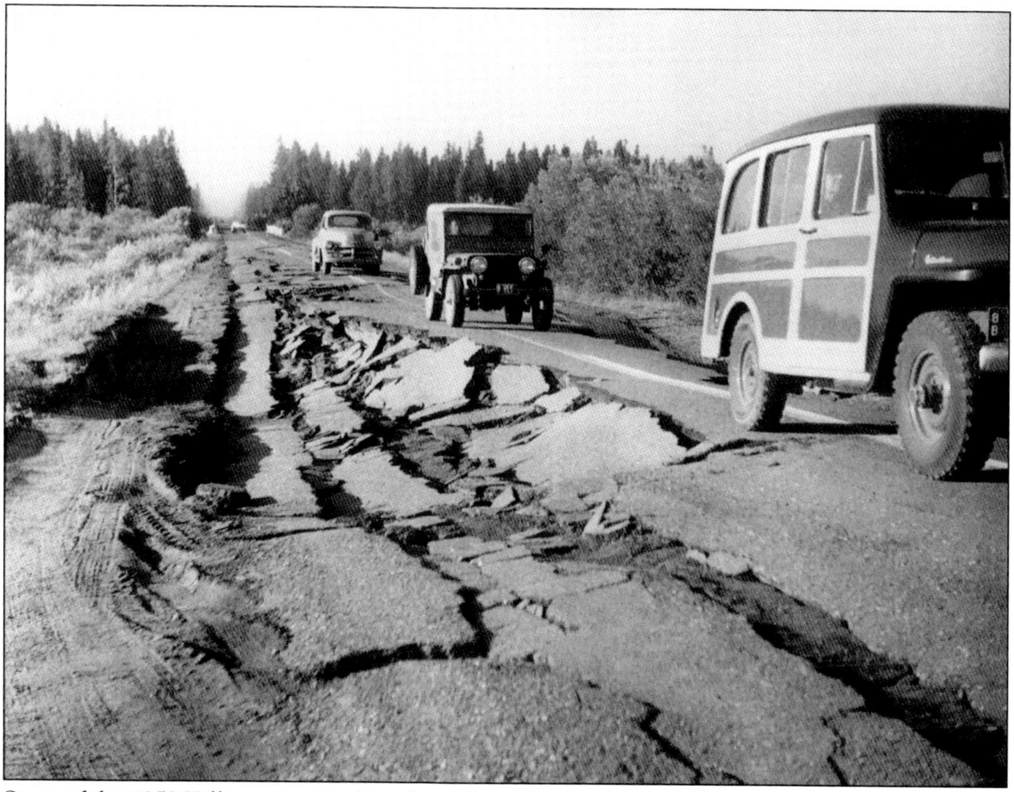

Signs of the 1959 Yellowstone earthquake and its aftershocks could be seen throughout southwest Montana and eastern Idaho, like this crumbled portion of broken highway leading out of West Yellowstone toward Island Park. The tremor that shook Idaho Falls at 11:37 p.m. on a Monday night caused no damage here, but "residents rushed from homes in awe and partially evacuated downtown hotels and motels," the newspaper reported. As the daily newspaper was closest to the disaster area, *Post-Register* staff members banded to cover it.

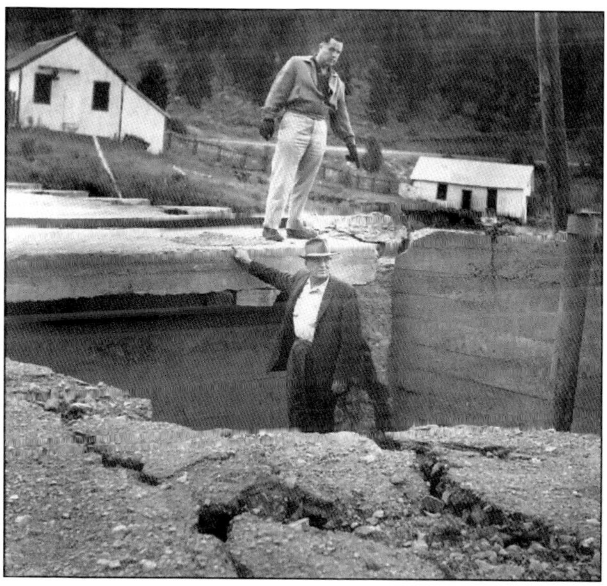

Twenty-five years after the earthquake, the *Post-Register* reported that "there haven't been any long-term negative effects on the area," according to then–Yellowstone Chamber of Commerce president Andie Evge, but survivors like Harold Ball said other earthquakes made them a little more nervous. "I got kind of a horrible feeling when the Challis quake hit last October," Ball said in 1984. The photograph at right ran with the caption, "Yellowstone area residents study quake damage."

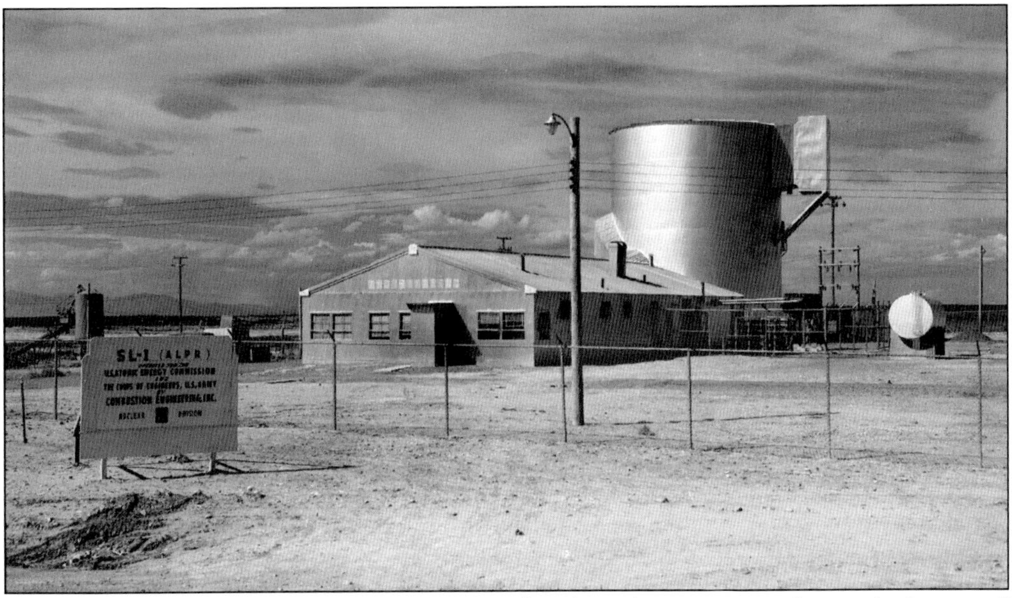

On January 3, 1961, America's first nuclear accident brought rescuers to this steel silo just off Highway 20 about 40 miles west of Idaho Falls. Volunteers in protective suits found a body and another badly injured man still alive. Two site doctors stripped him of his clothing, working by the side of the road under car headlights in 20-below-zero temperatures. The National Reactor Testing Station night nurse, Hazel Leisen, entered the ambulance and tried resuscitation. "She never hesitated," recalled Robb Brady, the *Post Register* reporter who interviewed her afterward. "She knew the risks and still went right after the revival effort. Quite a gal. A Nightingale story." It was six days before workers located and removed the third body, which had been impaled by the control rod on the ceiling of the steel reactor building. Leisen and a health physicist who supervised recovery operations died a few years later of suspicious cancers, and six of the rescuers, including Leisen, received the Carnegie Medal of Heroism. A total of 32 site workers were cited.

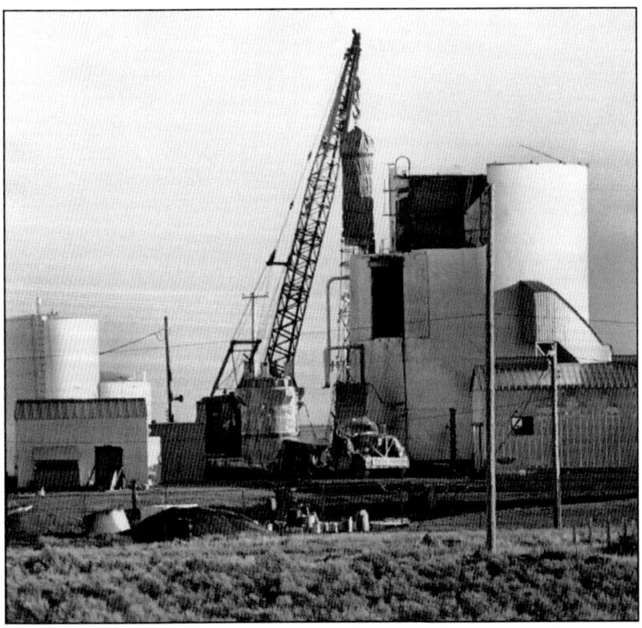

A crane removes part of the nuclear reactor core through a hole cut in the top of its containment silo at the SL-1 facility in 1961. Rather than risk further contamination from moving radioactive debris, much of the SL-1 facility was dismantled and buried there.

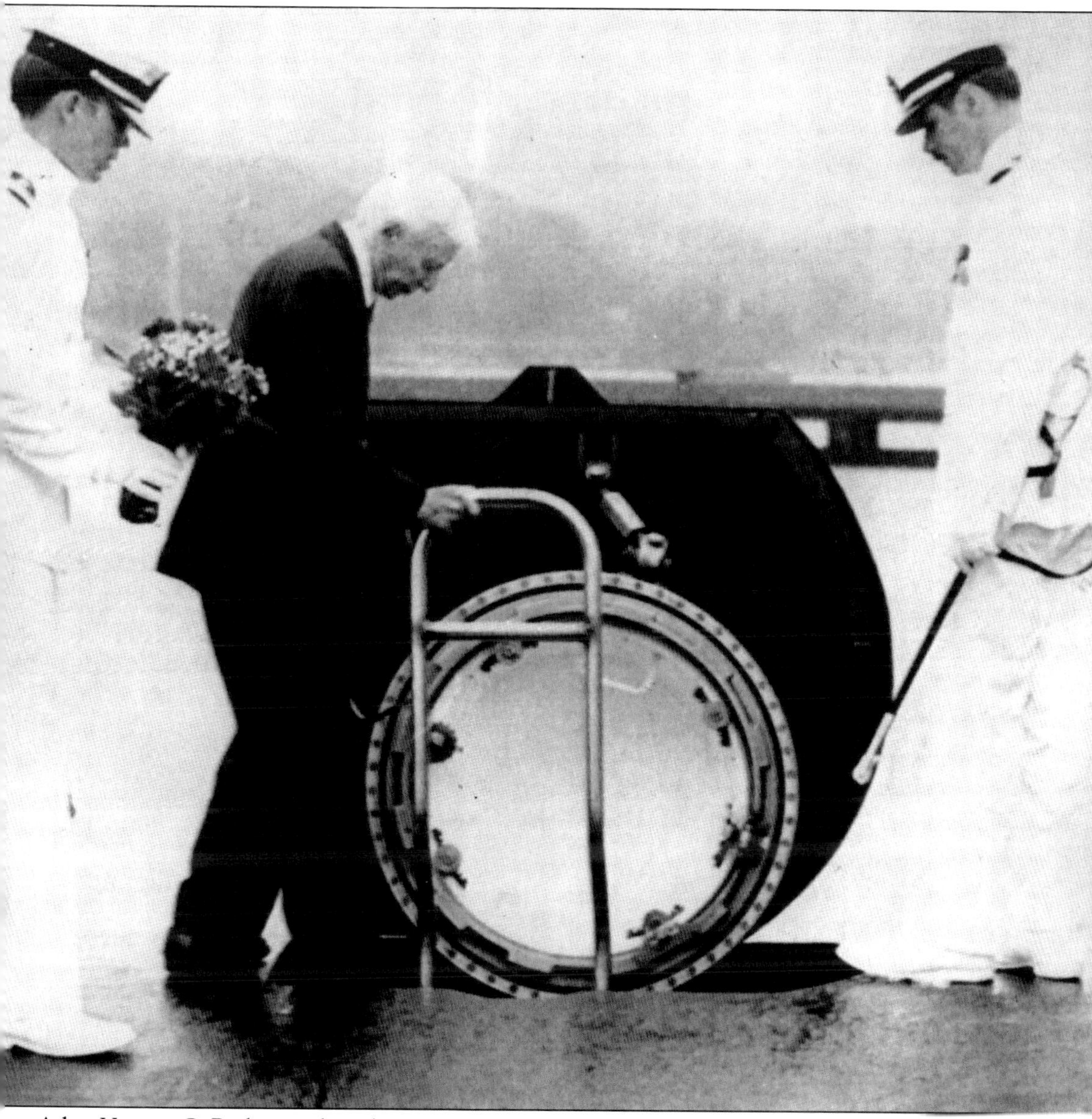

Adm. Hyman G. Rickover, the salty engineer who goaded the navy into the nuclear era through prototypes developed at the site, was a stern taskmaster who routinely worked seven days a week—and expected associates to do the same. Reporter J. Robb Brady recalls Rickover's frequent visits to Idaho Falls, when Rickover would summon reporters to his room at the Hotel Rogers for a late-night briefing. "He'd tell us, 'I'll take care of publicity, you guys get the job done,'" recalled Max Johnson, former site manager who worked closely with Rickover for 10 years. "He knew how to release information selectively so it would have the most impact." Johnson said his most vivid recollections were of the Nautilus prototype trials in the mid-1950s: "I remember his leadership . . . the joy and satisfaction he got out of the success out here in the desert. Our endurance runs were spectacular." This photograph shows Rickover inspecting the USS *Rickover* submarine named for him in 1984; he died in 1986, four years after being forced to retire at age 82. (Associated Press.)

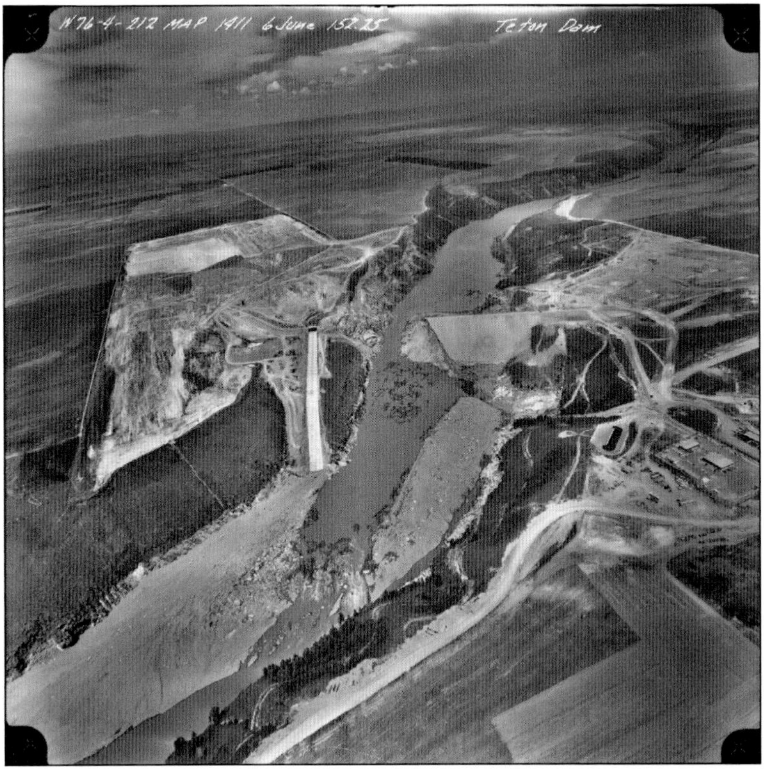

On June 5, 1976, Idaho's worst disaster struck when the Teton Dam collapsed while filling from its first spring runoff. This view is looking upstream one day after the collapse, which sent an enormous wave of water and debris downstream and did billions in damage to the Sugar City, Rexburg, Idaho Falls, and Blackfoot areas. (U.S. Army Corps of Engineers.)

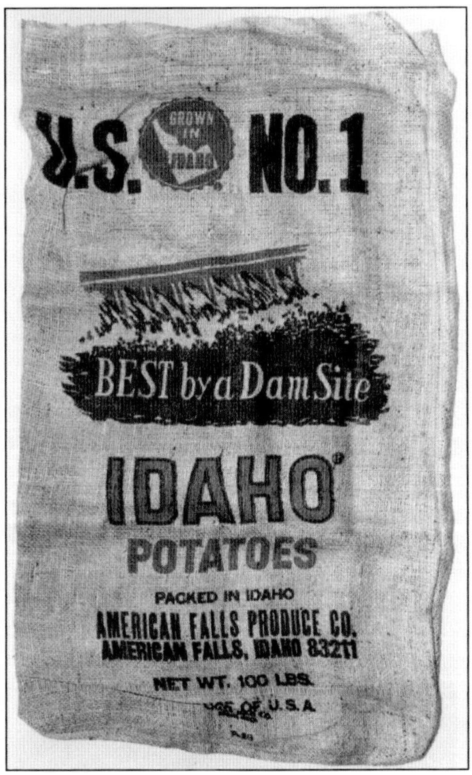

An ironic stamp on potato sacks used to sandbag homes along the river in Idaho Falls referred to the American Falls dam downstream, not the failed Teton Dam. The older concrete dam on the lower river presented no danger of failing from upstream flooding.

Georgia Ricks probably did not envision spending her summer break cleaning up from the dam failure at the home of her parents, Mr. and Mrs. Norman Ricks. Rexburg residents shoveled endless mud and debris in the aftermath of Idaho's worst disaster.

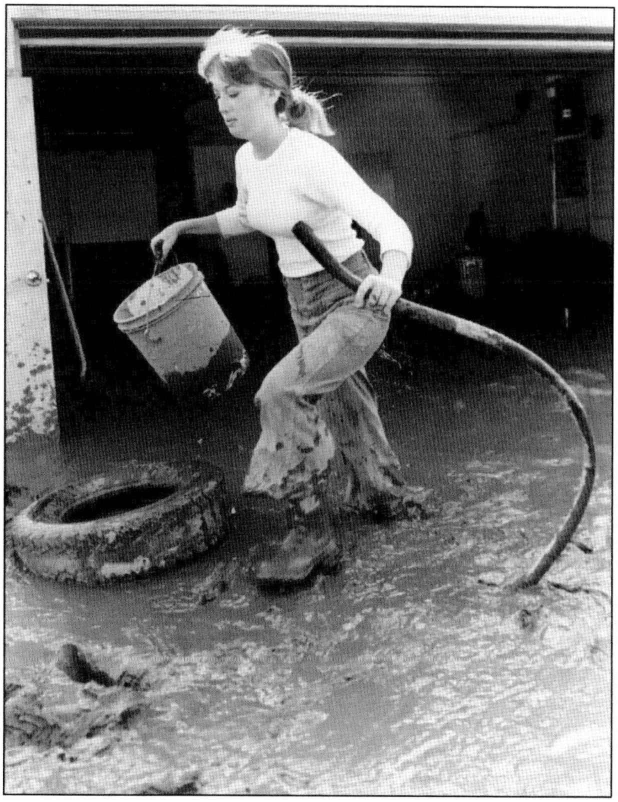

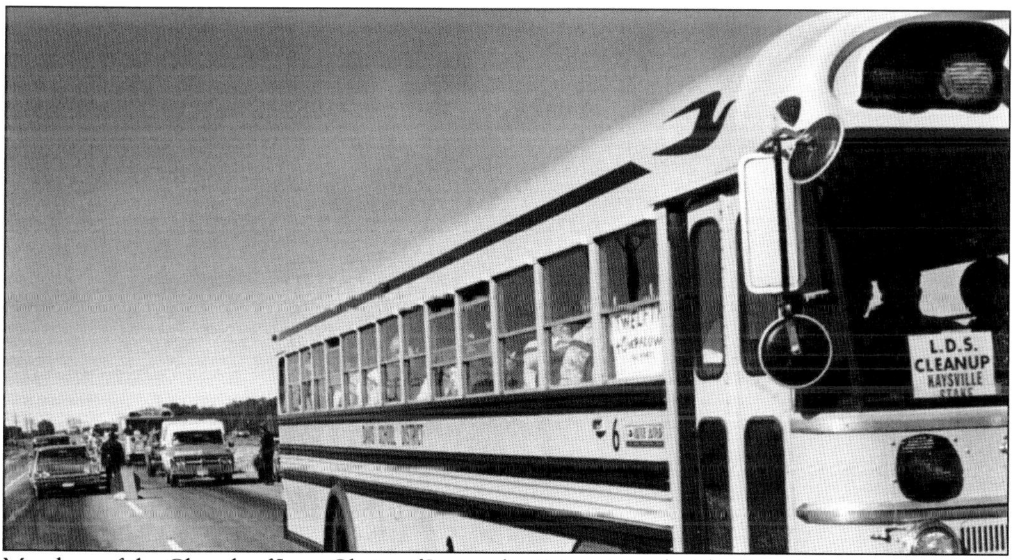

Members of the Church of Jesus Christ of Latter-day Saints joined with others in an interfaith effort to clean up from the Teton Dam disaster. Ricks College, built on a hill above the city of Rexburg, was largely spared and became a rallying point, providing emergency services and temporary food and housing for both displaced dam victims and volunteers who came to help.

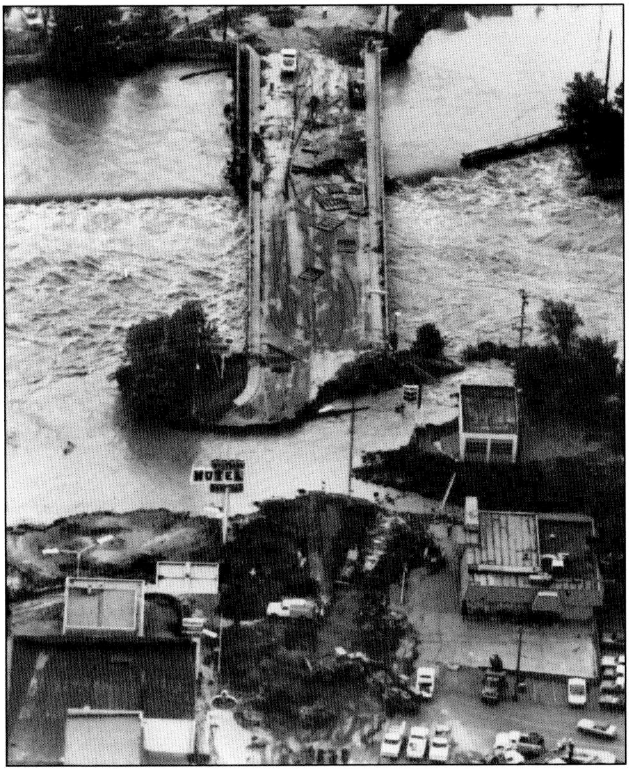

Sugar City and Rexburg got the worst of it, but floodwaters hit Idaho Falls hard as well. To protect the Broadway Bridge, a path was bulldozed for floodwaters, seen to the left. In the photograph below, water along River Parkway was kept at low depths, thanks to sandbagging efforts. Thousands of volunteers showed up to help, working through the night. (Robert Bower.)

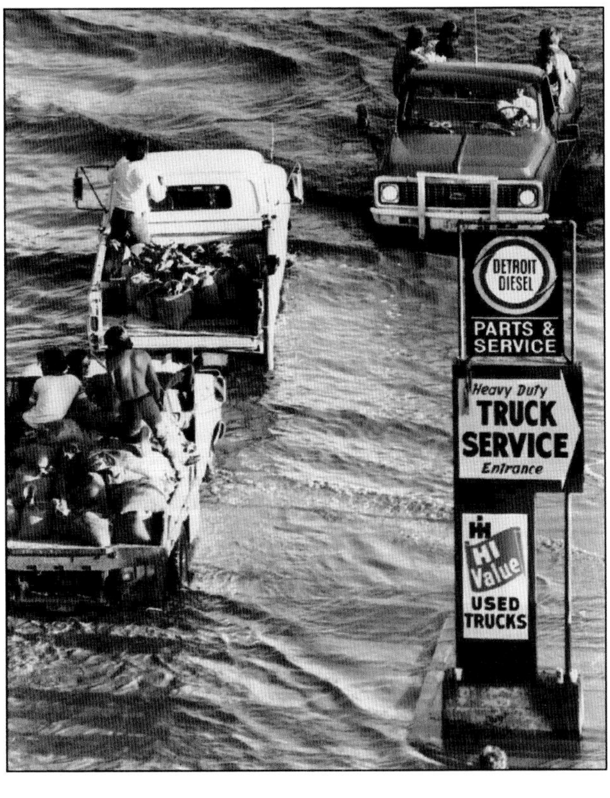

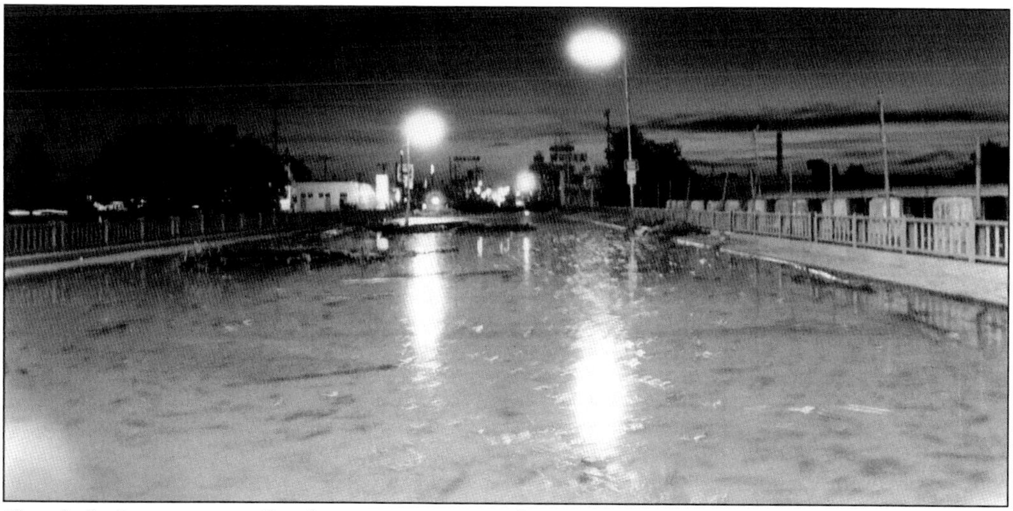

Shortly before cresting, floodwaters came over the top of the Broadway Bridge in Idaho Falls, inundating the falls the city was named for. The bridge held. (Robert Bower.)

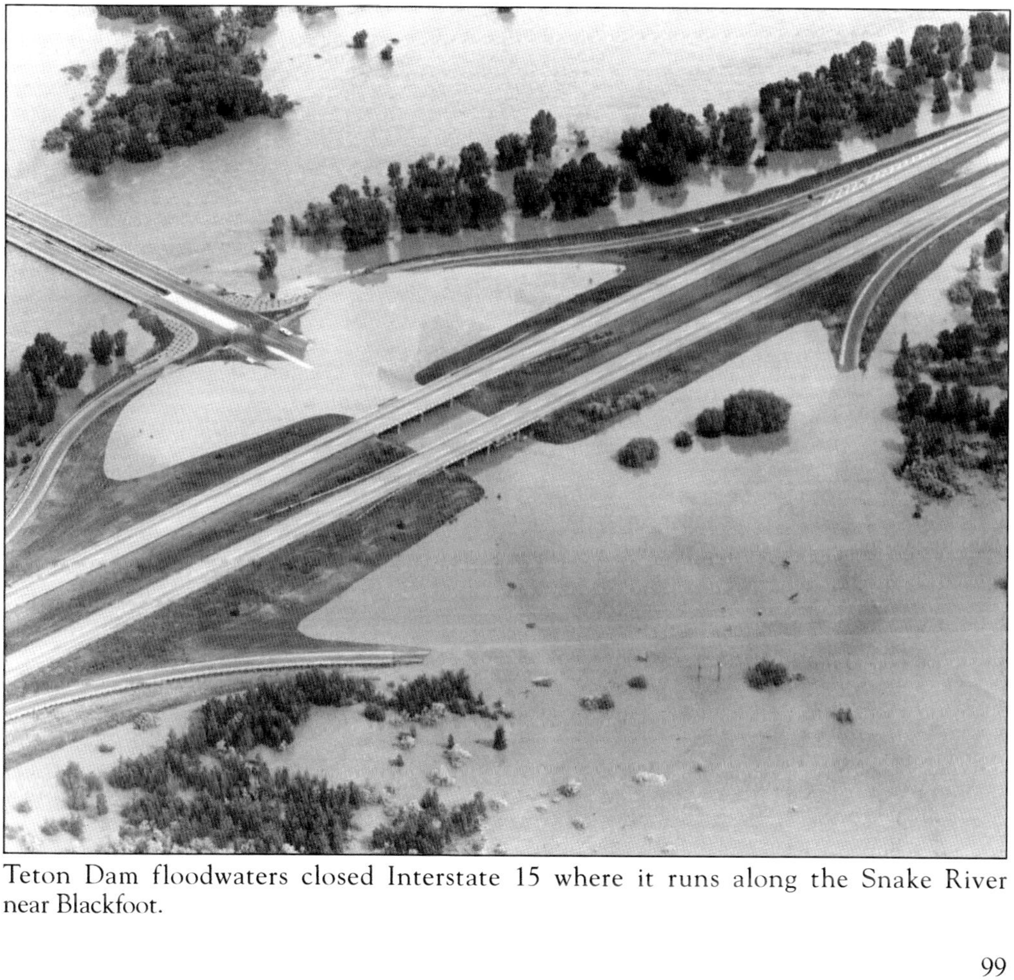

Teton Dam floodwaters closed Interstate 15 where it runs along the Snake River near Blackfoot.

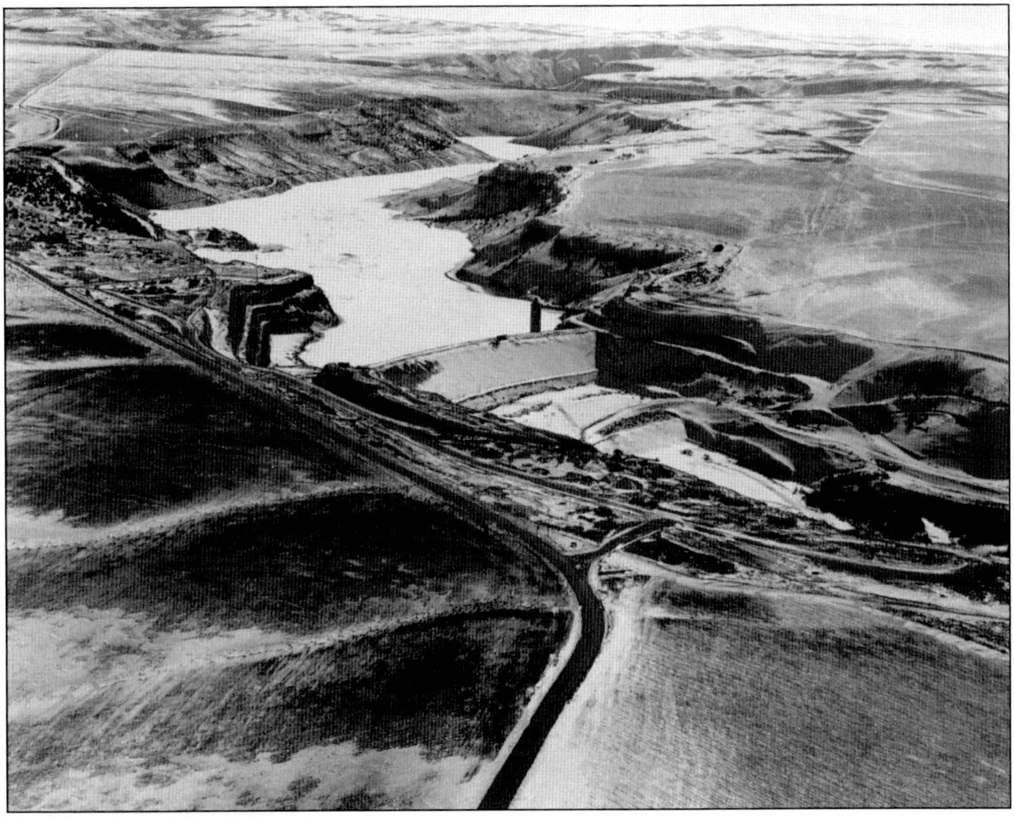

Following the Teton Dam's collapse, worries momentarily centered around the similarly constructed Ririe Dam on the South Fork, a different tributary of the Snake, as it filled with spring runoff. But fears were groundless. (U.S. Army Corps of Engineers.)

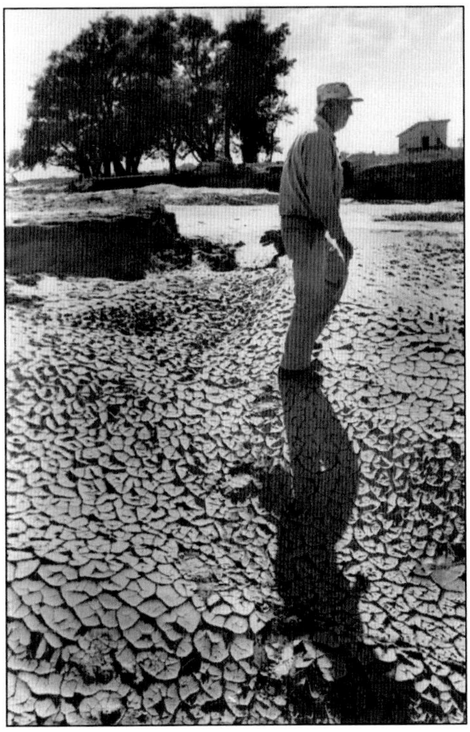

Following the Teton Dam failure, Wilford farmer Carl Smith tours what once was a potato field. The small town of Wilford at the mouth of the Teton Canyon took a direct hit from the wall of mud and debris. Smith had potatoes coming up on good level ground; after the flood, it dropped off five feet in places and was washed to gravel.

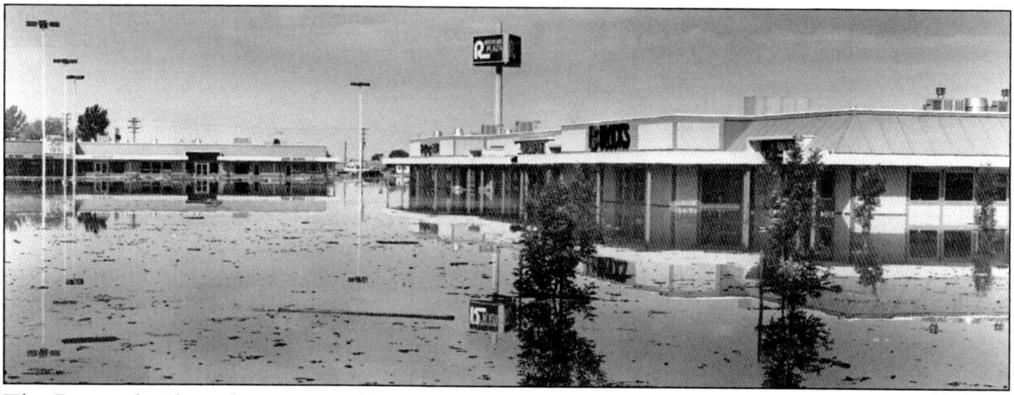

The Riverside Plaza shopping mall in Blackfoot, some 75 miles south, was under water several days after the failure of the Teton Dam.

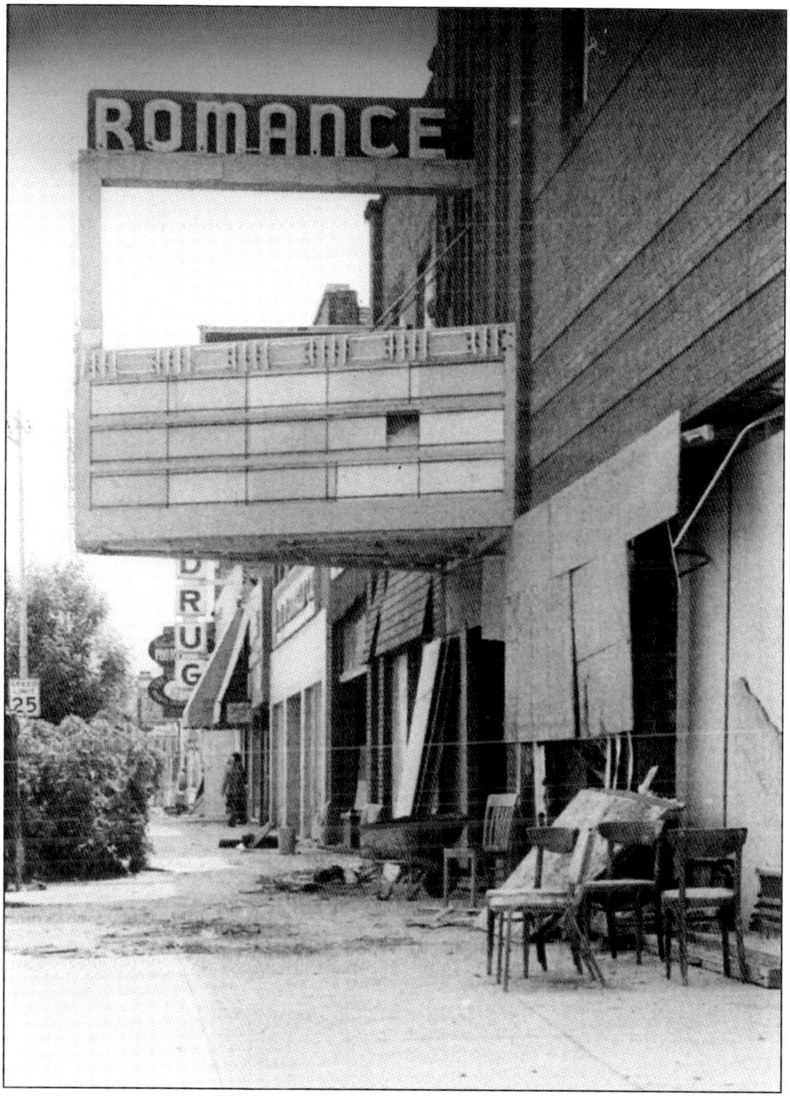

The show was over, for a while at least, at the Romance Theater in downtown Rexburg after floodwaters receded, leaving the town's main street businesses filled with mud and debris.

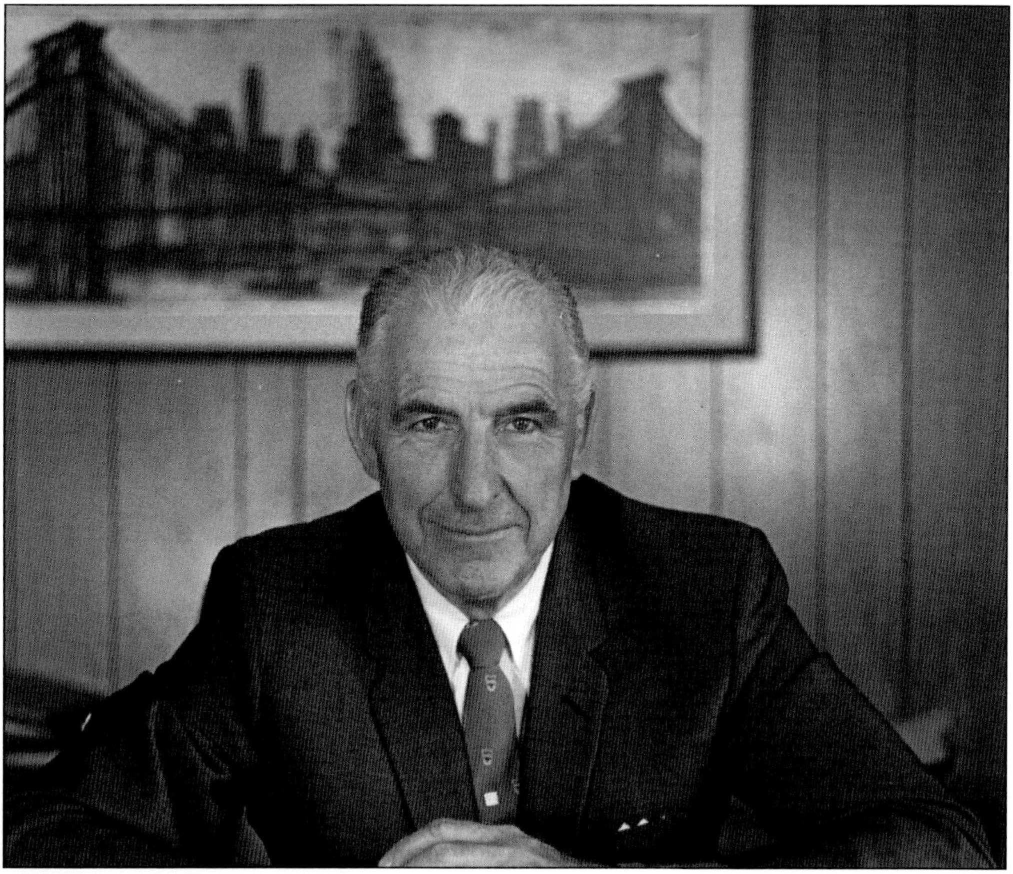

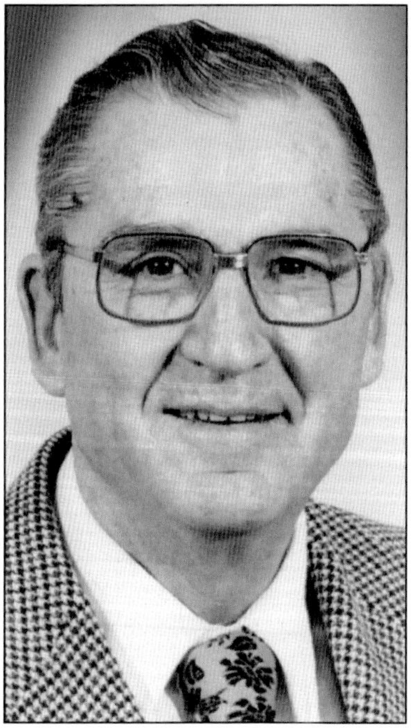

J. Robb Brady's sons, Jim Brady (above) and J. Robb Brady Jr. (left), grew up with relatives after their father died in 1926 while at his desk at the newspaper. Both sons went to Notre Dame University, as did Jim Brady's grandson Jerry Brady later on. Jim returned to help with the family business in 1933 but grew interested in the new mediums of radio and television. He started KIFI-TV8 and served as corporate head. J. Robb Jr. graduated with a degree in journalism and started at the family newspaper as a reporter in 1941. He served as publisher from 1977, on the death of Edwin F. McDermott, until 1988.

Nine

LESSONS FROM THE PAST

While E. F. McDermott built the paper, the younger son of J. Robb Brady had been quietly rising through the ranks of his father's newspaper. Hiring on in 1941 as a reporter, J. Robb Brady Jr. worked as sports editor, city editor, and finally managing editor. Along the way, he won a national AP award for his reporting on the January 1961 reactor accident that killed three people at the National Lab.

Through the early 1970s, political editor Ben Plastino ran roughshod over the concerns of those who had predicted the failure of the Teton Dam. In promoting the project, the Bureau of Reclamation had stacked the statistics. Scientists ripped those numbers to shreds, and independent geologists pointed out that the dam foundation would be resting on dangerously weak rhyolites instead of on bedrock. But this was still William Wheeler's paper, one that had never seen an irrigation project it didn't like.

As predicted by others, the Teton Dam failed, catastrophically, on June 5, 1976, forcing boosters like the *Post-Register* to eat their words. One year later, E. F. McDermott died and J. Robb Brady Jr. was named editor and publisher.

Having learned some of the hardest lessons about progress by covering a nuclear disaster and a dam failure, Brady began to temper the *Post-Register*'s cheerleading for progress. Long the region's leading booster, the *Post-Register* also became a voice of dissent calling for moderation of the region's historic belief in progress at all costs. Eastern Idaho's leaders were not bred on robust public debate, and this feisty editorial voice was unseemly. Brady deflected much of the criticism by virtue of his unfailing kind manners and gentle wit.

For years, the newspaper's "Sunday" edition had really been produced and distributed on Saturday mornings, which omitted most Saturday sports results, especially during college football season. Former sports editor Brady moved the Sunday paper to a true morning publication schedule in 1985, a foretaste of when the newspaper would convert all of its publications to a morning edition.

Beloved by the newspaper's staff for legendary acts of personal generosity, J. Robb retired in December 1988. He continues to write for the opinion page, and the Idaho Conservation League's top award is named for him in recognition of his early calls for wilderness protection and vigilant oversight of mining and logging.

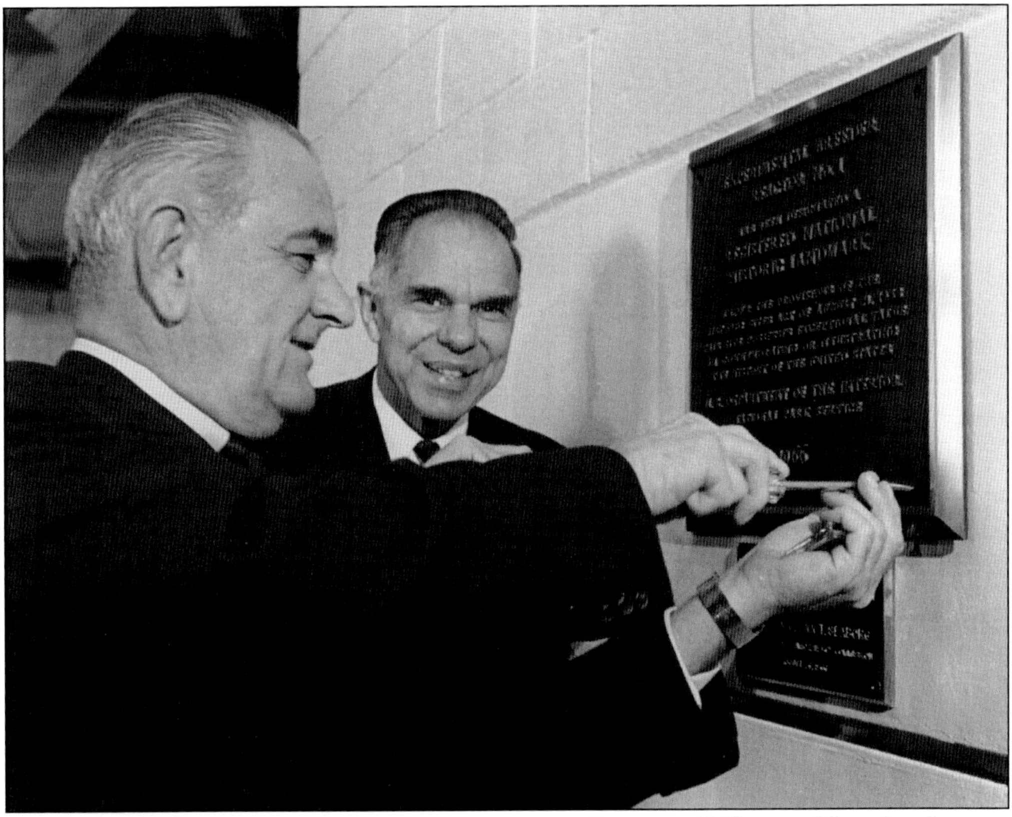

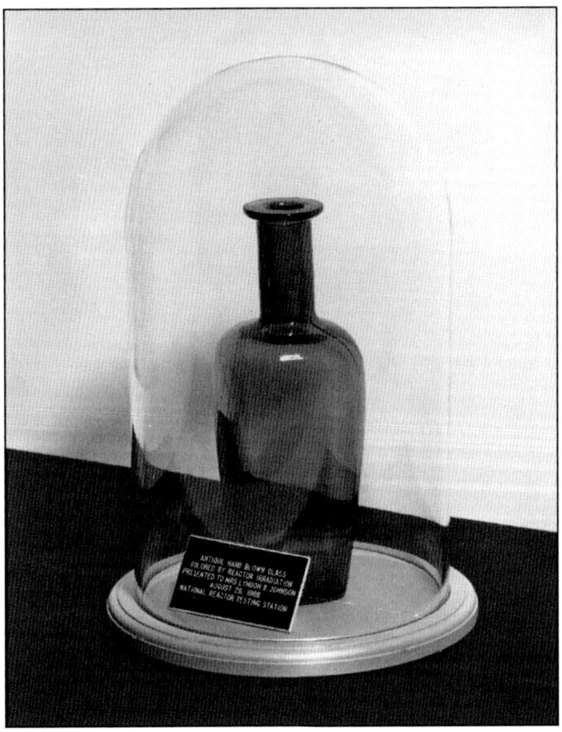

During a 1966 visit of Pres. Lyndon Johnson, he ceremonially affixed a plaque dedicating EBR-1 as a national monument and spoke about the promise of nuclear power.

This bottle was produced for Sage Brush Tonic Company of Shoshone in 1906, a short-lived hair preparation made from sagebrush and advertised as "the Indian's gift to the White Man—Did you ever see a bald-headed Indian?" The antique bottle was changed to a rich amethyst hue by exposure to extremely high gamma radiation at the Materials Testing Reactor in 1966 and presented to Lady Bird Johnson during LBJ's visit to the National Reactor Testing Station.

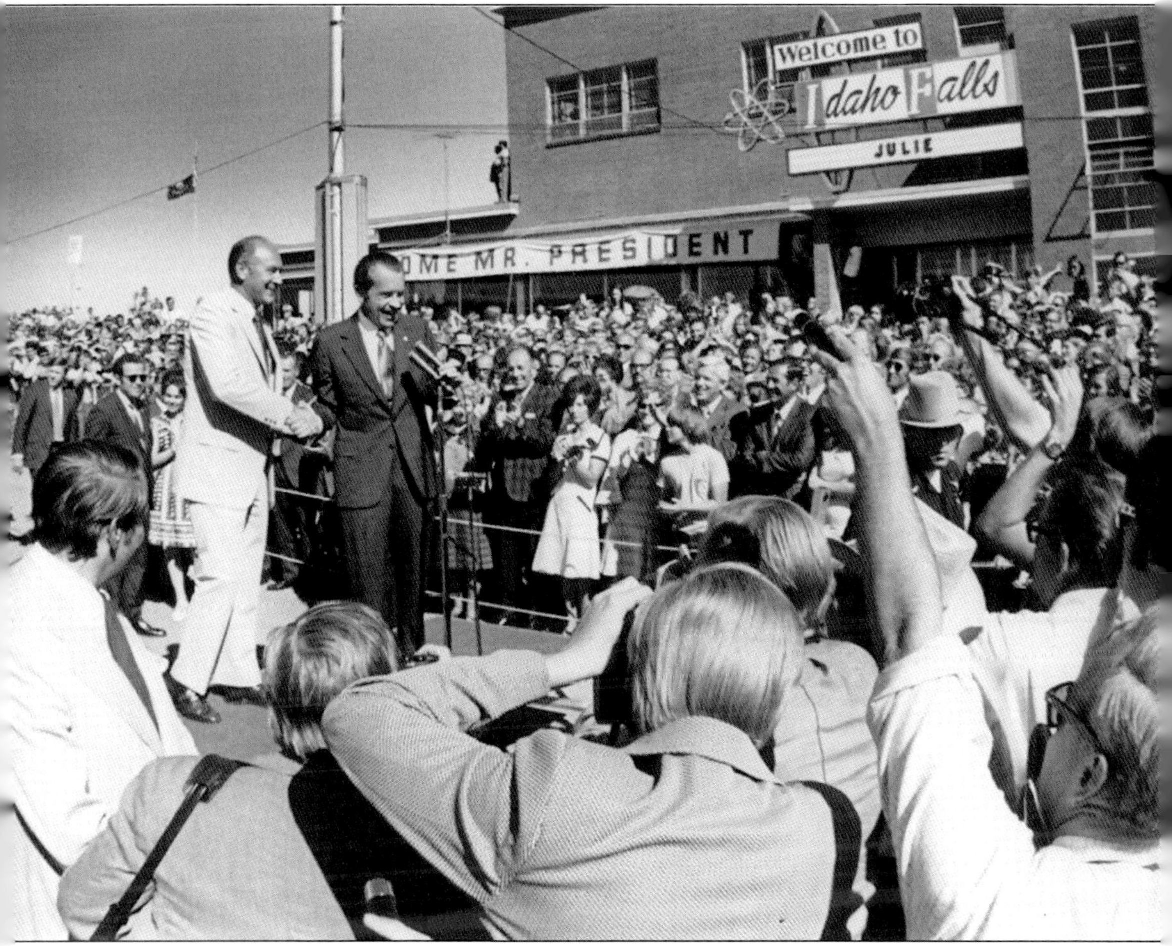

An airport full of spectators and officials greeted Pres. Richard Nixon as he stopped for a short talk on his way to Grand Teton National Park in 1971. Nixon is greeted by Democratic governor Cecil Andrus.

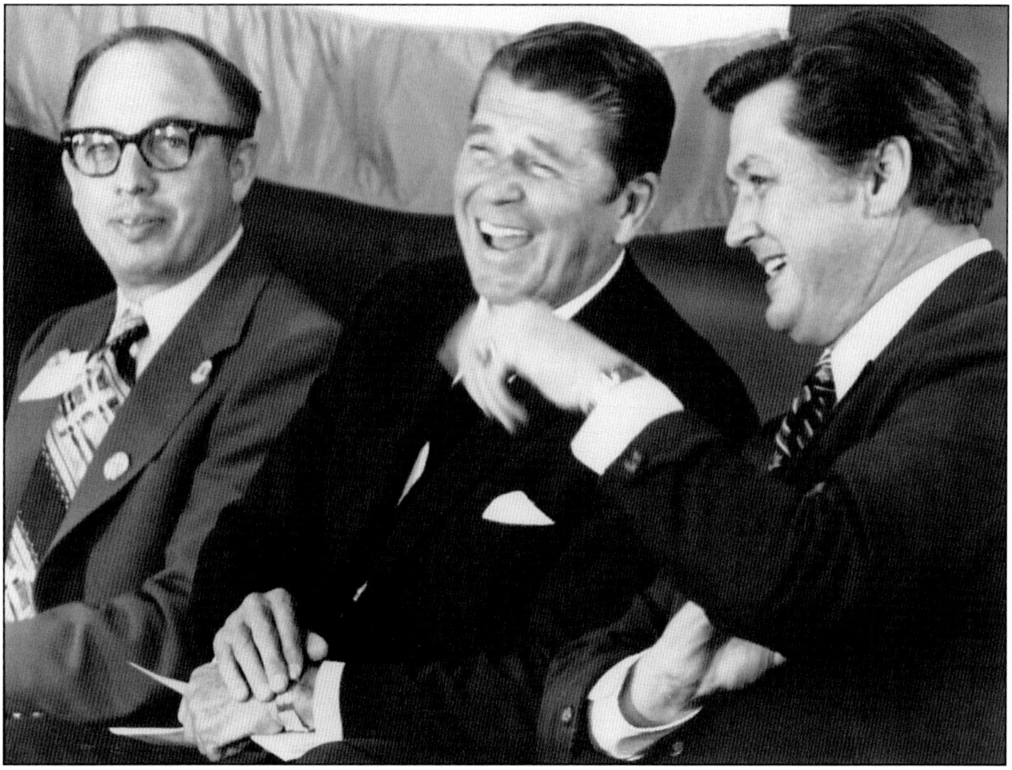

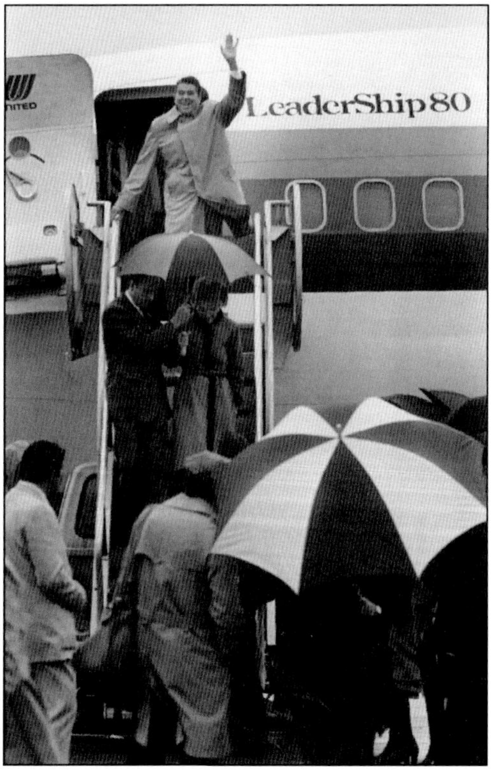

Ronald Reagan made two visits to eastern Idaho prior to becoming president in 1981; in the above photograph he is shown with the late Dennis Olsen (left) and former U.S. representative George Hansen (right) on May 12, 1976, at the Idaho Falls High School gym. In photograph to the left, he arrives on a rainy October day at the Idaho Falls airport just before the 1980 election.

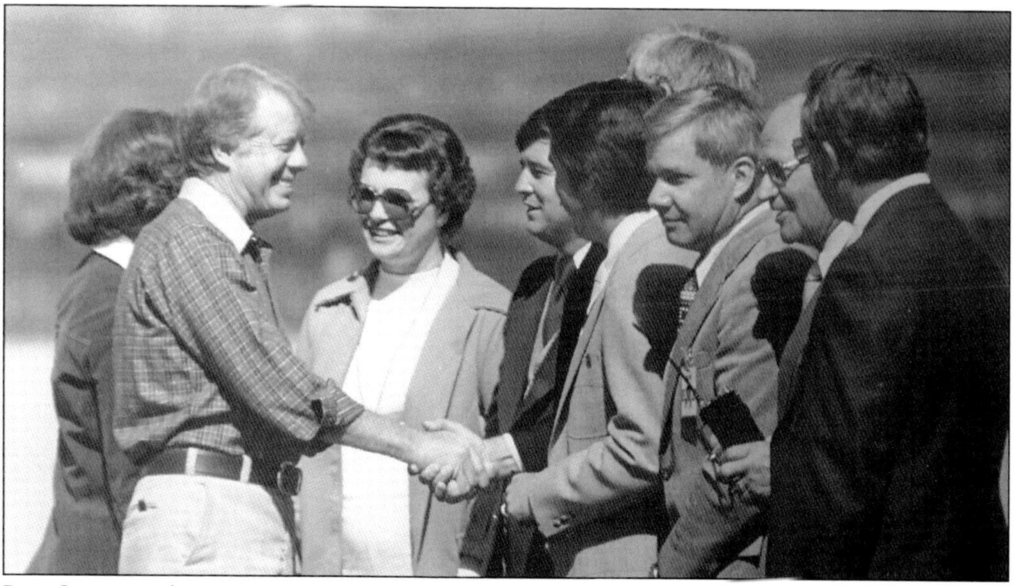

Pres. Jimmy and First Lady Rosalynn Carter are shown here being greeted by local dignitaries, including Idaho Falls mayor Tom Campbell in about 1980. As a U.S. navy officer, Carter qualified for nuclear power training school in Idaho but resigned a year before the *Nautilus* was launched in 1954.

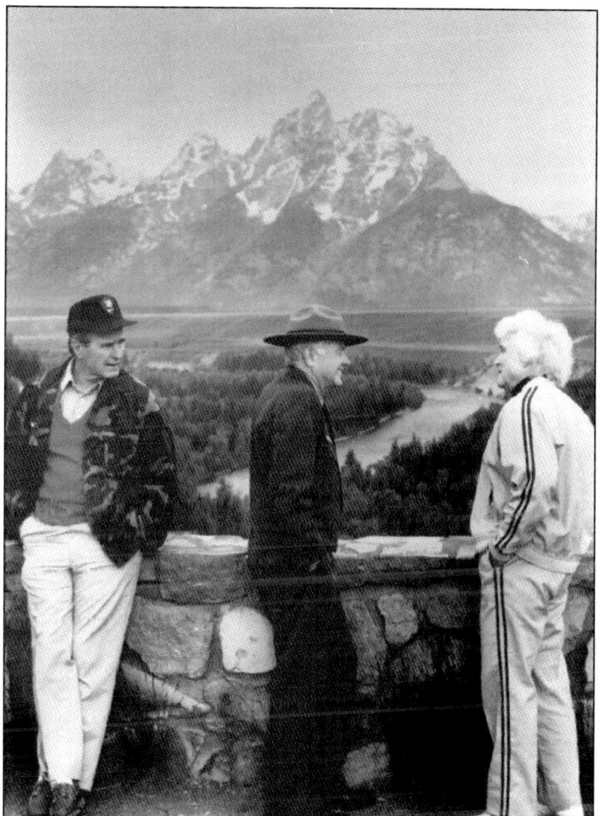

Pres. George Bush (left) and Barbara Bush enjoy a visit with a Grand Teton National Park ranger in 1987. Bush's successor, Bill Clinton, visited the park twice during his eight-year presidency. George W. Bush has not visited, though Vice President Dick Cheney is a Jackson Hole resident.

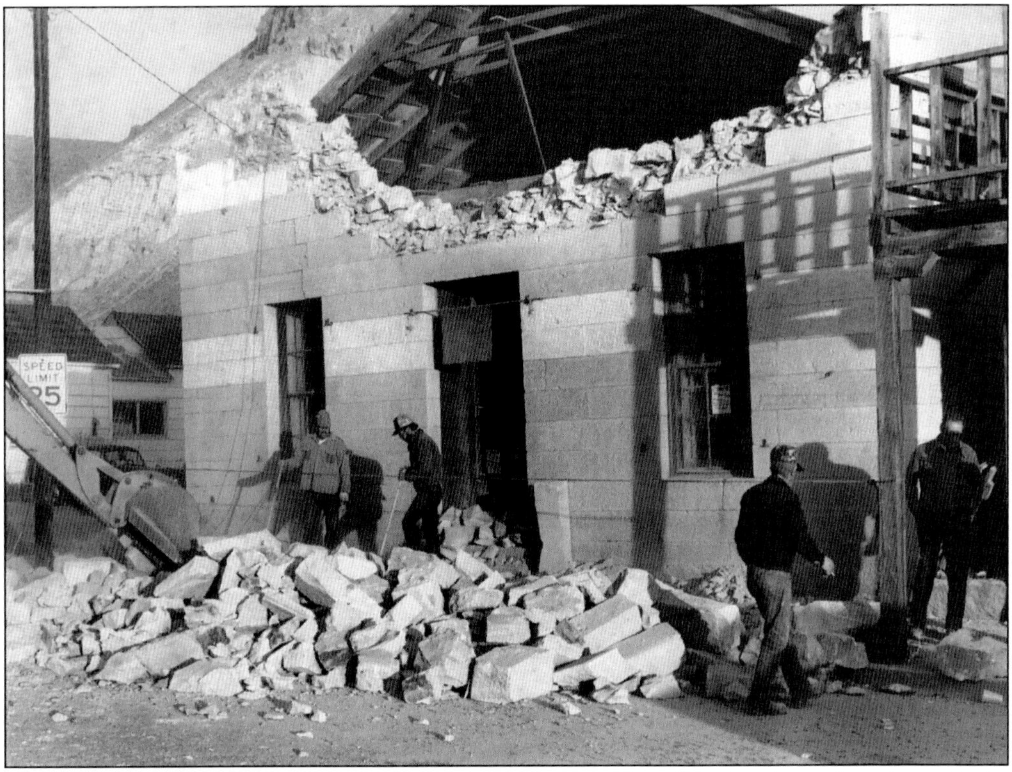

Another deadly earthquake rocked central Idaho on October 28, 1983, causing the deaths of two young schoolchildren. The two were struck by falling bricks while walking along Challis's main street.

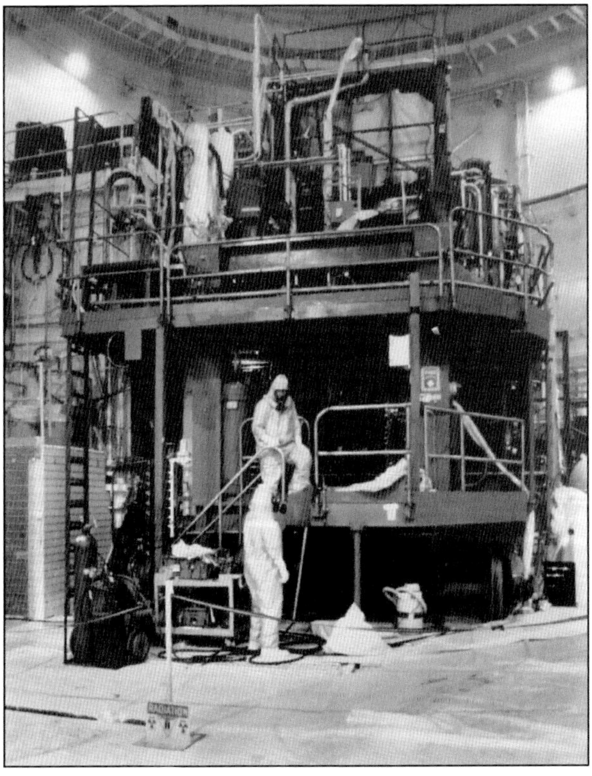

Workers dismantle the Loss of Fluid Test Facility, or LOFT, the last reactor allowed to melt down for experiments at the INL. The meltdown occurred in 1985.

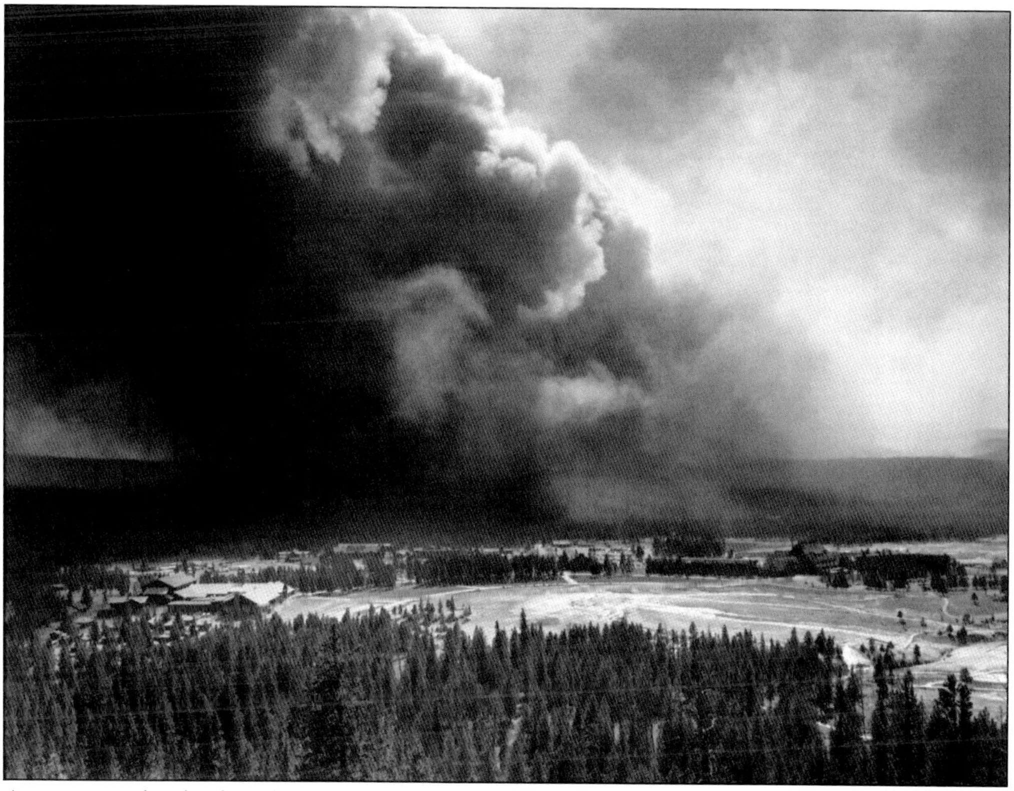

An ominous bank of smoke towers over Old Faithful Lodge and the famed geyser in 1988, during a summer when nearly 800,000 acres—36 percent of the park—was affected by wildfires that burned out of control all summer. The Yellowstone fires started with smaller individual fires in Island Park and the Madison Plateau and joined as increasing winds and drought whipped the flames into firestorms. The fires almost destroyed Old Faithful Inn and finally caused the park to be closed to all non-emergency personnel for the first time in its history.

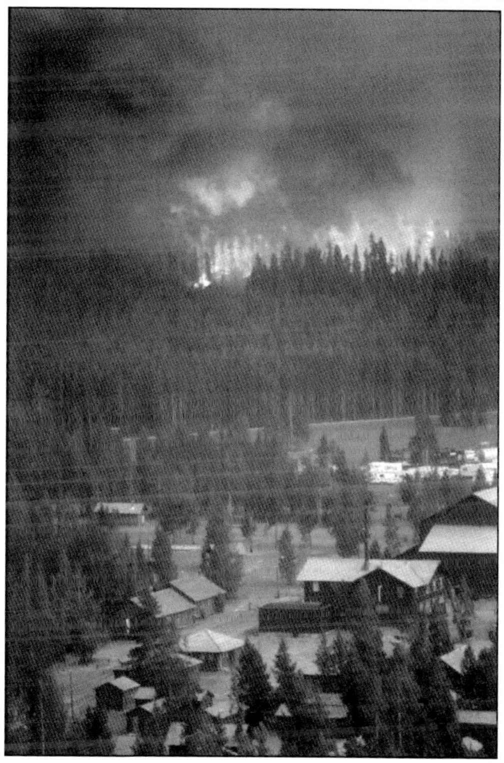

Fires that had been burning to the east and south of Old Faithful Inn turned toward the lodge and cabins as the wind shifted and a firestorm developed. Burning embers rained down on the upper geyser basin, and extensive damage was only averted by the frantic efforts of firefighters and another change in the wind. (Robert Bower/*Post Register.*)

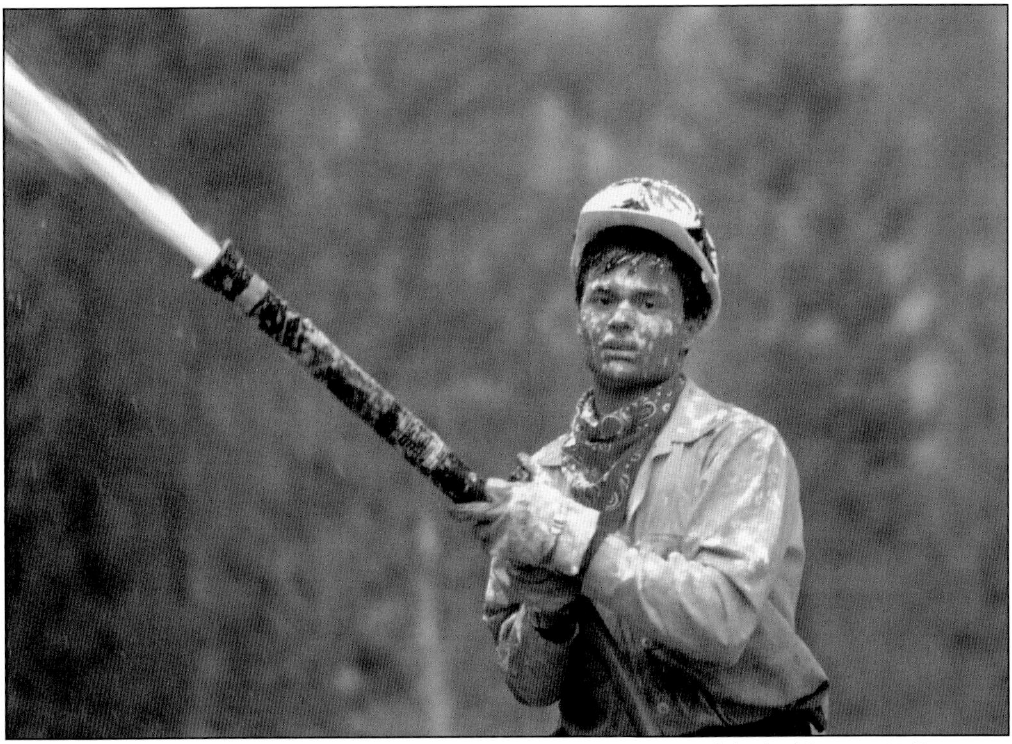

Exhausted firefighter Gary Wegner sprays fire retardant foam on one of the buildings in Yellowstone National Park's Grant Village. This July 1988 picture by *Post Register* photographer Robert Bower was released to the AP, ran in *USA Today*, and was even the subject of discussion on National Public Radio. It helped bring the world's attention to the plight of Yellowstone in the summer of 1988. By the time fall rain and snows put out the flames, more than 10,000 firefighters had battled the fires.

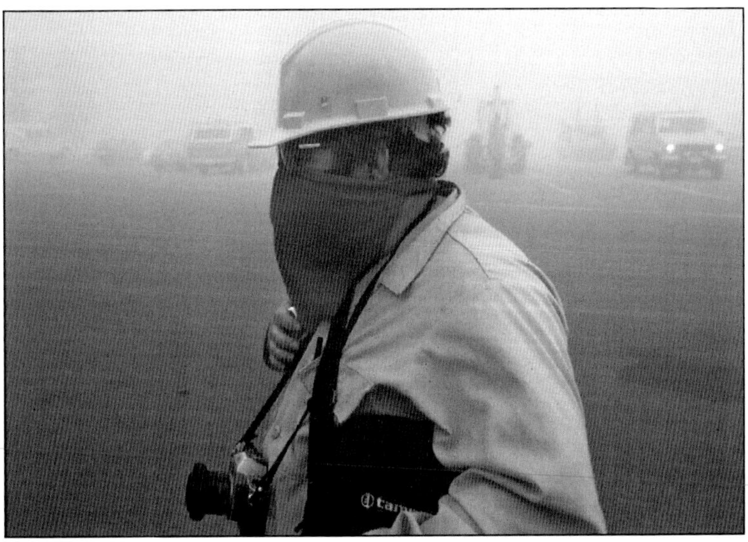

Smoke that blinded the eyes and choked the lungs was common across Yellowstone National Park during the summer of 1988. *Post Register* lead reporter Rocky Barker regains his composure in the Old Faithful parking lot after fleeing the firestorm as it swept across the upper geyser basin on September 7, 1988. (Robert Bower.)

Winds were a problem all summer, but when exceptionally high winds pushed the fires on August 20, 1988, more than 150,000 acres were charred in a single day and firefighters were forced to retreat. (Randy Hayes.)

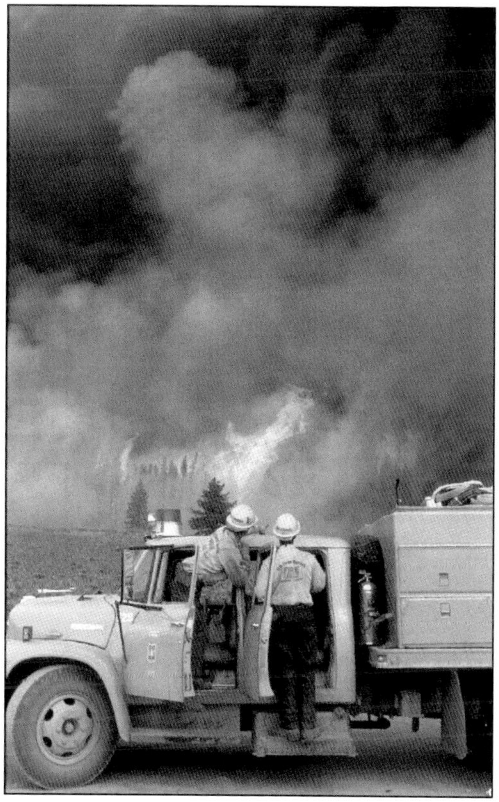

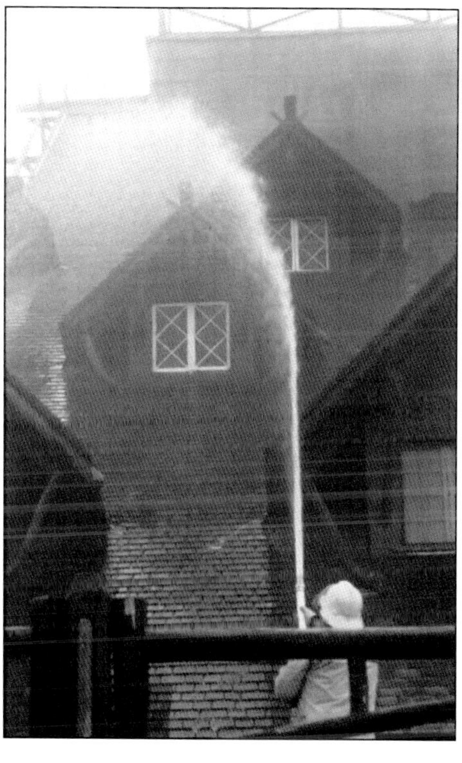

A firefighter sprays down the roof of the historic Old Faithful Inn during the firestorm that rained burning embers on the Old Faithful area on September 7, 1988. Thanks to the efforts of hundreds of firefighters and a measure of luck, the Inn and nearly all of the buildings in the area were saved. On the 20th anniversary, the *Post Register* and Associated Press took a retrospective look at the lasting legacy of the Yellowstone fires. (Robert Bower.)

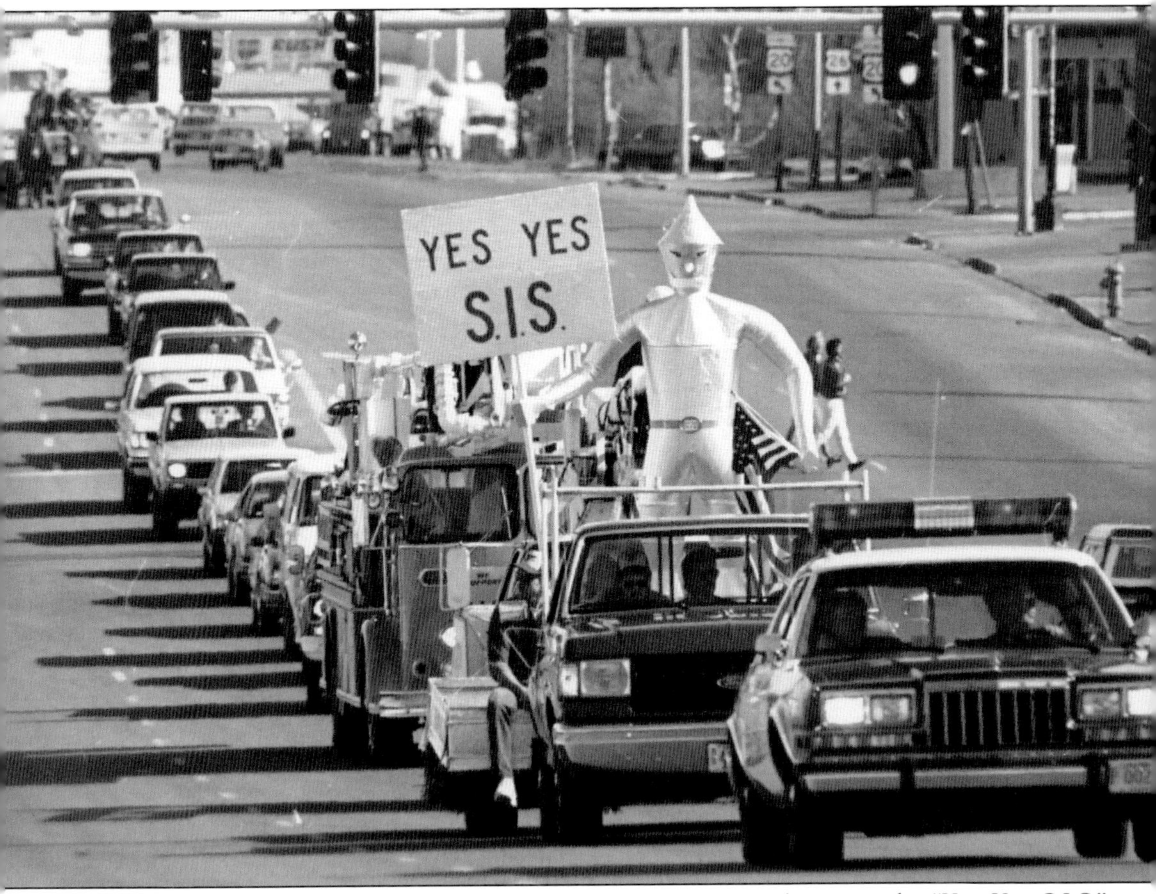

Among the many protests over military nuclear projects over the years, the "Yes, Yes, S.I.S." was a pro-nuclear demonstration in Idaho Falls in 1988. Plans to build a $1.2-billion plutonium refinery in the desert west of town brought out 450 vehicles to parade through the city showing support. Considered vital by the Reagan administration, the Special Isotope Separation project was scrapped early in 1990 by the Bush administration.

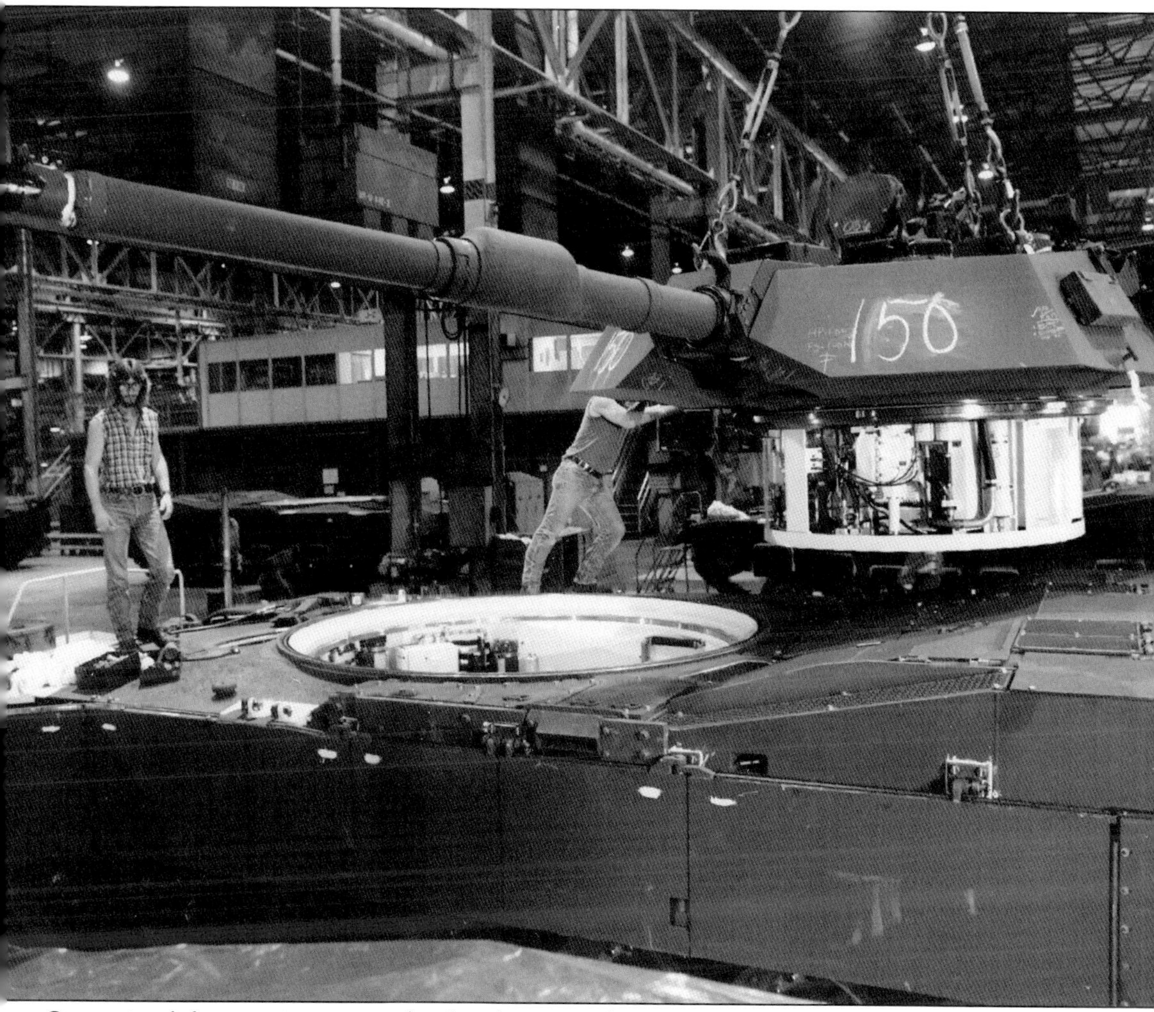

One major defense project materialized at the site in the 1980s: in 1983, the army began making an armor package using depleted uranium for its main M1-A1 Abrams Main Battle Tank. Known as Project X, the package was battle-tested in the 1991 Persian Gulf War and came through with flying colors. (INL.)

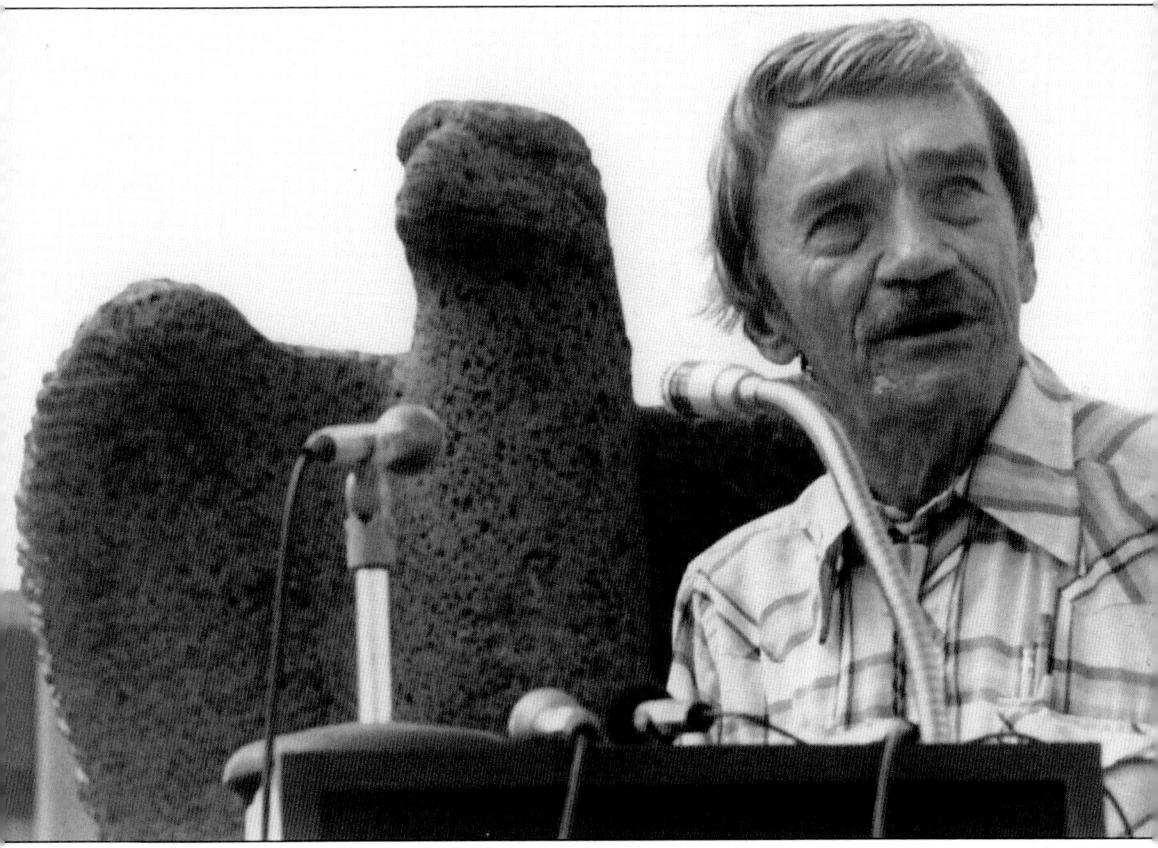

Post-Register history editor Joe Marker was a fixture at the newspaper for decades. Author of *Eagle Rock, U.S.A.*, Marker collected photographs and tidbits in his frequent history columns for the newspaper. Most of his collections found their way to the Bonneville County Historical Society, including pictures taken by his grandfather, Alma Marker, an early-day photographer and music store proprietor. Here he is shown speaking at dedication ceremonies for the Eagle Rock statue in downtown Idaho Falls, a depiction of the eagle for whom the early town was named carved out of solid basalt.

Unique businesses seemed to pop up from time to time in the 1980s, like DWI (right) and the Bakery Boutique (below). Tom and Heidi Tobin offered anyone who had had a few too many at their local tavern a ride home: Tobin would ride his collapsible moped to the patron's car, put the bike in the trunk, and drive him or her home for a fee. The full service bakery also offered home delivery of a custom-designed bikini cake with a kiss from a bunny-clad Rebekah Hansen. Neither flash of entrepreneurial inspiration lasted.

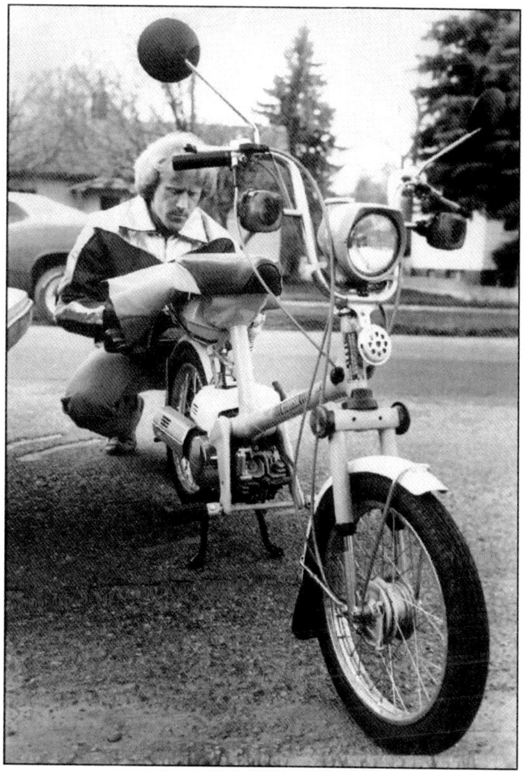

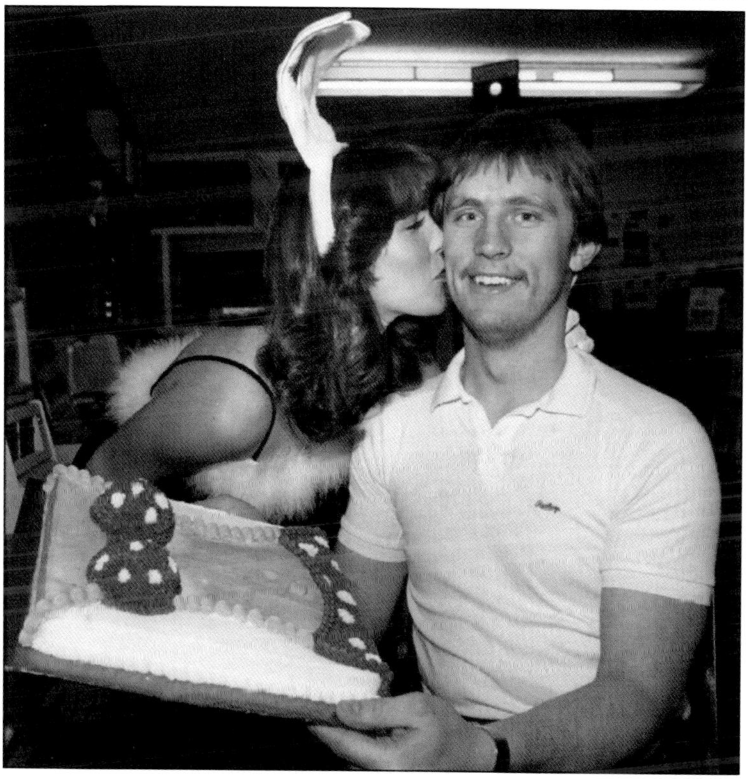

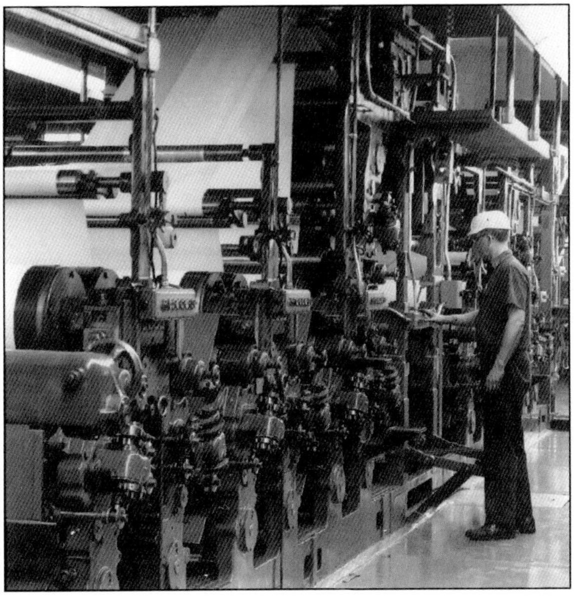

This Goss Urbanite offset press was installed in 1977 as an eight-unit press capable of producing up to 64 pages but had little color printing capability: each color added in a four-color printing system reduced the capacity of the press by eight pages. The press was upgraded to 13 units over the years. In 2005, the press was moved to the paper's new $6-million production and packaging facility. In 2009, it will be replaced by another Goss printing press, a full-color Magnum 4 capable of better color registration, faster printing times, and reduced newspaper waste. In fact, with rising newsprint costs, the $2-million, 48-page press is projected to pay for itself in newsprint savings over time.

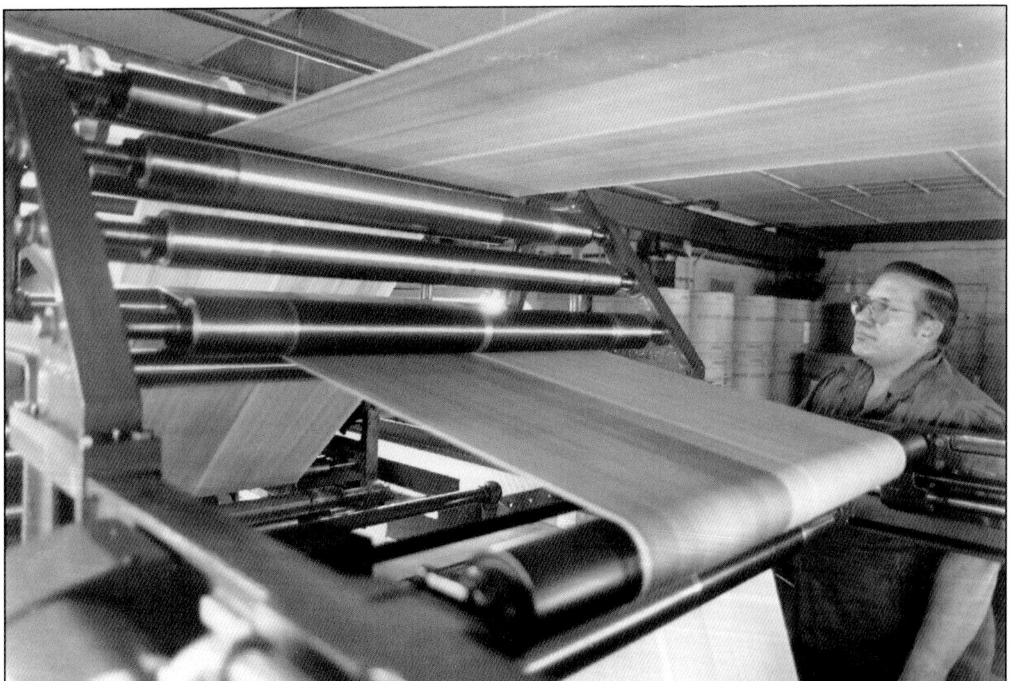

Pressroom foreman Ralph Ockerman checks the paper tension of the "web" in this 1987 photograph. Half-ton rolls of paper were stacked in the background, and this press used a lot of them.

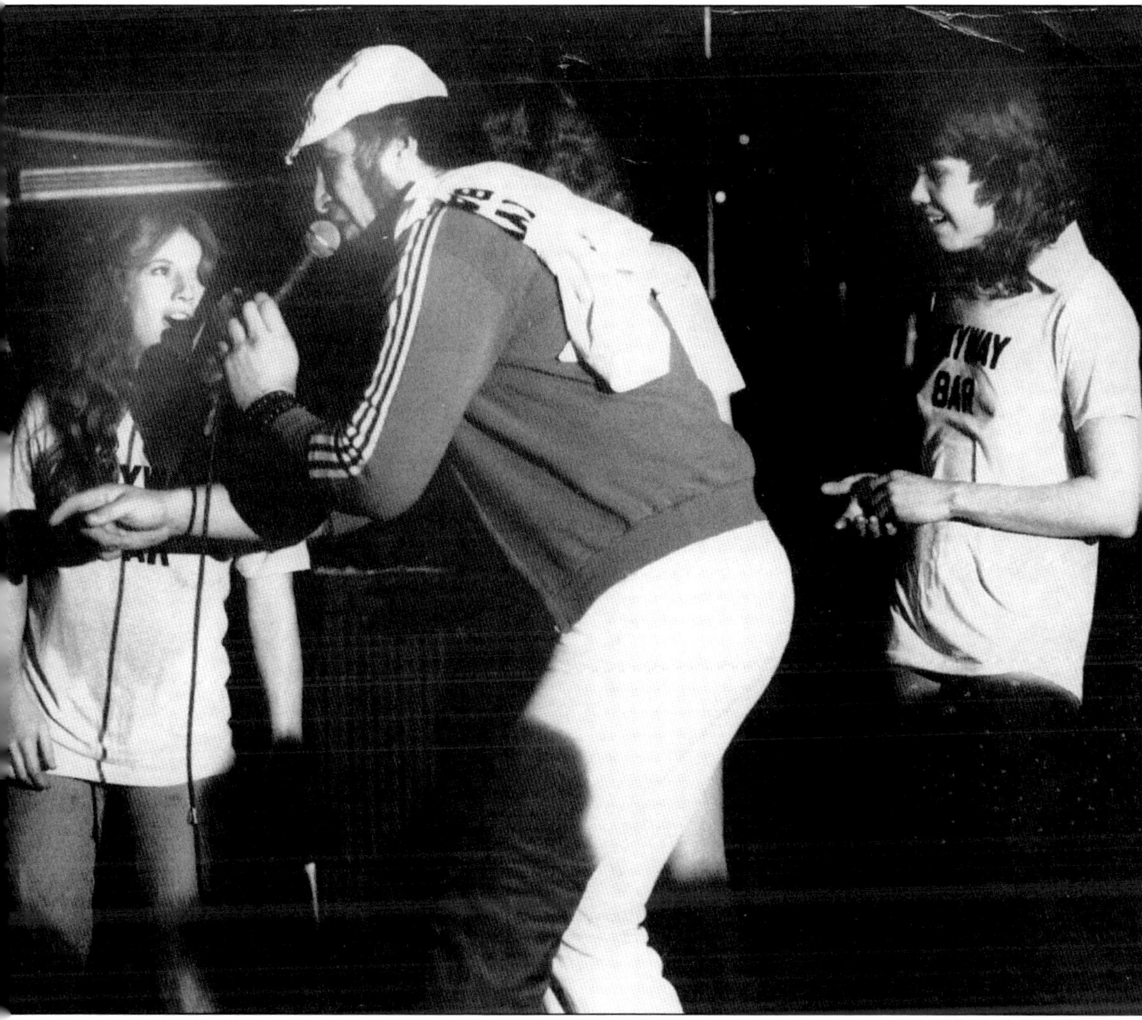

Society's boundaries were continually tested as Idaho Falls continued rapid growth in the 1970s and early 1980s. In 1973, city fathers attempted to block showings of the controversial Marlon Brando movie *Last Tango in Paris*. In 1982, a lounge owner was slapped with a fine for conducting a wet T-shirt contest.

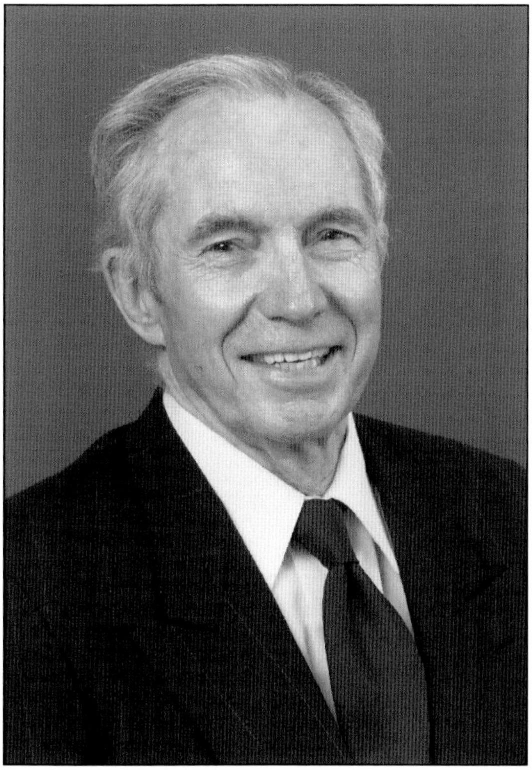

Post company president Jerry M. Brady became publisher when his uncle, J. Robb Brady Jr., retired. Robb still writes for the opinion page. Before his return to Idaho in 1984 to run the television station after his father's death, Brady had worked for two decades in Washington, D.C. As a young lawyer, he worked for Sen. Frank Church. He was a manager at the Peace Corps and at a third-world development agency before going into private practice specializing in energy law. Brady ran for governor as a Democrat in 2002 and again in 2006.

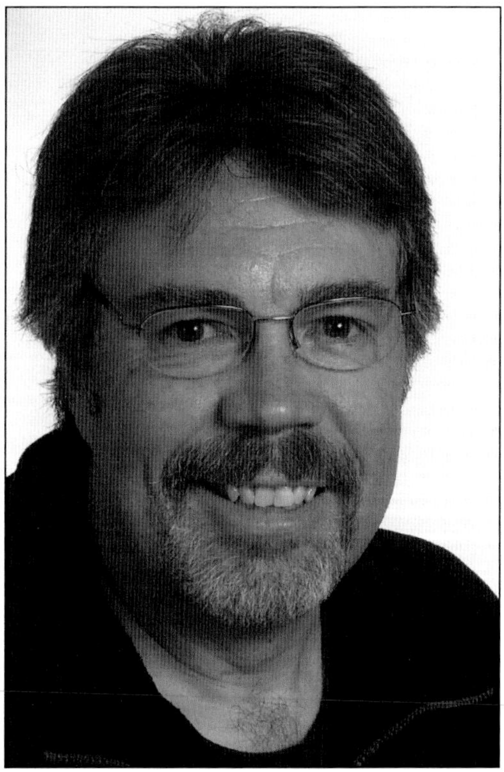

Roger Plothow has been publisher of the *Post Register* since 2002. A former executive editor of the newspaper, he came back as general manager in 1998 and has led the paper through modernization of its production system and a $6-million plant expansion.

Ten

New Era of Change

When J. Robb retired, he sold his shares to a family trust controlled by his nephew, Jerry, who had been managing KIFI-TV since 1984. On that day, it was one of just 450 independent papers left in America.

Jerry Brady pledged the *Post Register* would remain independent and locally owned. He spent thousands on market research and pushed a series of four managing editors to modernize the paper's writing and reporting. Circulation increased and in the early 1990s The *Post Register* was the fastest-growing afternoon paper in America. By then, the paper had built a reputation for its reporting on environmental issues. It won local and national awards for special projects, including a yearlong look at the Snake River.

On May 3, 1997, the *Post Register* switched to a morning publication schedule. Brady gave almost unlimited coverage to the community's efforts to restore the Colonial Theater. He served on community groups and worked to rein in the cost of health care. Concerned by the shrinking workforce at the nuclear laboratory, Brady put up company money to hire an economic development expert, launching the Eastern Idaho Economic Development Council. At about the same time, he had pushed a small team to launch the *Post Register*'s Web site, the second such newspaper Internet service in Idaho.

Keeping his promise to protect local ownership, Brady in 1998 sold 49 percent of the company to his employees under an Employee Stock Ownership Plan, or ESOP, financing the sale from the paper's profits while the company received some tax advantages.

Jerry Brady, meanwhile, had caught his family's political bug and announced he would run for governor in 2002. The editors constructed guidelines to protect the newsroom's independence from even the appearance of interference from the publisher-turned-candidate. Brady, a Democrat, lost to incumbent Republican governor Dirk Kempthorne and returned to work as president of the Post Company, with a new publisher, Roger Plothow. He ran again, and lost again, in 2006. Jerry Brady announced the sale of the company-owned television station KIFI-TV8; the sale went through in August 2005 and was announced that spring.

The *Post Register*, meanwhile, purchased the *Challis Messenger* in 2004, followed by the *Shelley Pioneer* and the *Jefferson County (Rigby) Star*, and operates a weekly agricultural publication, *Farm & Ranch*. The paper's Web site won national awards for its pioneering work on pay-for access Web publishing.

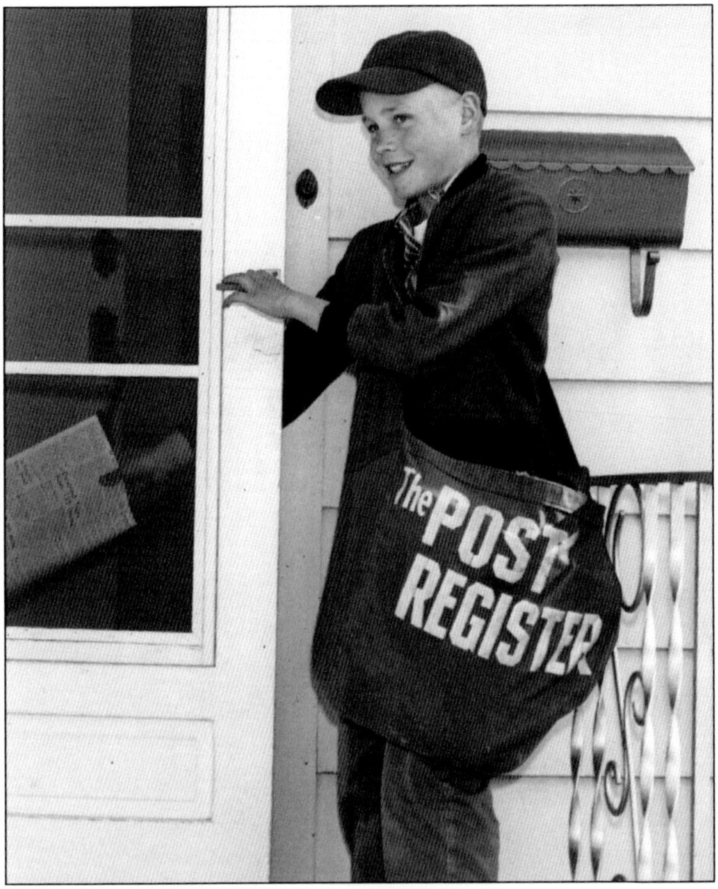

The combined efforts of the newspaper's staff eventually fall into the hands of paper carriers and delivery personnel, who are pledged to deliver the *Post Register* by 7:00 a.m. on the front porch each morning, seven days a week. The photograph to the left shows carrier Phillip Carr in 1959, son of Dr. and Mrs. T. H. Carr of Idaho Falls; the photograph below shows carrier Chris Miles using his bicycle to shorten delivery time on his west side route in 1984.

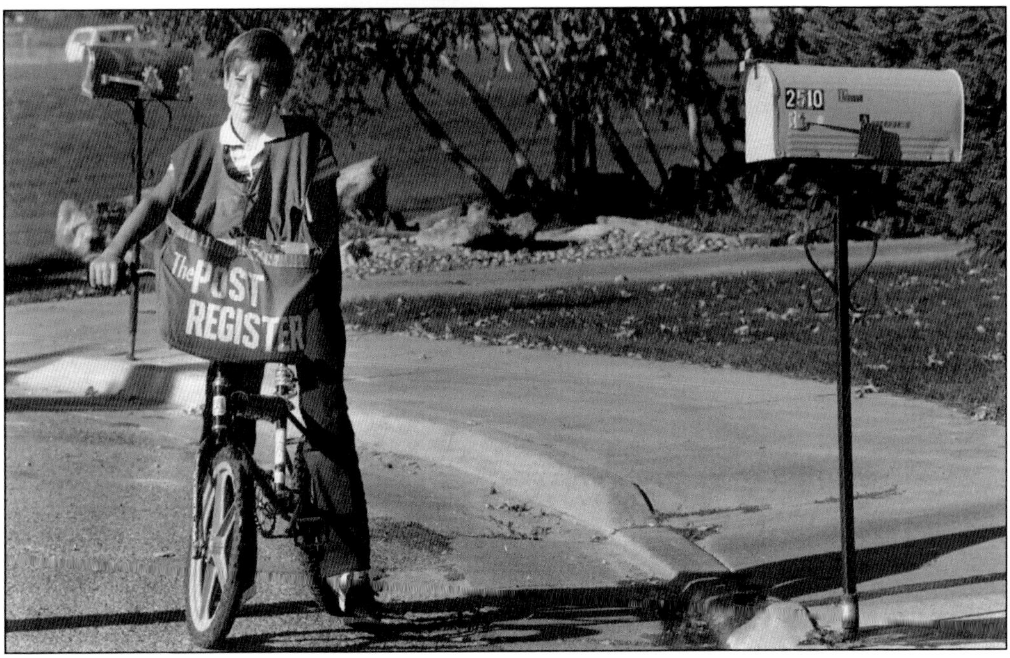

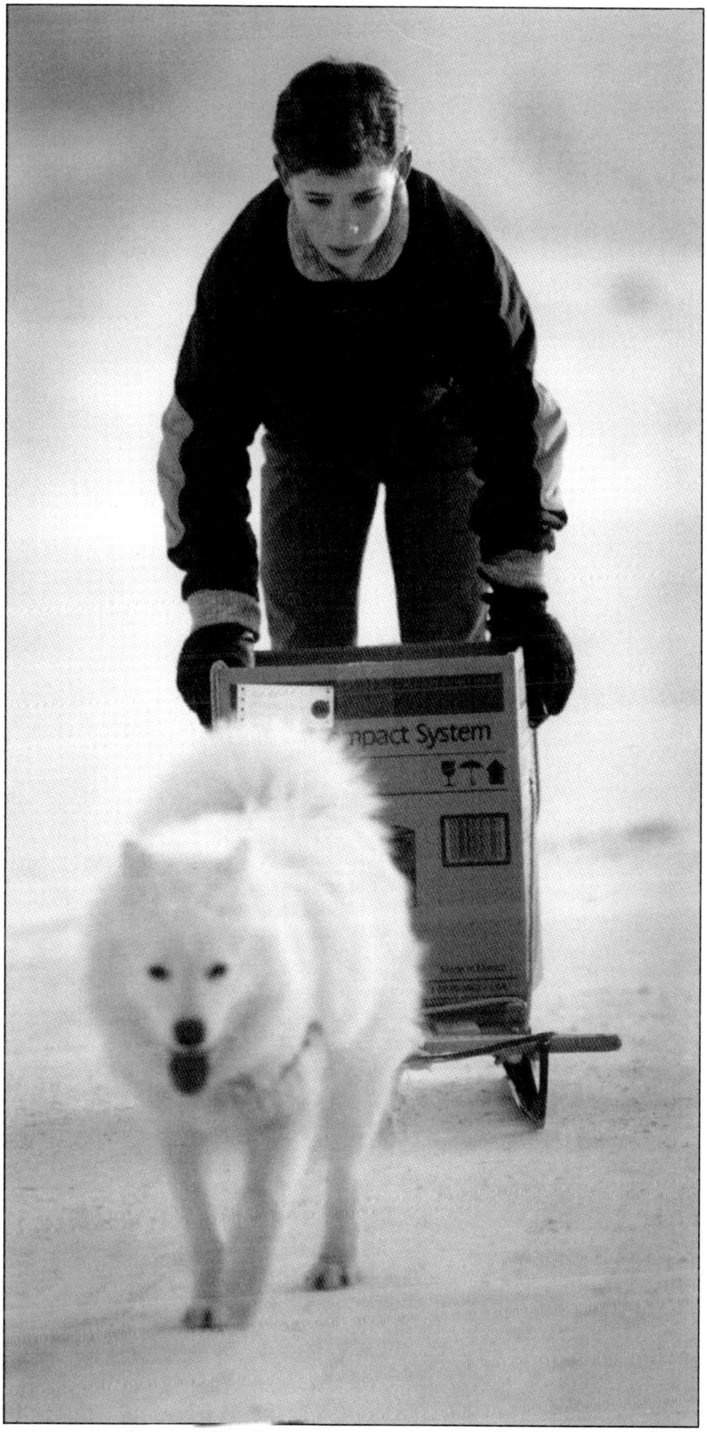

In 1997, the *Post-Register* changed back to morning delivery (the *Post* began as a morning daily in 1905), and its youth carrier force began to change as they dropped out, citing cold weather and dark mornings. This photograph shows an unidentified carrier using the family dog to pull a sled filled with papers.

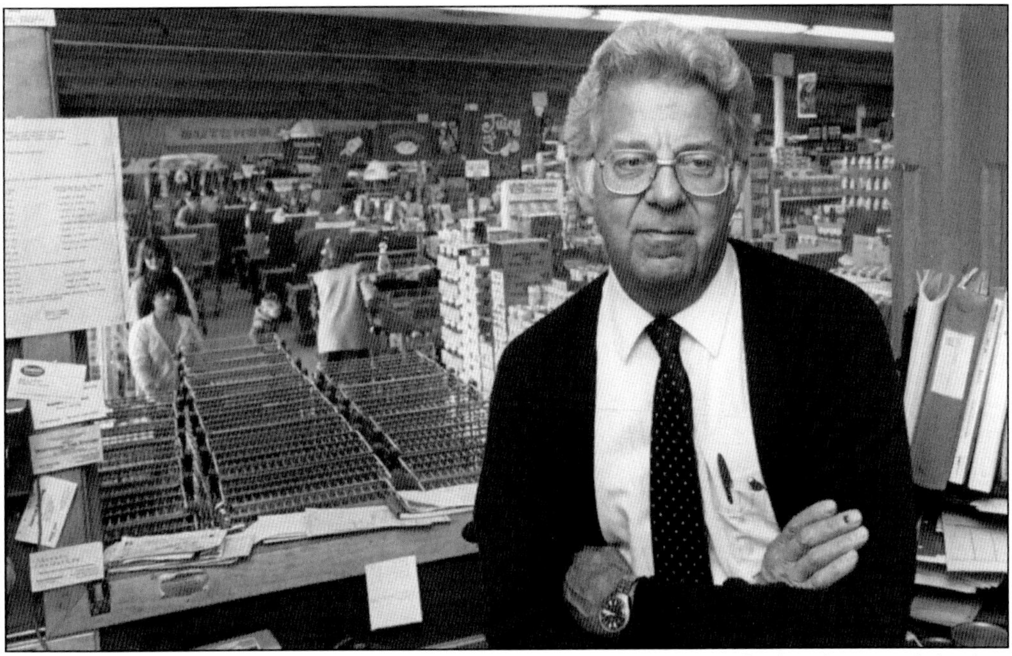

Superstores finally reached into downtown Idaho Falls in 2008 with the closing of the last independent downtown grocery, Saving Center on Memorial Drive. Vern Kelsch owned and operated the store and a second Saving Center on Seventeenth Street that closed a few years ago (now Hastings Bookstore). The *Post Register* reported in 1989 that the store was holding its own, with competitive prices and good promotion work. But the opening of the city's second Wal-Mart Superstore a few blocks away, and Kelsch's desire to retire, helped spell the end of a 60-year-old downtown business.

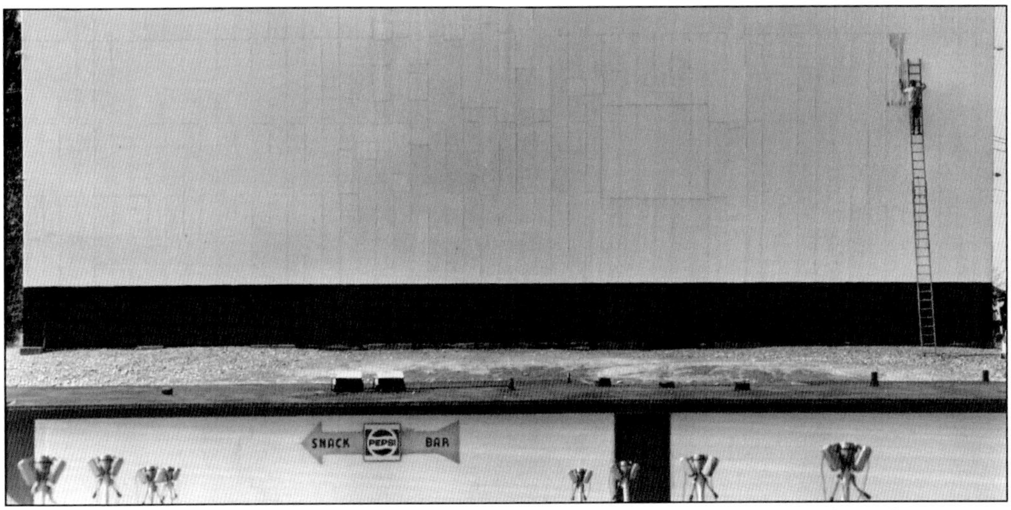

With outdoor theaters regaining popularity across the country, Idaho Falls went through a summer in 2008 without a drive-in movie. The Motor-Vu on the north side of town and the Sky Vu on the south have been operating since the end of World War II; this screen at the Sky Vu, shown undergoing repairs in 1989, was built in 1949 and enlarged in 1953. The owner of both screens decided not to reopen them in 2008 but left open the possibility that one or both screens would reopen for the 2009 summer season.

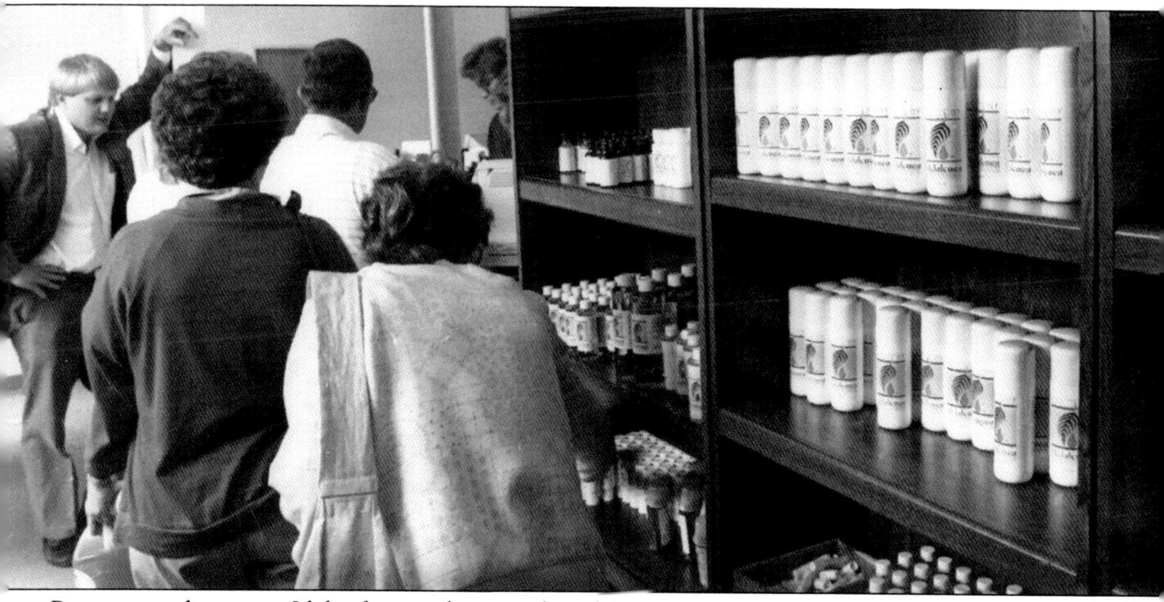

Potatoes made eastern Idaho famous, but it is the oil from a tea tree that fuels Idaho Falls–based and homegrown Melaleuca, Inc., with 2007 sales of more than $859 million. The company started as Oil of Melaleuca, Inc., in 1984. The firm's sales grew to $90,000 during its first month in operation, and the Ball Brothers brought in their friend Frank VanderSloot, who reorganized the company as Melaleuca, Inc., in 1985. By 1994, Melaleuca became an international firm with a rapidly expanding suite of health and beauty products, adding the Nicole Miller Skin Care line. A history of the company by R. M. Barry, *Built on Solid Principles: The Melaleuca Story*, was published in 1999. In the 1988 photograph above, distributors select products to fill orders from the shelves in the company's Idaho Falls office.

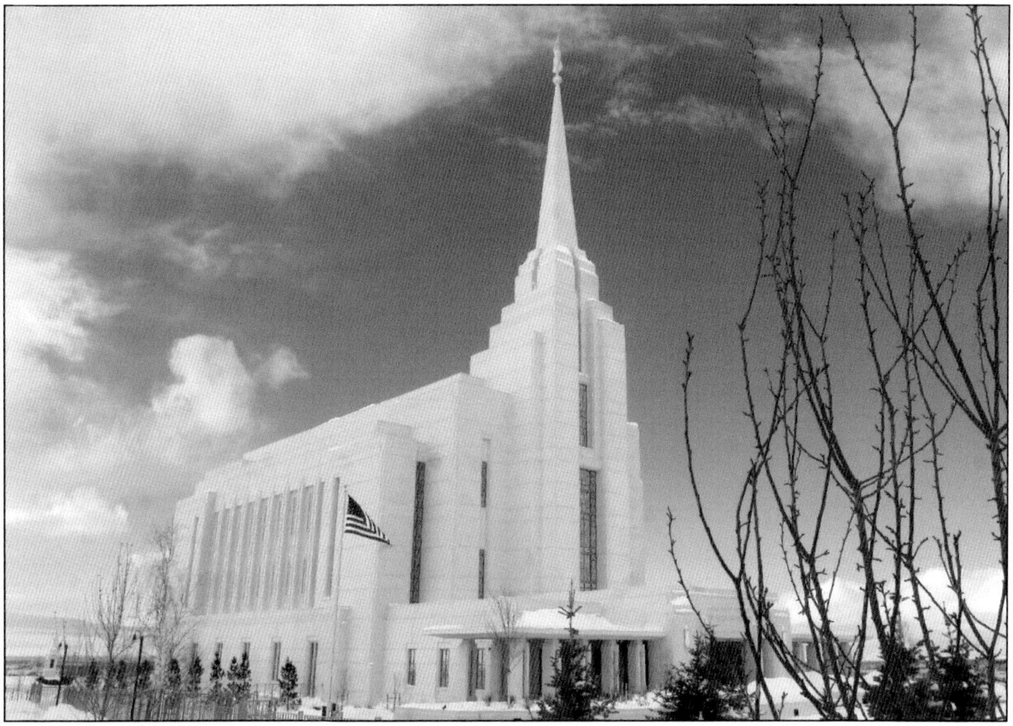

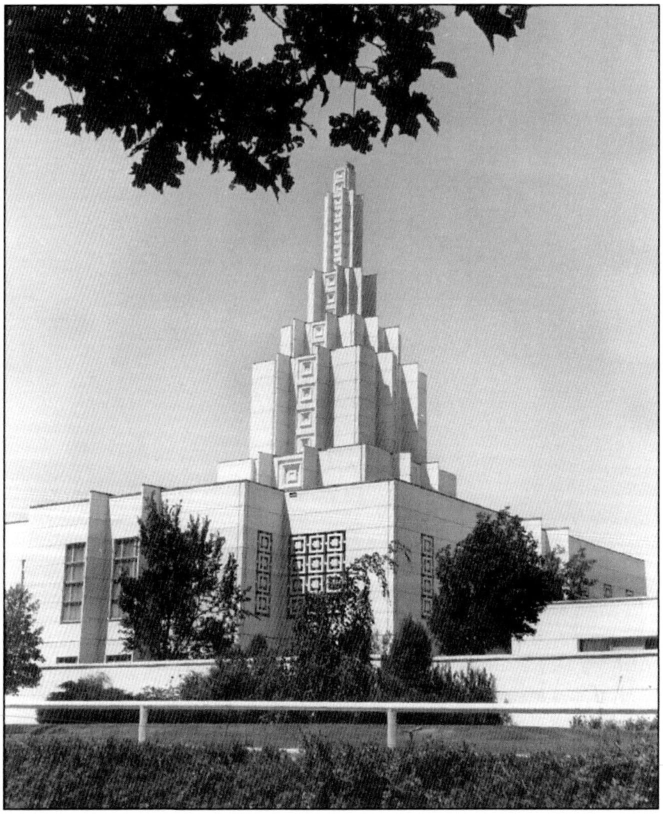

Eastern Idaho received its second LDS Temple in 2008 when the Rexburg Temple of the Church of Jesus Christ of Latter-day Saints was dedicated by Pres. Thomas S. Monson. It is the third LDS Temple in Idaho. The state's first LDS Temple at Idaho Falls was dedicated in 1945, adding an enduring landmark to the Idaho Falls Skyline (left).

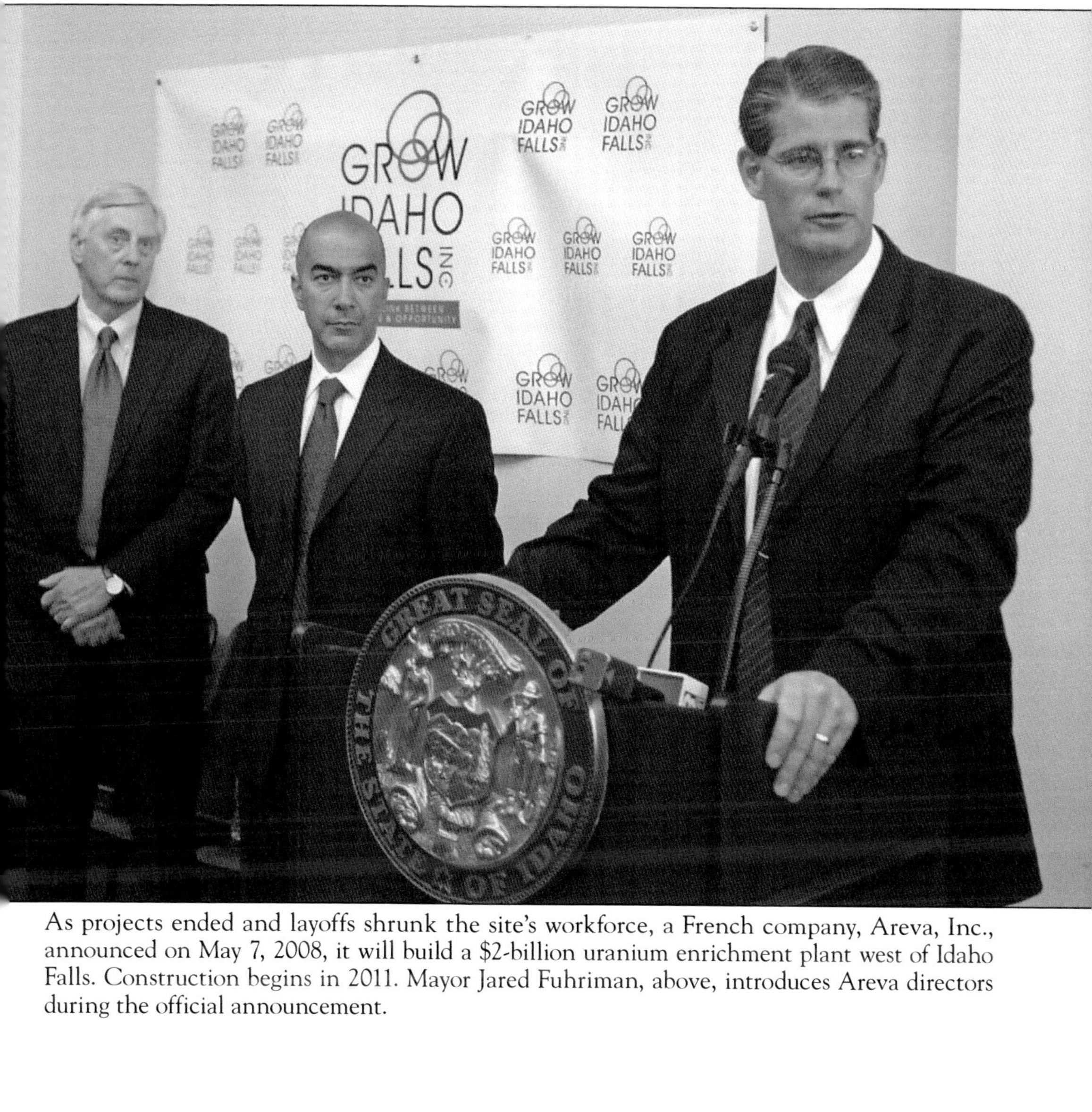

As projects ended and layoffs shrunk the site's workforce, a French company, Areva, Inc., announced on May 7, 2008, it will build a $2-billion uranium enrichment plant west of Idaho Falls. Construction begins in 2011. Mayor Jared Fuhriman, above, introduces Areva directors during the official announcement.

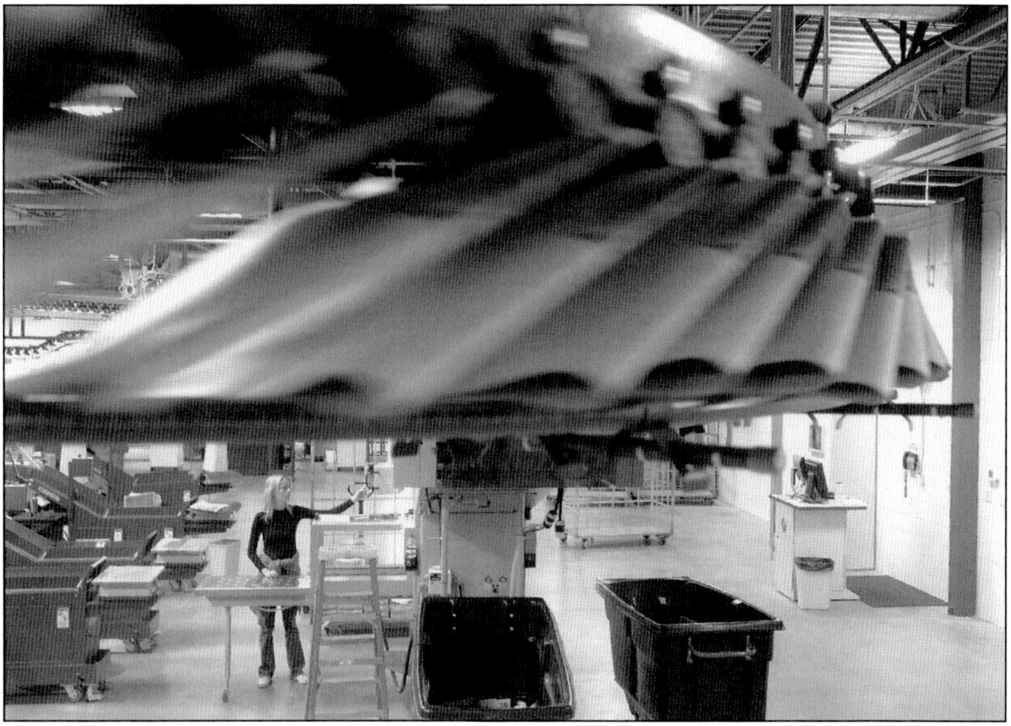

The *Post Register* moved into its $6-million production and packaging facility in 2005. Besides achieving direct-plate printing technology, the new facility allows for much faster and more precise packaging and distribution of the daily newspaper. The new press will be a 17-unit Goss Magnum configured with four four-high color towers and one black unit. It will include splicers to avoid stopping for roll changes, digital inking technology to improve registration and general reproduction, tensioners to reduce paper stretch during a run, and a new folder. It is at least the newspaper's fifth Goss press since 1919.

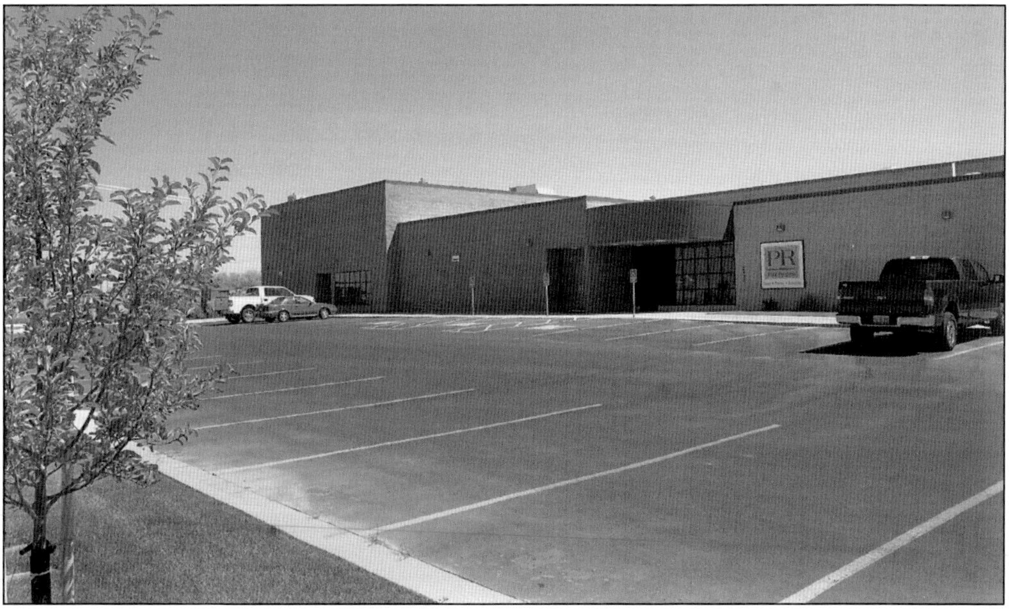

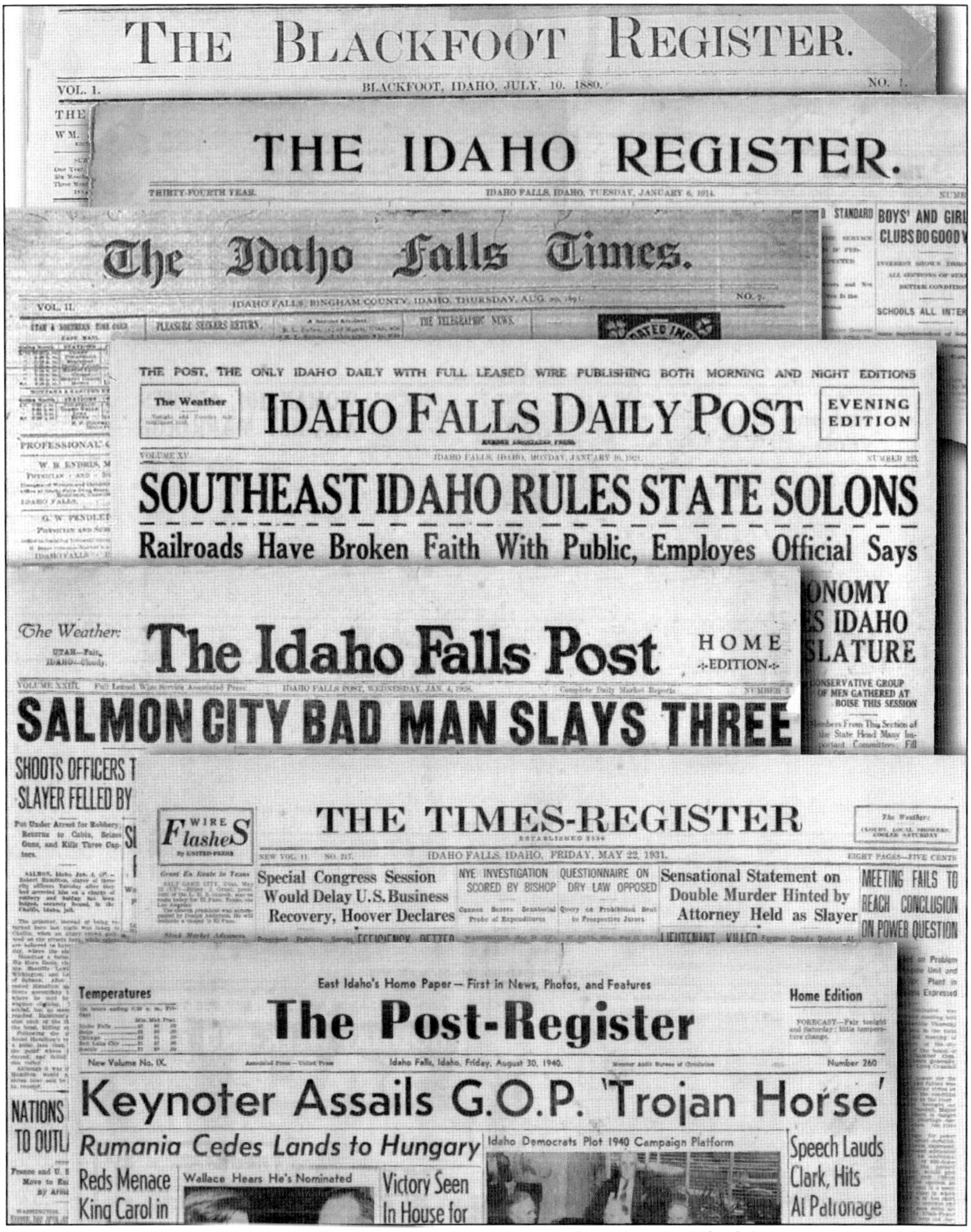

The six newspapers of Idaho Falls can trace their lineage back to the *Blackfoot Register*, published in 1880. When editor William Wheeler moved the paper to Eagle Rock in 1884, he changed its name to the *Idaho Register*. In 1890, Sam Dennis and Rufus Bonney launched the *Idaho Falls Times*, which had a rocky time against the Republican paper at first but wound up buying the *Register* 30 years later. The *Idaho Falls Daily Post* emerged in 1905; after a few years as a morning publication, it reverted to evening paper. The "Daily" was dropped when the *Post* shortened its publication schedule for a while. The *Times-Register* was formed in 1920 when the *Register* was purchased by Dennis and William Snyder. The *Post* and the *Times-Register* merged in 1931, moving into the *Post*'s offices at Capital Avenue and A Street under the leadership of E. F. McDermott.

ACROSS AMERICA, PEOPLE ARE DISCOVERING SOMETHING WONDERFUL. *THEIR HERITAGE.*

Arcadia Publishing is the leading local history publisher in the United States. With more than 4,000 titles in print and hundreds of new titles released every year, Arcadia has extensive specialized experience chronicling the history of communities and celebrating America's hidden stories, bringing to life the people, places, and events from the past. To discover the history of other communities across the nation, please visit:

www.arcadiapublishing.com

Customized search tools allow you to find regional history books about the town where you grew up, the cities where your friends and family live, the town where your parents met, or even that retirement spot you've been dreaming about.

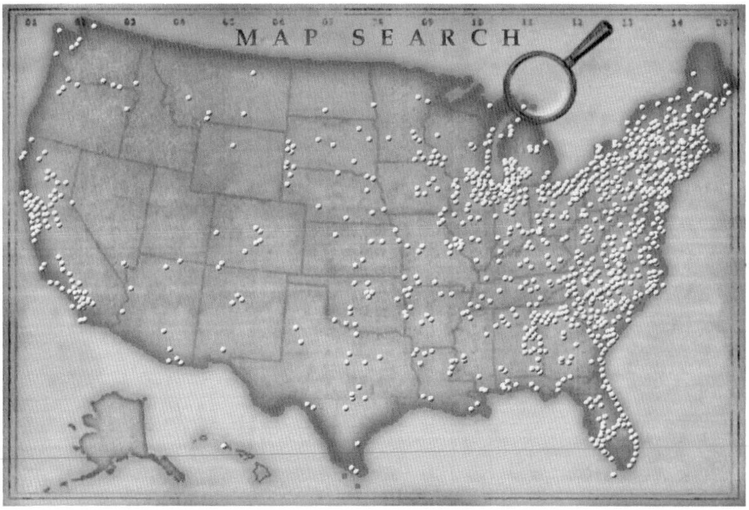